39x 10/19

THE DARK AGES

BOOKS ON HISTORY

BY ISAAC ASIMOV

———————————

THE GREEKS

THE ROMAN REPUBLIC

THE ROMAN EMPIRE

THE EGYPTIANS

THE NEAR EAST: 10,000 YEARS OF HISTORY

THE DARK AGES

BY ISAAC ASIMOV

HOUGHTON MIFFLIN COMPANY BOSTON

To my daughter Robyn,
who could brighten any age, however dark

CONTENTS

4 THE MEROVINGIANS

5 THE MAYORS OF THE PALACE

6 FROM MAYOR TO KING

GERMANS VERSUS ROME

FIRST COLLISION

About 1000 B.C., a group of uncivilized tribesmen — tall, light-skinned, and savage hunters of game — lived north and south of the mouth of the Baltic Sea, in lands which we would now describe as Denmark, southern Sweden and Norway, and northern Germany. Where they came from, nobody knows.

Their language was different from the languages spoken by the tribes to the east and south, and we group the tribesmen together for this reason.

Many centuries later, the Romans encountered a tribe descended from these primitives (and still quite primitive even then). This tribe called themselves by a name that sounded to the Romans like "Germani." The Romans applied this name, eventually, to all tribes speaking the language of the Germani, and we speak of them as the Germanic tribes therefore.

Even today, we call their descendants Germans and their nation Germany. The Germans, however, call themselves Deutsch (from an old word that may have meant "people") and their nation Deutschland.

The Germanic tribes are among those who are often referred to in history books as "barbarians."

To the civilized Greeks and Romans in the south, anyone who did not speak Greek or Latin was considered a barbarian; that is, he seemed to make unintelligible sounds like "bar-bar-bar." The word wasn't necessarily meant to be insulting. After all, the inhabitants of Syria, Babylonia and Egypt were barbarians in this sense, and they were just as cultured and learned as the Greeks and Romans, and had been so for a longer time.

The Germans were barbarians in this sense but they were also uncivilized. In later centuries, they helped destroy parts of the Roman Empire and their lack of appreciation of culture and learning gave the word "barbarian" its present meaning — that of uneducated and uncivilized.

The only importance of the German tribes to the rest of the world at this early time lay in the accidental fact that along the southern shores of the Baltic Sea, some sixty million years before, huge forests of pine trees had existed. Those forests died long before man came upon the earth and that variety of pine tree is extinct, but while those trees lived, they produced enormous quantities of resin.

Hardened pieces of this ancient resin can be found in the ground and are washed up from the sea by storms. It is a translucent substance, yellow to orange to red-brown in color, beautiful in appearance and soft enough to be easily carved into attractive shapes. This material (now called amber) was greatly valued as ornaments.

Amber passed from hand to hand, and in southern Europe people far more advanced than the dwellers in the northern forests must have come across specimens and longed for more. An amber trade route was established and the products of southern Europe, exchanged for amber, drifted northward.

It was probably as a result of the amber trade that the Germans first became dimly aware that somewhere far to the south were regions of wealth.

Knowledge of the barbarian north was just as dim to the civilized south. About 350 B.C., the Greek explorer Pytheas of Massilia (the modern Marseilles) ventured out into the Atlantic and explored the northwestern shores of Europe. He brought back much interesting information to the book-reading public which then, as always, made up but a small fraction of the population. The time was soon to come, though, when knowledge of the Germans was to impress itself on the average man in far more direct fashion.

In early centuries, the German tribes did not practice agriculture but lived by hunting and by keeping herds of cattle. The northern forests could not support many people living in this fashion, and even when the population was still very thin by modern standards, the land was already overpopulated.

Tribes would fight each other for land to support the growing population and one side would lose, naturally. The losers would wander off in search of better pasture and more game, and so there came to be a slow drift of German tribes out of their original homeland.

Gradually, the Germans pushed southward, and westward along the North Sea coast. By 100 B.C., they had reached the Rhine River on the west and had occupied most of what is now Germany.

Ahead of them, they pushed or absorbed a group of people who had earlier dominated wide stretches of northern and western Europe, and who spoke a group of related languages called Celtic. To the west of the Rhine, for instance, were the Celtic tribes who inhabited a land called Gallia by the Romans and Gaul by us.

As the Germans moved west and south, they must have heard more and more of the rich and wonderful lands to the south. By 150 B.C., the great civilization of the Greeks was in decline but Italy was rapidly rising in power and wealth. The city of Rome in central Italy was busily establishing its rule over the entire Mediterranean area.*

The south must have seemed incalculably rich to the Germans — a wonderful place for possible loot. The pull of the south was combined with unusually hard times in the north, for in what is now Denmark, the chronic overpopulation was made worse by great damage from storms and flooding.

Hordes of tribesmen, men, women and children, began to rumble southward in unprecedented numbers in 115 B.C. The Romans later called this horde the Cimbri. (The Danish peninsula, which we call Jutland, still bears the older name of Cimbrian Peninsula, in consequence.)

In the course of their drift southward, the Cimbri were eventually joined by other tribes whom the Romans called Teutones. This particular tribal name was eventually applied to all Germans, so that one may speak of them as Teutons or as the Teutonic peoples. We may also speak of the Teutonic languages, which include all those descended from the language spoken by those old Germans — English is one of them!

(It is not at all certain, by the way, that the Cimbri and Teutones — despite the latter name — were actually German. Though that is the traditional view, many modern historians think they were Celtic in part, or even entirely.)

* For details, see my books *The Greeks* (Houghton Mifflin, 1965) and *The Roman Republic* (Houghton Mifflin, 1966).

It is not very likely that the advancing Cimbri were a really formidable host. They were short of metal, so that they were unarmored and had few swords. What weapons they did carry were much inferior to those of the Romans. What is more, they lacked discipline or any sense of ordered tactics.

Their only hope of overcoming the Romans was to catch them by surprise and then come thundering down at them with ferocious yells in the hope that the first shock of contact would throw them into disarray and send them running.

This worked very often. In the first place, the tribes formed a numerous host, for they all fought — women and older children as well as men. Then, too, the Germans made a fearsome sight, with their long shaggy hair and their primitive garments. They were tall as well — much taller and stronger, individually, than the men of the Mediterranean lands.

The Roman troops might easily have overcome the barbarian hordes if they had stood firm and remained cool; but all too often, they broke and ran at the first charge. Then the tribesmen found it easy to pick off the running soldiers one by one and massacre them.

Rumors of the southern march of the Cimbri spread ahead of them and, as is almost always true of rumors, were exaggerated with the telling. The Cimbri were said to number half a million or more; their height, strength, and ferocity were described in superlatives. The Roman army sent northward to meet them beyond the Alps listened to these tales and were terrified and half-defeated before contact was ever made.

The Cimbri met that army in 113 B.C. and broke it easily. Before them now lay the Alps, undefended. The simple tribesmen, however, had no clear notions of geography. Why try to pick one's way through those towering peaks when one could veer off westward and skirt the mountain rim? Off they went into Gaul.

Three separate battles between the Cimbri and the Romans took place in Gaul, and the Romans lost each one. By 105 B.C., all Rome was in absolute panic. In heroic wars over the past two centuries, she had defeated every other nation of importance around the rim of the Mediterranean, but before these ill-armed barbarians she seemed helpless.

Undoubtedly, if the Cimbri had now marched into Italy, they would have had looting beyond their wildest dreams and the history of the world might have been altered. But again, one direction seemed like another to them and, fortunately for Rome, the tribes marched off westward into Spain, where they fought Celtic peoples not much less primitive than themselves.

This gave Rome time, and the man for the occasion appeared. He was a rough, practically illiterate soldier named Gaius Marius. He was made the virtual dictator of Rome and he set to work beating an army into shape and seeing to it that it was trained to stand firm before the wild barbarian charge.

By 102 B.C., when the Cimbri returned from Spain and finally seemed about to make for Italy at last, Marius was ready for them. The barbarians marched in two contingents, one of which was wiped out almost to a man in southern Gaul. The other managed to make its way into Italy, but in 101 B.C. it was annihilated in the Po Valley.

The menace had vanished entirely and Rome went into spasms of joy. For the moment, Marius was their godlike darling. No one at the time could possibly have foreseen that these battles between Romans and barbarians were only the first of a many-centuries war.

GERMAN RECOVERY

For a time, the Germanic tribes remained penned east of the Rhine and north of the Alps. But population pressure continued to mount. If Rome was too tough, there were easier pickings to the west. Warily, Germans moved into Gaul.

Leading the invasion was a tribe living in the southwest corner of the Germanic territories. Modern Germans call them Schwaben but the Romans called them Suevi and to us they are the Sueves.

A generation after the defeat of the Cimbri, a German chieftain, whom the Romans called Ariovistus, ruled over the Sueves. As early as 71 B.C., he began to raid westward across the Rhine, coming to control more and more Gallic territory. There seemed every reason to suppose that all of Gaul would fall to him, but then Rome interfered. In 58 B.C., a Roman army marched northward into Gaul under the leadership of the greatest general the Romans were ever to have — Julius Caesar.

For a brief time, Roman and German met again in a contest over Gaul, but no man at that time could have beaten Caesar. He hurled the German forces over the Rhine and then crossed it himself, marching through Germany territory in two separate raids as a gesture of force, though he carefully refrained from forcing Ariovistus into a pitched battle on German home territory.

Gaul became a Roman province and now the German tribes faced Rome not only on the south but on the west as well.

Nor did Rome seem disposed to stop. Caesar was assassinated in 44 B.C., but his great-nephew eventually seized control of Rome, established the Roman Empire, and ruled it under the title of Augustus.* Augustus' stepson, Drusus, led an army across the Rhine in 12 B.C., and by 9 B.C. he had reached the Elbe, 250 miles to the east. For twenty years the Romans stayed between those rivers, gradually calming the country and introducing it to Roman ways.

For a while it seemed that Germany, like Gaul, might be absorbed into Roman civilization, but the Germans rebounded

---

* For the story of Rome under Augustus and his successors, see my book *The Roman Empire* (Houghton Mifflin, 1967).

and recovered. They found their leader in a young warrior, Arminius (the Latin form of the German name, Hermann). He had learned Latin, had become Romanized, and had even gained Roman citizenship, but he remained a German at heart.

He lured the Roman general who had succeeded Drusus as head of the province deep into the forests in A.D. 9.* There he launched a sudden surprise attack, and in three days three Roman legions were totally destroyed.

The rest of the Roman forces had to fall back. They tried to hold on to the North Sea coastline but even that was eventually given up. They retired west of the Rhine, which remained the Roman-German frontier for over four centuries. Rome made no further attempt to conquer and civilize the Germans — something which turned out, in the end, to be bad for the Romans, and for the Germans, too, and perhaps for the whole world.

The Germans were naturally of particular interest to the Romans. Other barbarian tribes had been conquered and absorbed in Spain, Gaul, and even Britain. The Germans, however, had maintained their independence and had beaten the Romans in doing so. The Romans were therefore curious about them.

Nearly a century after the Roman defeat by Arminius, a historian named Cornelius Tacitus seems to have traveled through Europe. He may have visited Germany or have talked to people who had. At least, after returning home he published a short book on the Germans in 98. That book, only about fifty pages long, remains our chief source on the Germans of the Roman period.

By that time, the Germans had settled down to an agricultural way of life. Tacitus described them as tall, vigorous and warlike, delighting in hunting, fierce and cruel, but honorable

---

* Years that follow the birth of Jesus are often given the initials A.D. ("Anno Domini" or "year of the Lord") to distinguish them from the years B.C. ("before Christ"). In this book almost all the dates are A.D. and they will henceforth be given as mere numbers.

and hospitable. It is hard to know exactly how far to trust Tacitus in his descriptions of German manners and government, however, for he was not an impartial observer. He was a severe critic of the Roman society of the time, feeling it to be decadent and vicious. He therefore used the Germans as an example of "noble savages" with all the manly virtues the Romans lacked. He spoke of their independence of spirit, of their love of liberty, of the way in which they early trained their children to hardihood and the use of arms, of the way in which their kings were elected by bands of warriors, and of how individual chieftains of renown might gather followers about them. People have tried to trace later notions of feudalism and democracy back to German tribal customs, but as long as we must rely on Tacitus we can't be sure what is really so and what he was merely presenting as a suitable moral lesson for his Roman audience.

Tacitus warned that the vigor and independence of the German people would yet make them a menace to a softening and declining Rome, and in that, at least, he was all too right. Rome remained strong in Tacitus' lifetime, to be sure, for it was then coming under the rule of a line of strong and capable Emperors. In the reign of the last of these, Marcus Aurelius, troubles began to mount.

There was war in the east, and although the Romans were victorious, the soldiers brought back with them a deadly plague that ravaged the entire Empire in 166 and weakened it permanently. It must have penetrated Germany, too, but the concentrations of population were smaller there and it must have spread less easily and done less harm proportionately.

A German tribe in southern Germany, called the Marcomanni by the Romans, seized the time of Roman confusion under the blows of the plague to cross the Danube River and advance southward. Marcus Aurelius spent the rest of his reign fighting them. Indeed, he died at the city now known as Vienna, while still at war with them.

Marcus Aurelius' unrelenting defense succeeded in pushing the Marcomanni back across the Danube and preserving the Empire. From that moment on, though, there was no chance of peace. The German peoples were constantly alert, watching the Roman Empire across the Rhine and the Danube; watching, waiting and striking at the first sign of weakness.

Nor did it matter how often they might be defeated, for they had only to retreat into the forests where the tired Romans hardly ever dared follow them — and where they could resume their watch for the next moment.

What's more, the Romans were losing one of their greatest advantages. Until Marcus Aurelius' time, the Germans had remained split into a large number of mutually hostile tribes. Even when one of the tribes attacked Rome, the other tribes could always be bribed to remain neutral or even to fight on the Roman side.

Now, however, the German tribes were beginning to form confederations and to join into larger, and more formidable, unions. The Marcomanni joined a loose confederation of tribes across southern and southwestern Germany. They were called the Alemanni by the Romans, clearly from the German word meaning "all men." It would seem that the Alemanni hoped to form a completely united Germany — something which never came to pass in ancient times. (The name is still preserved in the French word for Germany, "Allemagne.")

The Alemanni pressed into Gaul in 233, when the Roman Emperor of the time, Alexander Severus, was absent in the far east on another of the numerous wars in that area. When Alexander returned, he tried to drive them off and failed. He then attempted to bribe them to leave Roman territory, and his soldiers used that as an excuse to assassinate him.

This ushered in a period of fifty years of Roman anarchy, during which it seemed that the Empire would break apart forever and that large parts of it would fall to the Germans. It was at this moment that one of the most famous of all the German tribes, the Goths, appeared on the scene.

ROMAN RECOVERY

The Goths seem to have originated in what is now southern Sweden. The name may mean "the good people" and it would, of course, be applied by the Goths to themselves. People generally think highly of their own qualities.

By the time of Tacitus, groups of Goths had migrated across the Baltic to northern Germany. That might, indeed, have set off a kind of domino movement, for the Goths would displace the people already living there, who would drive southward, displacing others, until in southernmost Germany, the Marcomanni would feel pressed into invading Rome at the first good opportunity.

The Goths continued moving southward and eastward, out of Germany proper and into the lands occupied by the less warlike Letts and Slavs. They moved up the Vistula River and down the Dniester (through what is now Poland and southwestern Russia) until they reached the area north and northwest of the Black Sea. This was land well suited to agriculture. (Today it includes the lush fields of the Ukraine and Bessarabia.)

The Goths now found themselves on the northeastern borders of the distracted Roman Empire.

The Romans had pushed north of the Danube and had occupied Dacia (modern Rumania) a century and a half before, not long after the time of Tacitus. Dacia remained, however, thinly and insecurely held. The Goths raided it repeatedly and the looting was good. They even built ships, launched themselves on the Black Sea, and sailed across it to harry the coasts of Asia Minor and the Balkans.

All the borders of Rome were caving in and a series of short-lived Emperors could do little about it. Their hardest efforts only made matters worse, it seemed. In 248, Decius became Emperor and he hurried to take the field against the Goths who were devastating the provinces south of the Danube. For his pains, he was defeated and killed in 251, the first Roman Emperor ever to die in battle.

But Rome held on and the clouds seemed to begin to lift ever so slightly in 268, when Claudius II succeeded to the throne.

The Gothic menace had grown worse by then. A large fleet of vessels carried numerous Goths across the Black Sea, through the Bosporus and into the Aegean. They landed in northern Greece and marched inland to Naisus (the modern Nish, in eastern Yugoslavia). Never had the European East been so nearly in a state of collapse.

Claudius II met the Goths at Naisus, however, and after a long and bloody battle, defeated them utterly. Claudius proudly took the name of Gothicus as a title of honor, but his triumph was short-lived. He died of the plague the year after.

His successor, Aurelian, was another capable Emperor who went far toward restoring the integrity of the Empire. He realized, however, that Dacia at least could not be held and that province was given up forever. The Goths promptly took it over. For a century, though, they were firmly held beyond the banks of the Danube.

To the north of that river, however, was space enough. Indeed, the Goths now formed two kingdoms: an easterly one to the north of the Black Sea in what is today the Ukraine, and a westerly one west of the Black Sea in Dacia.

The tribes north of the Black Sea called themselves the Ostrogoths, those west of the Black Sea, the Visigoths. It seems natural to interpret these names as "East Goths" and "West Goths" but that is not apparently their real origin. The best guess now is that Ostrogoth means "splendid Goth" and Visigoth means "noble Goth." There was no limit, apparently, to the high opinion the Goths held of themselves.

This Gothic realm was not occupied entirely by the Goths, of course. The bulk of the population consisted of downtrodden, long-suffering Slavic peasants. The Goths were a thin ruling aristocracy making up a warrior caste. This was the first example of what was to become commonplace among a whole series of German kingdoms outside Germany during the next five centuries.

While the Goths were spreading over the east, a new group of German tribes was heard of along the Rhine. They called themselves the Franks. There are a number of theories as to the origin of the name. It could mean "free," "spear," or "brave." Whatever it meant, the Franks were, of course, praising themselves.

During the period of Roman anarchy, the Franks and Alemanni knifed separately into Gaul and devastated it despite a defeat handed them by the Roman Emperor Probus in 276.

In 284, at last, the period of anarchy came to an end. A new Emperor arose, Diocletian, who reorganized the Empire politically, economically, and militarily. He did so at great cost and Rome staggered to her feet rather than sprang to them. But she was on her feet, however painfully, and the barbarians drew away — temporarily.

For a while, the Roman revival seemed to glitter and grow splendid. In 300, another strong Emperor, Constantine I, established on the Bosporus a new great capital which he named Constantinople after himself. To many, it must have seemed that the Empire was eternal, and yet it was really far gone in internal decay. Its economy was weakening steadily and its population growing demoralized.

Worse yet, it was hagridden by civil war.

Diocletian had sought to make the burden of Empire easier by establishing two co-Emperors, one in the east and one in the west. Theoretically, they ruled over a single Empire, but historians from this time forward speak of an Eastern Roman Empire and a Western Roman Empire. The Eastern Empire was much the wealthier, the more cultured, and the more populous of the two.

Such a division of the Empire worked well when it worked at all, but it didn't always. Often the co-Emperors and their prospective heirs intrigued against each other and led armies against each other to the harm of all. Making matters worse, there was the rival Persian Empire in the east. Warfare with Persia might sink to a smolder, but it never went out entirely.

The Germans had only to keep on waiting.

After the death of Constantine, the Empire went through a period of civil war. Even after it was reunited under Constantius II, a son of Constantine, it remained involved in a long and largely unsuccessful war with Persia. The western regions were left unattended, and in 355, the Franks and Alemanni were busily cutting through Gaul again.

Constantius sent a cousin, Julian, to Gaul. The young man was a scholar without military experience and with a completely inadequate army. To the surprise of everyone, he revealed an unexpected capacity for war.

Skillfully, he outmaneuvered the bumbling German forces, retaking cities and inflicting considerable damage on them. Finally, in 357, he met a main German army on the upper Rhine, near what is now the city of Strasbourg. He was outnumbered three to one and seems to have hesitated to attack until he was pushed into battle by the eagerness of his own troops. Roman discipline and order prevailed over German numbers, and at little cost to his own troops, Julian inflicted a tremendous defeat on the enemy.

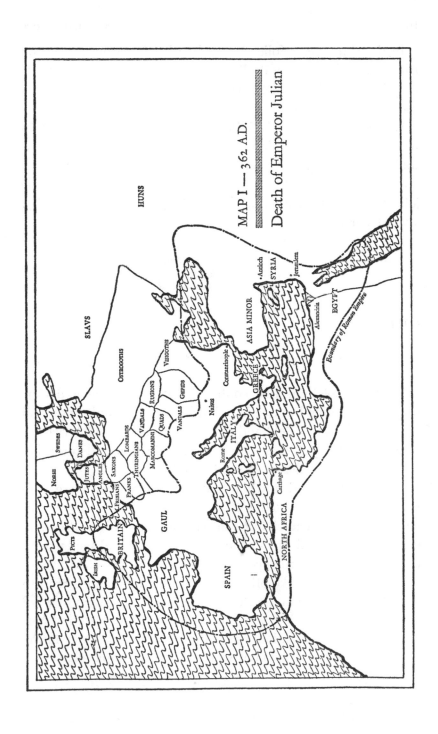

MAP I — 362 A.D.

Death of Emperor Julian

In the three years following, Julian led his army across the Rhine to raid Germany itself three times. He defeated and utterly humiliated the tribes. To his men, he seemed to be Julius Caesar come back to life.

When the Emperor Constantius, growing jealous, tried to weaken Julian by withdrawing some of his troops, the excited soldiers declared their general Emperor. Another civil war was about to start, but Constantius died before battle could be joined, and Julian, after a short reign, died in a campaign against Persia.

CHRISTIANITY

We must not think that contact between Romans and Germans was nothing but one long battle between civilization and barbarism, between light and darkness. There were intervals of peace during which there were communication and trade between the two peoples — even friendship.

Germans migrated into the Empire, where they were welcomed as mercenary soldiers. It had grown increasingly difficult to recruit Roman civilians into the army. Long centuries of peace had deprived them of aptitude for war and made them uncomfortable and unhappy with the hard military life.

The Germans, on the other hand, tall, strong, and inured to hardship, found life in the Roman army actually a step upward from that to which they were accustomed. They were fed better than before and had all the material comforts. Then, in the course of the numerous civil wars, they had ample chance to gain women and loot.

Indeed, when Julian fought the Franks, his own army consisted largely of German mercenaries, so that it was not Roman against German at all. It was very largely German against German.

Julian carried this tendency a step farther by agreeing to settle whole groups of Germans in Gaul, soon after his great victory over them at Strasbourg, in return for their agreement to serve in the Roman army. This was a precedent which turned out to be disastrous for Rome.

In short, the distinction between Romans and Germans was beginning to blur. The Roman Empire was beginning to take on a German coloration all along its northern edge. In return, the Germans themselves were slowly beginning to pick up Roman ways, through trade and through the return of compatriots who had served the Romans and lived among them.

Most important of all, the Germans were beginning to pick up a Roman religion.

In the time of Augustus, a new religion, Christianity, had arisen. It began as a dissident Jewish sect but quickly developed into a way of thought acceptable to non-Jews. Little by little, despite periodic persecution, it gained power in Rome. By 300, perhaps one-quarter of the Roman population was Christian in fact or in sympathy. The Christians were still a minority but they were a dedicated and vocal one. The pagan majority was largely indifferent and apathetic, and was sinking steadily in importance.

The Emperor Constantine I, a clever politician, saw this clearly. He became Christian in sympathy and by the end of his reign, Christianity was virtually the official religion of the Roman Empire.

But since Christianity considered itself to be a universal religion, it did not restrict itself to Roman dominions. There were Christians in Armenia and Persia to the east of the Empire and there were even drives to convert the German barbarians.

A Goth named Ulfilas (the Latin form of the Gothic name Wulfila, or "wolf cub"), having visited Constantinople in 332, was converted to Christianity. Returning to his homeland, he began tirelessly to preach Christianity to the Goths and to make a few converts.

For his purposes, Ulfilas invented an alphabet and produced a written form of Gothic. He prepared a translation of the Bible in Gothic (censoring out some of the passages dealing with descriptions of warfare on the grounds that the Goths needed no stimulation in that direction). Small fragments of that translation still exist and are virtually the only records we have of the now-extinct Gothic language.

Ulfilas' progress was slow, but he laid the groundwork. While the Germans remained outside the Empire, they stayed overwhelmingly pagan. But they knew of Christianity, were inoculated with it, so to speak, and when the tribes finally broke into the Empire, they quickly adopted the imperial religion.

Eventually, Christianity was so successful as to wipe out most of the signs of the Germans' pagan past. Little remains. The Icelandic literature (in Iceland, Christianity did not win its victory till after 1000) preserves some of the "Norse myths" and sagas, which lack the grace of the better-known Greek myths and which reflect the harsher environment of the north.

The names of some of the gods and goddesses — Odin (or Wodan), the chief of the gods; Thor, the god of storm and thunder; Tiu, the war god; Freya, the goddess of love and beauty — still live on in the English names of the days of the week (Tuesday, Wednesday, Thursday, and Friday). We still read the dramatic tales of Thor's lost hammer; of Loki's evil brood, including his daughter Hel, who ruled the underworld and gave us our name for it; of the death of Baldur.

The gods are mortal, and there is a circumstantial tale of their death at the great final battle against the giants and the other forces of evil. This is entwined with the tale of Sigurd, or Siegfried, which is best known today in the version given us by the German musician Richard Wagner, who wrote four connected operas on the subject in the 1850's.

The oldest surviving piece of Germanic literature is *Beowulf*. This is usually considered an English classic because the sole surviving manuscript from early times happens to be an Anglo-Saxon version. The manuscript dates back to 1000 but represents a version that may first have been put in written form as early as 700.

The scene of the epic is in Denmark and the hero, Beowulf, is of a Swedish tribe, so that the original story may well date back to very early days before the southern migration had altered the primitive German way of life. There is a thin Christian overlay in the versions that reach us, but it is superficial. The poem is essentially pagan.

Some of the pagan beliefs of the Germans live on to our day and have so woven themselves into the fabric of our lives that few realize they are remnants of a pre-Christian past. Some, in fact, have worked themselves into the very heart of Christian religious customs. What would Christmas be without the Christmas tree — which is of completely pagan origin? So are the mistletoe and the yule log (the very word "yule" is from the Gothic name for December).

There was an important catch, though, in the conversion of the Germans.

Christianity existed in numerous varieties, and in Ulfilas' day there were two chief sects. One, originally preached by a priest named Arius (and therefore called Arianism), stressed the all-importance of God. Jesus was considered human, a created being subordinate to God. The other view was that God, Jesus, and the Holy Spirit were three completely equal aspects (a "trinity") of a single Being. The latter view was adopted by a large gathering of bishops and was therefore considered the official doctrine of the "universal" Church. Those who believed it came to be called Catholics, from the Greek word for universal.

Although the Catholic viewpoint was official, the Arians supported their own position throughout the fourth century. There was deep hostility between the two sects and ferocious mutual persecution at times.

As it happened, Ulfilas was converted to the Arian version and he in turn preached Arian Christianity to the Goths. It was to Arianism that the Goths were converted, and in succeeding centuries, other German tribes were similarly converted. As Arianism became more and more to be associated with Germans, it grew less and less popular with Romans, who gradually became just about unanimously Catholic.

This conversion of Germans to Arianism was perhaps not entirely a matter of the sheer accident that Ulfilas had happened to become an Arian. The German tribes, living under a primitive form of monarchy, in which the king was in clear view and was not much greater than his warriors, favored a version of Jesus that did not place him too far above his people. They saw Jesus as a tribal leader.

The Romans, however, were used to Emperors, who were withdrawn from common view and who were fenced in by a wall of ritual and custom. They were accepted as almost more than human and, indeed, in pagan days had been considered divine. The Romans were therefore readier than the Germans to accept Jesus as a divine Emperor and the Imperial Ruler of the Universe, rather than as merely a petty king.

Whatever the reason, however, the conversion of the Germans to Christianity served to mark them off from the Romans. They were divided, rather than united, by a common religion and this, as we shall see, was a matter of first importance to the subsequent history of Europe.

THE HUNS

It is conceivable that the European melting pot might have continued to simmer after the reign of Julian. More and more, Roman culture and religion might have flowed out into Germany while German mercenaries moved into the Empire. There might have been a slow amalgamation of the two groups of people and eventually Europe might have become a kind of Roman-German mixture through a more or less peaceful vanishing of differences.

The chances were probably small that this could have happened, but in order for even so small a chance to be realized, Europe would have had to be left alone.

It was not. Europe is not an island but a large peninsula jutting out from the western edge of the huge land mass of Asia. Asia was then, and still is today, the great population-reservoir of the human race. Its central tracts are semi-arid grasslands that support hardy nomadic herdsmen, speaking "Altaic languages" such as Turkish and Mongolian.

Like the Germans, the central Asian nomads pressed outward whenever the population rose beyond the capacity of the land to support it, or when a series of dry years suddenly lowered that capacity. The nearest civilized area that might be raided with profit was the huge rich land of China in east Asia.

China, weary with fighting off the raiders, whom they called Hsiung-nu, built the Great Wall some time before 200 B.C. It was a huge, well-manned barrier, stretching for thousands of miles along the nation's northern borders. It improved Chinese defenses and served to ward off many raids, but (like all passive defenses) it sometimes failed at crucial moments.

When China went through a period of strength and when its defenses held, that was bad news for western Asia, for then the Hsiung-nu and other Altaic tribes, finding their raids blunted against the Great Wall, turned west.

In the fourth century, such a westward turn was taken — the greatest that civilized Europe had yet seen. About 370, the hordes of the Hsiung-nu (called Hunni by the Romans and Huns by ourselves) plunged out of central Asia. They probed at India, as rich and populous as China, but that land had a natural wall in the Himalayas, the mountain range that was infinitely more effective than any wall of masonry that man could build.

They turned west again where neither masonry nor mountains existed to stop them and where the west Asian tribesmen could offer only negligible resistance. In a short time, they found themselves on the eastern border of the large Ostrogothic kingdom.

The Ostrogoths had been expanding northward under the greatest of their early kings, Ermanaric. He drove his armies and his control northwestward back to the Baltic and east to the Don River. All of what is now East Germany, Poland, Lithuania, White Russia, and the Ukraine was Ostrogothic.

Legend made Ermanaric a cruel and bloody tyrant who achieved a phenomenal age, sometimes given as 110. This need not be taken literally but he may well have lived to be seventy. In that era of short lives and early deaths in battle, anyone achieving old age would be a phenomenon indeed.

Actually, the Ostrogothic expansion could only have a weakening effect. It looks impressive on a map and it may well have swelled the Ostrogothic breast with pride to beat ragamuffin levies of poorly armed peasants, but it did not increase the numbers of the warrior caste. The Ostrogothic army, no stronger than before, was spread more thinly than ever, over a large territory containing mute hordes of suffering subjects who waited for any invader — *any* invader — to beat their arrogant overlords. (The new invader almost invariably turned out to be as bad as the old, but this was somehow never taken into account in advance.)

The Ostrogothic aristocracy, like other social groups of the sort who came after them, were without firm roots among the population. This meant that they could easily be defeated and replaced by another warrior caste. An entire kingdom could seem to be destroyed and to vanish from the pages of history in this way.

This is an illusion, however. The real population, the millions of slaving peasants, are there before the war bands (German or otherwise) come, remain under those bands, and still remain after the bands leave. The "kingdoms" that rise out of nowhere and then suddenly vanish are simply the names we give the temporary aristocracies and don't represent the real population at all — at least in those times of tribal wanderings.

Naturally, there is always some racial admixture. The ruling aristocracy can take native women either as wives or as casual friends. Occasional men of the lower classes might, through deeds in war, earn a place in the lower ranks of the aristocracy. Eventually, if a war band remains long enough, the admixture grows intimate and the rulers and ruled begin to identify themselves as countrymen with a common interest against foreigners.

There was no time for such an amalgamation, however, in the case of the Ostrogoths, for the Huns were at their doorstep, and the proud German warriors were about to find themselves outclassed.

The armies of the Greeks and Romans had been largely composed of foot soldiers, and the Romans had carried the organization of their infantry to a high pitch of versatility and excellence. The Roman legions were unmatched as a fighting force for six centuries.

The Greeks and Romans had cavalry, too, and ordinarily one might well think that a man on horseback could beat a number

of men on foot. He could move faster, charge with more ferocious effect, get away before a possible counterattack. This is
all true, but there is then the problem of staying on the horse.
Horsemen had to avoid too sharp a contact or too sudden a
turn or they would fall off. Cavalry could only be used spar-
ingly as a support for the infantry that carried the brunt of the
fighting.

The German war bands borrowed the Roman style of fighting as best they could. They, too, used infantry as the mainstay
but they were never quite as disciplined as the Romans, and the
latter, when well led, usually won the battles.

But here came the Huns rolling in from Asia: small, bandy-
legged men, no match at all, individually, for the tall, muscled
Germans. They were innocent of agriculture and of formal
warfare, they were nomads and herdsmen who were coming
west with their families, their tents, their herds — all their
earthly goods.

They came on horseback, each man riding an incredibly
hardy pony, rough, shaggy and unbeautiful, but capable of answering any demands put upon it. And those ponies were
equipped with something the European horses did not have —
stirrups.

Centuries before, the nomadic horsemen of the steppes had
invented efficient metal stirrups to suspend from the saddle.
With each foot thrust into a stirrup, a horseman had a firm seat
and need fear no fall unless the horse itself stumbled. With
feet securely planted, horsemen could release clouds of arrows
with deadly aim, could veer and turn, halt and dash ahead, maneuver as no cavalry had ever maneuvered before.

This the Huns did to perfection. Their speed of movement,
their sudden charges, their equally sudden retreats ending in
another charge, were something Europeans had never seen.
Even the skillful Persian horsemen could not match the Huns.

And against these horsemen the Ostrogoths could only place
their spear-wielding footmen, who proved just so many targets

for arrows. The Huns simply rolled over them, hardly knowing anything was in the way, and the Ostrogothic kingdom vanished in a day. The old king, Ermanaric, who had raised his realm to the height of its power, now saw himself dashed to complete defeat. There was nothing left for him but suicide. As for the Huns, they took over the land ownership, the tribute, and the military responsibilities. The peasantry remained in place with no voice in anything, and where the Ostrogothic kingdom had covered a large patch on the map of Europe, there was suddenly a Hunnish kingdom instead.

Those Ostrogoths who survived and did not succeed in fleeing westward had to continue as warriors — the only job they knew — and had to serve under Hunnish officers. They became part of the Hunnish army and learned to fight from horseback.

Nor did the Huns stop. They reached the Dniester River, which served as a boundary between the Ostrogoths and Visigoths. They pressed beyond, entering the Visigoths' territory and defeating them as they had earlier defeated their eastern cousins. They swept into the plains of what is now Hungary, and by 380 they controlled a realm that stretched from the Alps to the eastern shores of the Caspian Sea. For half a century they rested, ruling over Germans and Slavs.

In one respect the Visigoths had an advantage over the Ostrogoths. The Visigothic kingdom, in what had once been Dacia, bordered on the powerful Roman Empire, which lay just across the lower Danube. In 375, with the Huns at their backs, some eighty thousands Visigoths humbly asked permission to enter the Empire as refugees.

Roman officials had several choices. They might cold-bloodedly have refused permission and allowed the Visigoths to be cut to pieces or enslaved by the pursuing Huns. The officials might, on the other hand, have granted entry to the Visigoths and enlisted them in the Roman army, where, by good treatment, they might have become loyal soldiers.

The Romans did neither. They were soft-hearted enough to

allow the Visigoths entry and then hard-hearted enough to mistreat them. The Romans disarmed the Visigoths, held their children as hostages, sneered at them as cowards who had fled the Huns, and then attempted to fleece them by selling them food at exorbitant prices.

It might not have been so bad if the Romans had really thoroughly disarmed the Visigoths, but that had been bungled, too. The angry Visigoths found arms enough to turn on their tormentors and ravage the province for food and further arms. Before the Romans knew what had happened, they found they had given entry not to a gang of fugitives but to a hostile army.

At that time, the Eastern Roman Emperor was a man named Valens, a not very capable hothead. He might have waited for reinforcements from the young Western Emperor, Gratian, but Valens was sure he would have no trouble and plunged ahead. Perhaps he hungered to become a new "Gothicus."

The Visigoths, however, were not the Goths of old. They had learned something important from the Hunnish enemy, the value of the strong metal stirrup. They had commandeered horses and had built up a cavalry. Indeed, their forces included some Huns who had drifted across the Danube to join the Visigothic band.

Unfortunately for the Visigoths, their cavalry was out foraging for food when the Roman army approached the rebellious host at Adrianople, only a hundred miles east of Constantinople. The Visigothic leader, Fritigern, could not fight the legionaries with his foot soldiers only, so it was necessary to delay battle. The only way he could do that was to offer to surrender while sending out messengers to order his cavalry back in a hurry.

Valens was perfectly willing to accept the surrender and set hard terms. Fritigern agreed to them but raised small points and argued them tirelessly. For several hours, the Roman soldiers stood, armed and impatient, under a hot sun without water, while the leaders talked and talked and talked, and Fritigern watched anxiously for the cloud of horsemen on the horizon.

Finally, some of the infuriated Romans began fighting without waiting for orders, but battle had barely been engaged when the Gothic cavalry raced onto the scene and fell upon the surprised legions. Already weary and dispirited, the Romans could put up little resistance. In attempting to back away from the horses, their formation was thrown into utter disorder and they became nothing but a crowded mass to be cut down helplessly. The army was wiped out, and Valens himself was killed.

The Battle of Adrianople was a key event in history. It represented the first complete breach of the northern boundaries of the Roman Empire, for the Visigoths were never pushed out again.

In addition, the Roman legions had been smashed and were never again an effective fighting force. It was the horseman and his stirrup that now gained the upper hand and in this form of fighting the barbarian was superior to the Roman.

The forces of civilization began to recede.

2

THE GOTHIC KINGDOMS

ALARIC THE BOLD

Despite Fritigern's victory at Adrianople, his later successes were sharply limited. He could raid and ravage at will, for the Romans would not meet him again in an open fight. They would lock themselves inside their fortified cities and these Fritigern could not take. For that, he needed complex siege machinery which the Visigoths did not have.

Unable to fight effectively, the Visigoths were ready to consider some arrangement and the new Emperor, Theodosius I, was ready to negotiate with them. He assigned the Visigoths land south of the Danube, displacing the older Roman landowners who had already been killed or forced to flee in any case.

The Visigoths, willing to settle down and enjoy the life of landed proprietors, turned Christian in increasing numbers until paganism virtually vanished among them.

They gave as well as took. While they learned to speak Latin and to live in civilized manner, they also introduced a new form of dress.

Throughout the ancient civilized world, men and women alike had worn flowing clothing, which we would today describe as robes, skirts, or dresses. When this drapery got in the way of work, it could be raised out of the way and bound in a belt or sash. (This is what was meant by the expression "to gird one's loins.")

In the colder north, however, bare legs were no fun, and for the sake of warmth, the tribespeople wore heavier, closer-fitting robes. For women these were fine, but they only got in the way of men in battle, especially if the warriors were horsemen. Therefore, the robe was split and each leg was separately encased, so that the result was what we now call trousers. This barbarian invention was introduced into the civilized world only in the time of the decline of Rome and has stayed with us to this day.

The Visigoths had turned Arian Christian, and partly because they had done so, Arianism grew much less popular among the Romans themselves. It became a German religion in Roman eyes, and if the Romans dared not oppose the barbarian armies militarily they could at least express their national feelings by refusing the German religion. Theodosius was the first Roman Emperor to be wholeheartedly Catholic. He suppressed not only the open profession of paganism in the Empire, but Arianism as well — among the Romans, that is, for there was nothing he could do about the Germans.

Theodosius, in addition to granting land to the Visigoths, carefully cultivated the friendship of their chiefs. After Fritigern's death, a man named Alaric became chief of the Visigoths and Theodosius made sure that Alaric remained a friend of his.

Indeed, the time had now come when the Germans were not only serving in the army ranks, but were officers as well, even generals. After all, an army made up almost entirely of barbarians would best obey a barbarian leader.

One such leader, an ally of Theodosius in his dealings with the Visigoths, was a Frank named Arbogast. Theodosius placed Arbogast in charge of the military forces in Gaul and he became the virtual overlord of the western half of the Empire.

Theoretically, a teen-ager, Valentinian II, was Western Emperor, but the worst of making a general the number two man in the government is that he has the power to make himself number one if he wishes. When Valentinian II grew old enough to demand an active share in the government, he died suddenly, in 392, and most people were certain he had been assassinated at Arbogast's order.

The Frankish general promptly raised a harmless scholar to the post of Emperor and then began to make a strong effort to abolish Christianity and restore paganism. Though Theodosius was willing to swallow the death of his colleague, he could not endure this attack on religion. A civil war followed, and in 394, Theodosius' barbarian soldiers completely defeated those of Arbogast, who killed himself.

Once again (and for the last time) a single Emperor ruled over the length and breadth of a Roman Empire that was still intact.

Theodosius could not do without German warriors, however, since scarcely any other kind existed within the Empire. He relied heavily on one Flavius Stilicho, who is thought to have been a member of a German tribe called the Vandals. Now coming into prominence for the first time, the Vandals had been defeated by the Visigoths in the days before the Hunnish invasion and numbers had made their way into the Roman Empire. Presumably Stilicho was one of these, or the descendant of one of them.

When Theodosius I died in 395, he divided the Empire between his two young and incapable sons. The older, Arcadius, became Eastern Roman Emperor; the younger, Honorius, Western Roman Emperor. Each was put under German guardianship: Stilicho was in control in the West, while a warrior named Rufinus ruled in the East.

Alaric the Visigoth, who had counted on his friendship with Theodosius to insure him a huge inheritance, was most indignant at being left with no more than he already had. He therefore gathered his Visigothic clan about him and marched on Constantinople. Failing to take the city, he moved into Greece, ravishing at will.

This was the first example of something which the Roman provinces were now to become constantly familiar with — a chieftain's war band. The bands were rather like modern street gangs multiplied many times — lawless, destructive, and held together by personal loyalty to a commander. When the commander enforced strict discipline, the situation wasn't too bad; when he didn't, the results were nightmarish.

The war bands were few in number. It is estimated that the population of the Roman Empire was about sixty million at this time, and that all the Germans who invaded the Empire from beginning to end could not have been more than ten million. However, a war band consisted almost entirely of wild warriors who knew how to handle their weapons and had no hesitation in doing so, whereas the people they met were mostly peasants and citizens who knew nothing about organized fighting. In very much the same way a modern street gang can terrorize an entire section of a city, though the people they terrorize may outnumber them fifty to one.

But where were the Roman armies, whose duty it was to protect those terrorized citizens? Doing nothing, and worse than nothing, unfortunately.

Either Rufinus or Stilicho might have taken care of Alaric, but the two barbarian rulers of the Empire were far too busy intriguing against each other. Eventually, the Eastern Empire got rid of Alaric, not by defeating him in battle, but by bribing him to march westward into the Western Empire.

In 402, and again in 403, Alaric entered northern Italy and each time he was defeated by Stilicho.

This did not, however, cancel out the disastrous defeat of the Romans at Adrianople a generation before. In the first place, the Visigoths were not driven out of the Empire, merely out of Italy. In the second place, the victory over the Visigoths was as ruinous in its way as the earlier defeat had been.

The Romans had a long frontier and for three centuries now they had been desperately trying to guard it. The Germans had a tremendous advantage here. The Romans had to guard it *all;* the Germans merely had to choose some weak point, any weak point, and concentrate their forces there. The Germans might be fewer in numbers altogether, but at whatever point they chose, they would have local superiority.

With increasing difficulty, the Romans had wearily plugged each gap and stemmed each leak. And now, when Stilicho flung back Alaric, the border broke once and for all. Stilicho had been obliged to call in his armies in Gaul to fight Alaric, and left behind, guarding the crucial Rhine River, was nothing but a skeleton force.

On the last day of 406, the Rhine was stormed by the German tribes. The southern confederation of the Alemanni (or, at least, those among them called Sueves by the writers of the time) punched into Gaul over the upper Rhine. They were accompanied by Vandals and also by a non-German tribe, the Alani (originally an east European people who had fled westward before the Huns).

The only Roman troops that could be gathered to oppose them were the legions on the island of Britain. These legions, however, had set up a rival Emperor of their own. In 407, the would-be Emperor brought his troops into Gaul, not to fight the

Germans but to strike a bargain with them whereby they would get land and he would get their support. He was captured and executed by other Romans and his troops dispersed. All that had been accomplished was the complete abandonment of Britain after over three centuries of Roman occupation — and Gaul still remained helpless.

Stilicho might possibly have stabilized the situation, but the weak Emperor Honorius feared his strong general more than he feared the barbarian armies. Perhaps he remembered the death of Valentinian II at the hands of Arbogast the Frank a decade and a half before, and determined to strike first. In 408, he arranged to have Stilicho assassinated, and the last hope for the salvation of the Western Empire vanished.

The Sueves and Vandals ravaged across the full breadth of Gaul and entered Spain in 409. There was nothing to stop them.

What's more, in the chaos that followed the death of Stilicho, Alaric decided to lead his Visigothic band into Italy again. There was now no strong general to oppose him. In fact, many of Rome's own troops, who were of barbarian origin after all, indignantly deserted to Alaric's side after the assassination of their leader.

Alaric marched southward toward Rome, and Honorius and his court fled to the city of Ravenna, 180 miles to the north. In a way, Honorius seemed to be hurrying toward the enemy, but Ravenna was well fortified, surrounded by difficult marshland and well-nigh impregnable.

Alaric found himself at the very walls of Rome and attempted to negotiate good terms for himself as the price of the city's safety. The Roman civic leaders, in their panic, were ready to promise anything, and Alaric held off. However, Honorius and his court, safe in Ravenna, would yield nothing. Eventually, in 410, Alaric lost patience and sent his war band into the city streets.

For three days, the Visigoths occupied Rome, but little damage was done to it. Alaric and his troops seemed awed at the very name of Rome and acted more like gawking sightseers than anything else.

The psychological damage was enormous, though. Rome had been taken, however gently. Eight hundred years before, when Rome was but a village, the Gauls had taken it. Since then, no foreign army had passed its walls — until now. Its image was ruined forever.

After leaving Rome, Alaric led his band southward, apparently with some plan to cross into Africa, where he might set up a permanent kingdom. He reached the tip of Italy's "toe" and prepared a fleet to carry him across the sea, but his ships were wrecked in a storm and he abandoned the notion.

He marched northward again, but died almost at once, in the same year in which he had taken Rome. The Visigoths, forced to bury their leader in a strange land, diverted the current of a stream near the city of Cosenza in the Italian toe. They buried him under its bed, then allowed the waters to return, and killed the peasants they had forced to do the work. The secret hiding place would now be safe from disturbance.

THE KINGDOM OF TOULOUSE

The Visigoths, now under the leadership of Ataulf, the brother-in-law of Alaric, continued to wander northward, looking for a place to settle.

They were no longer quite the people their fathers had been, who a generation earlier had fled across the Danube before the Huns. Forty years of exposure to Roman civilization had softened them into an appreciation of the culture. They wanted land and power, but were satisfied to have it along with the acceptance of the imperial ideal.

So eager were the Visigoths to be Roman that Ataulf kidnaped and married Galla Placidia, the sister of the Western Emperor, Honorius. The Visigoths undoubtedly felt pleased and honored at this marital coup. It is a measure of the weakness of the Empire that the Emperor could not prevent his sister from being forced into marriage with a barbarian.

Considerations of politics may even have recommended the marriage as a good move for the Romans. The imperial government realized the attraction Roman culture had for the Visigoths and tried to make use of that. To have the Visigoth leader tied to the imperial court by marriage could be useful.

The Romans could not defeat the multiplicity of barbarians who were now infesting the western provinces, but why could they not use one set of barbarians against another? One set would surely be destroyed, and perhaps the two might fight each other into mutual destruction.

The Visigoths were therefore given the title of "Roman allies" and encouraged to pass through Gaul and into Spain. There they could fight against the enemies of the Romans — the Sueves and the Vandals.

The Visigoths were only too glad to oblige. In 414, they moved into Spain and by 415 had virtually cleared the province of its earlier invaders. Some Sueves clung to the far northwest of Spain and some Vandals to the far south. Those, too, might have been wiped out, but the alarmed Romans, not anxious to see the Visigoths grow too powerful, intervened and coaxed them out of Spain.

The Visigoths were back in Gaul now and, with Roman approval, finally found the home they were looking for. In 419, they were given broad districts in southwestern Gaul and they made their capital at the city of Toulouse.

That same year, Theodoric I, a son of Alaric, began to rule over the Visigoths. He was the first Visigothic chieftain to be

more than a warlord. He was a king outright, ruling over what
came to be called the Kingdom of Toulouse and maintaining
that position for over thirty years.

The founding of the Kingdom of Toulouse was an enormously important event. For the first time, a German tribe had
established itself as an essentially independent kingdom within
the borders of the Empire.

To be sure, a stolid pretense was carried on by both sides.
The Roman Empire never admitted that its territory was lost
or that the Kingdom of Toulouse (or any other German kingdom later set up) was truly independent. The imperial view
was that the barbarians merely occupied Roman territory and
that they did this legally only insofar as they were Roman officials. The Emperor made the barbarian kings into "Roman
generals" and gave them other titles. The pretense always was
that the kings, whatever they did, were following imperial
orders.

And the German leadership played along with this. Theodoric called himself King of the Visigoths and, in theory, ruled
over his own compatriots only. The territory remained Roman,
in theory, and the Roman population remained under Roman
law, as administered by the Roman civil service. Theodoric
and the other German kings were always delighted to accept
Roman titles, however empty they were. (It was many centuries before the people of Europe could bring themselves to
admit that the Roman Empire no longer really existed. Its
ghost continued to haunt the world right down into modern
times.)

In one respect, the Visigothic rule could not be shrugged off.
The Visigoths took for themselves two-thirds of the land of the
kingdom, leaving only the remaining third to the older Roman
ruling class. As usual, though, it made little difference to the
peasantry who the landlords were. Indeed, if the Visigoths established a stable government with a reasonably efficient administration (as they did), the peasants were better off under

them than under feeble Romans who could not protect them against raiding barbarians.

The example of Toulouse was not lost on other tribes. The Sueves who remained in northwestern Spain and who had survived the earlier Visigothic attack, now set up a kingdom of their own there on much the same terms as that of Toulouse.

The Vandals in southern Spain seized upon a chance offered them by two intriguing and quarreling Roman generals. They hired themselves out to one of the generals and were ferried over to North Africa in Roman ships, in 429. There, under their capable leader Gaiseric, they took over the land for themselves. The Vandal kingdom was centered about the great city of Carthage, which fell to them in 439. The Vandals and Sueves also adopted Arian Christianity soon after their irruption into imperial territory.

Indeed, it is easily possible to underestimate these early invaders of the Empire. They were not as bad as they were pictured by the Roman writers of the time, whose feelings were tinged by national and religious enmity. All were eager to adopt Roman ways and in some ways they tried to improve society. Gaiseric, for instance, closed the bawdy houses in Carthage and tried to establish a more puritanical way of life.

THE HUNS AGAIN

There was still hope, then, that Rome might withstand the shock of the invasions, that the invaders might be digested and made into Romans, and that the Emperors might rule as before. The great barrier was religious. The Germans were Arians, and to the Roman population, which was so overwhelmingly Catholic, this was much worse than the fact that they were Germans.

Yet even that might have eventually been smoothed over. If only history could be made to stop at some point, then almost any change could be absorbed.

But history won't stop. Rome was falling apart, and faster than one set of invaders could be Romanized and absorbed, new sets of invaders, raw and barbaric, plunged inward. These new waves might have come on their own, but actually they were pushed, for once again the Huns were on the march.

After their conquest of the Ostrogothic and Visigothic territories a half century before, the Huns had remained quiet. In 433, however, a ruler named Attila reached the throne. Shrewd, ambitious, and by no means an utter barbarian, he embarked the Huns once more on an aggressive policy of expansion. Through most of his reign, he directed his attacks southward across the Danube and spread ruin and pillage among the provinces of the Eastern Empire, exacting much in the way of loot and tribute.

He then moved westward for mixed reasons. The Eastern Empire was anxious to bribe him to move on as they had once bribed Alaric to do, a generation before. Besides, the Eastern Empire was putting up a desperate defense and Attila rightly felt that the Western Empire, weaker and farther advanced in disintegration, would make much easier pickings.

He pushed his army westward across Germany, forcing some of the tribes to flee across the Rhine before him. Among these were the Burgundians, who had dwelt along the central Rhine and who now poured into southwestern Gaul, occupying the land around Lake Geneva. Farther north, the Franks crossed the lower Rhine and pushed into northern France.

In 451, the Huns themselves crossed the Rhine and for the first and only time in history, Altaic warriors were west of that river. (Europe was to tremble before invasions of other Asian warriors, including Mongols and Turks, but none were ever destined to move this far west.) At this moment, the Hunnish realm stood at its peak, controlling a swatch of territory across central and eastern Europe that was twenty-five-hundred miles wide. It almost equaled the Roman Empire in size, though it was far less populous, civilized and prosperous.

The Western Emperor at this time was Valentinian III and his chief general was Flavius Aëtius, a capable man who had spent much time with the Visigoths and, for that matter, with the Huns.

Aëtius had upheld the imperial burden in Gaul for years, maneuvering one set of barbarians into fighting another, so that no one group could grow too strong. He also engaged in vicious intrigues against other imperial generals, and it is hard to say whether he did more good than harm to Rome in the long run, for he never seemed to hesitate to put his personal welfare ahead of that of the government.

It was his rivalry with another general, for instance, that led to the establishment of the Vandal kingdom in North Africa and the loss, to Rome, of an important source of grain.

In his time, Aëtius had fought against the Visigoths and had cheerfully used Hunnish troops whenever they were willing to fight on his side. But now it was the Huns who were the chief enemy and Aëtius made a quick about-face. He made an alliance with his old enemy, the aged Theodoric I, king of the Visigoths, and together with other German allies, including the Franks and the Burgundians, they turned upon the Huns.

Nor was Attila's army exclusively Hunnish. He had many German allies and a strong Ostrogothic contingent, for the Ostrogoths had now been under Hunnish rule for eighty years.

Attila tried to split the forces against him by announcing that he had not come to fight the Empire, but only the Visigoths. He knew Aëtius well and felt that Aëtius could easily be made to fall back and let the Huns and Visigoths fight it out. For once, though, Aëtius did not take the dirty way out. He held firm.

Before the Imperials could reach him, Attila had moved to the very walls of Aurelianum (the modern Orléans) and had even gained a foothold within the city. He was forced to move back, though, when the Imperials arrived.

The armies met on the Catalaunian Plains (the chief city of that area is Châlons) about 120 miles northeast of Orléans. It was not so much a battle of Roman versus Hun, as Goth versus Goth.

Aëtius placed his own troops on the left of the line and the Visigoths on the right. Weaker allies were placed in the center where, Aëtius hoped, Attila (who always remained in the center of his own line) would launch the chief attack. And so it happened. The Huns struck at the center and drove inward, while the ends of Aëtius' lines closed upon them and surrounded them. When the battle broke off, the Imperials clearly had the upper hand.

Had the victory been properly pursued, the Huns might well have been wiped out and Attila killed. But Aëtius, the intriguer, felt that his first concern was to keep his allies from growing too strong. Theodoric, the old Visigothic king, had died in the battle, and Aëtius urged the monarch's son and heir, Torismund, to return quickly to Toulouse to secure the succession. The Visigoths were hastily pulled away from the site of the battle and their chance of expanding their own kingdom on the basis of the victory was lost.

This failure of Visigothic expansion suited Aëtius, of course. He was sure he could also count on a civil war to occupy Visigothic energies and he was right. Torismund mounted the throne but within a year was killed by his younger brother, who became Theodoric II.

Though Aëtius thus gained an advantage, he lost the short-term values. With his Visigothic allies gone, Aëtius lacked the strength to pursue the Huns. The result of the battle of the Catalaunian Plains was to force Attila out of Gaul, but entirely because of Aëtius' maneuverings, the battle did not end the Hunnish menace, as it might easily have done.

Attila was able to reorganize his army and catch his breath. In 452, he invaded Italy. He laid siege to Aquileia, a city at the northern tip of the Adriatic Sea, and after three months took and destroyed it. Some of the inhabitants, fleeing from the devastation, took refuge among the swampy lagoons to the west. This, the story goes, served as the initial nucleus of what later became the famous city of Venice.

Italy was as prostrate before Attila as, forty years earlier, it had been before Alaric. The Hun might have taken Rome as the Visigoth had, but he withdrew at the last moment. Some say it was because of Attila's superstitious awe of the aura of Rome and of Pope Leo I, who came to meet him in full papal regalia with the plea that Rome be left unharmed. Some, less romantic, say it was because of a sizable gift of gold that Pope Leo brought with him.

In any case, Attila left Italy. Back in his own barbaric camp in 453, he married again, adding one more wife to his numerous harem. He partook of a vast feast, then retired to his tent where during the night he died, apparently of a stroke, possibly brought on by too much celebrating.

His realm was divided between his many sons and broke up almost at once under the impact of a German revolt that erupted as soon as news of Attila's death spread. The Hunnish dominion collapsed and the Huns disappeared from history.

LAW AND LANGUAGE

Meanwhile, Aëtius, who had been unable to do a thing against Attila during his stay in Italy, found his own stock plummeting. The Emperor Valentinian III viewed him with suspicion (perhaps rightly so) and had him assassinated in September of 454, as, half a century before, Honorius had done away with Stilicho.

The results were just as disastrous. Aëtius' soldiers were driven to fury and two of them assassinated Valentinian in early 455. Rome was thrown into confusion and once again the way lay open for a conqueror.

This time it was Gaiseric, who had now been ruling over the Vandal kingdom in North Africa for a quarter of a century.

He was the only one of the barbarian rulers of fragments of the Empire to have developed a fleet, and he controlled a number of the larger Mediterranean islands.

Taking advantage of intrigue within the city, he led a fleet of ships to the mouth of the Tiber in June, 455. There was no opposition. The Vandals remained for two weeks, systematically removing all that was movable and valuable for carting off to Carthage. There was no useless destruction, no sadistic carnage. Rome was impoverished but, as after Alaric's sack, she remained intact. It is ironic, therefore, that the bitter Roman denunciation of the thefts of the Vandals have made the term "vandal" today synonymous with one who senselessly destroys — something which was precisely what the Vandals on this occasion did not do.

By now the Roman imperial government in the West had no strength at all. The Emperor had become a mere puppet of rival generals. Theodoric II of the Visigoths had all five fingers dipped into such intrigue. It is really a dramatic example of the turns of history. Eighty years before, the Visigoths had been refugees on the Danube. Now they were masters of a kingdom at the other end of the Empire and the makers and unmakers of Emperors as well.

Theodoric's intrigues weren't always successful, but that scarcely mattered. By helping to keep Rome in turmoil, he managed to expand his own kingdom. Aëtius' decision to sacrifice the victory at the Catalaunian Plains for the sake of preventing Visigothic expansion had bought Rome only a decade or so of time.

Now the Visigothic kingdom extended to the Rhone River on the east and to the Loire River on the north. A full third of Gaul was in Visigothic hands. What's more, Theodoric began expanding southward into Spain, too. In 466, however, he fell to danger from within. He was assassinated by his brother Euric, who became king by that most unanswerable of rights, the right of murder.

Under Euric, the Visigothic kingdom reached the pinnacle of its power. Virtually all of Spain fell under his control. The Sueves in the northwestern corner of that peninsula maintained a precarious independence but acknowledged his overlordship.

The independent status of the Kingdom of Toulouse was pushed forward another step. Euric found it uncomfortable to rule the kingdom under two sets of laws, one for the Visigothic aristocracy and one for the Roman subjects, and indeed it was a most inefficient arrangement. One law must hold for all.

But in this case, it was necessary to know what the law was, and Euric published the first written code of Visigothic law to apply uniformly throughout the land.

And as law became one, language was also becoming one. The Visigoths spoke a Germanic language to begin with, but they made up a minority in the Roman provinces they ruled over and could not hope to impose their language on their subjects. It was they, rather, who strove to adopt Latin; all the more so since Latin was the vehicle of the Roman civilization they admired so.

In the stress of the times, however, Latin was already beginning to break down into several dialects. The level of education was falling and Latin was losing some of its classic subtlety and intricacy. Naturally, the decay took different directions in different provinces. Furthermore, the German overlords, de-

prived of a classical education, were bound to speak a kind of
"pidgin-Latin" which varied from region to region.

These dialects slowly developed into the various Romance
languages: French, Italian, Spanish, Portuguese, and so on.

Latin itself was never forgotten, of course, and it remained
(and still remains) the language of the Catholic Church. For
many centuries there was the feeling that the "vulgar tongues"
(a phrase synonymous with "language of the uneducated")
were unsuitable for use by educated men.

But of what use was that? Since all the peasants, both men
and women, as well as the women of the upper classes, were
never educated, even the most saintly of churchmen and the
most rarefied of scholars could not make do on Latin alone. He
had also to learn the vulgar tongue, for who could go through
life without ever speaking to women?

In the end, therefore, Latin became a "dead" language, while
the vulgar tongues became living languages of great subtlety
and the vehicles of a rich literature.

There remained, though, the old sticking point of religion.
Though law and language were melting into one, the Roman
underlings were ardent Catholics and the Visigothic overlords
were Arians. Euric was, in fact, an unusually fervent Arian and
his Catholic subjects had reason to complain of persecution.

In 484, Euric died and his son Alaric II succeeded. In some
ways matters improved. In 506, Alaric presented a new code of
laws, based more closely on Roman rather than Visigothic customs, so that it proved more acceptable to his subjects. He was
also more tolerant in religious matters and persecution of Catholics ceased.

In fact, Alaric II seemed sincerely desirous of drawing all
those he ruled into common harmony. It would be pleasant if
he had succeeded, but it was too late. Events outside Toulouse,
as we shall see, were destined to blunt the Visigothic rise, and
the future of Europe lay elsewhere.

THE GREATEST OF THE GOTHS

During Euric's rule, the dominions over which the Western imperial government had any real power had shrunk to Italy itself. Its armies were composed exclusively of German mercenaries, but the Emperor, the government officials, and the Italian landowning class were still Roman.

The German mercenaries were gradually growing dissatisfied with this. In Gaul, in Spain, and in North Africa, their countrymen ruled. They had land and power. Why, then, in Italy, should they allow themselves to be governed by decadent Romans? What they wanted was land, and their leader, Odoacer, pressed that demand.

The Romans refused and Odoacer decided to take for himself what he wasn't being given. On September 4, 476, he forced the Emperor Romulus Augustulus (a completely powerless teen-ager) to abdicate. Odoacer did not bother to choose a new imperial puppet; he simply took over the control of Italy for himself.

It is for this reason that 476 is often given as the date of the "fall of the Roman Empire." That date, however, is a false one. No one at this period of time considered that the Roman Empire had "fallen." It clearly still existed and was the most powerful realm in Europe. Its capital was at Constantinople and its Emperor was Zeno.

Since there was no Emperor ruling in Italy, Zeno considered himself the sole Emperor ruling over the entire Empire, including Italy (and Gaul and Spain and Africa, for that matter). Indeed, Zeno bestowed the rank of patrician on Odoacer, who ruled Italy (in theory) as Zeno's deputy. Odoacer acknowl-

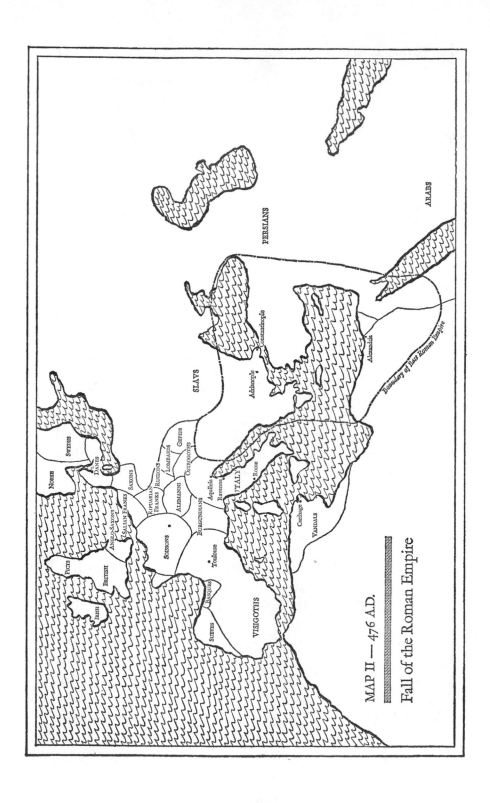

MAP II — 476 A.D.

Fall of the Roman Empire

edged Zeno's overlordship and never called himself king of Italy.

As Odoacer grew stronger, however, Zeno grew uncomfortable. He looked about for some tool that would neutralize the German ruler of Italy, and he found it in the Ostrogoths.

For eighty years, the Ostrogoths had been under the control of the Huns and had fought alongside them, notably at the battle of the Catalaunian Plains. With the breakup of the Hunnish realm after Attila's death, the Ostrogoths regained their freedom. They were converted to Arian Christianity and settled south of the Danube where, a century before, their Visigothic cousins had dwelt, and where now they, like the Visigoths before them, were a constant threat to the Eastern Empire.

In 474, a young man named Theodoric succeeded as tribal chieftain over the Ostrogoths. He had served as Roman hostage in Constantinople while a boy and there he learned to appreciate Roman culture. Now, as tribal leader, however, he had no hesitation in leading his men against the Romans and in doing so with considerable competence and success.

It seemed to Zeno, then, that he could kill two birds with one stone. He could deputize Theodoric the Ostrogoth and send him on the service of the Empire in war against Odoacer in Italy. In that way, he would certainly get rid of the troublesome Ostrogoths. With luck, the two barbarian groups might fight themselves to a standstill in Italy and he himself could regain the peninsula.

Theodoric was by no means reluctant to go, and in 488, he turned westward. The entire Ostrogothic nation followed him; not the warriors alone, but the women and children, too.

Theodoric fought two battles in northern Italy and was victorious in both. Odoacer was forced to retreat into the impregnable Ravenna with what forces he could salvage. The rest of Italy fell under Ostrogothic rule and even Sicily was taken by them from the Vandals. (Gaiseric was now dead and the Vandals were in decline.)

Only Ravenna held out, but it held out four years. Finally, in 493, Theodoric persuaded Odoacer to give in by offering a generous compromise. They were to rule jointly, as completely equal co-kings. Considering that Theodoric ruled the entire peninsula and Odoacer had but a single city, these seemed generous terms. Odoacer accepted.

The two rulers met gladly, feasted for days, and then when Odoacer was thoroughly relaxed, Theodoric had him stabbed. Some say the Ostrogoth did the job with his own hand.

This piece of treachery has been roundly condemned by historians since, but Theodoric might well have argued that he was justified in his act. A double rule would surely not have worked and would have led to civil war. Theodoric put an end to war and prevented future war by this act, and was able to bring Italy, quickly, under a peaceful and steady rule.

Theodoric knew he could offer such a rule and did, in fact, produce it, turning out to be the greatest of the Goths. During his thirty-three-year reign, Italy was a land of peace and prosperity. She had never "had it so good" in centuries.

Theodoric considered himself the guardian of Roman culture. He saw to it that Ostrogoths and Romans lived in amity and that the Romans were never mistreated by the Ostrogothic warriors. The Ostrogoths owned one-third of the land, but as far as possible this was taken from government land so that the Roman landowners were disturbed no more than necessary.

The Ostrogoths made up the army, but only Romans manned the civil service. Theodoric named the consuls who, in theory, ruled the city of Rome, but he was careful always to name Romans. Italy remained under Roman law and continued to adhere to Roman customs. The Pope, for instance, dated his documents by the years of reign of the Emperor in Constantinople as though he and not Theodoric were overlord of Italy, and Theodoric allowed it, preferring the substance of rule to the shadow.

Theodoric also saw to the physical betterment of Italy. By putting an end to war and devastation and by rigidly minimizing corruption he could, at the same time, reduce taxes and increase useful expenditures. He dredged harbors, drained marshes, rebuilt aqueducts, erected churches, and organized games in the circus. It was almost like the old days.

Because Zeno, the Eastern Emperor, had died before Theodoric had established his rule over Italy, he didn't see his apparently shrewd policy backfire, or witness the replacement of the strong Odoacer by the much stronger Theodoric. Zeno's successor, Anastasius, did witness it and had no choice but to recognize Theodoric's rule in 497.

In return, Theodoric tried to be a good neighbor to the Emperor at Constantinople. He extended his own power across the Alps to the Danube, and west of the Alps into southwestern Gaul, over regions he took from the Burgundians. He never took, or even threatened, an inch of the territory of the Eastern Empire, however.

Theodoric was an Arian Christian, of course, but he maintained a rigid policy of toleration, interfering in no way with the Catholic worship of his Roman subjects. Nor did he allow proselytization among them. In fact, when a papal election was disputed, both sides welcomed Theodoric's mediation, confident of his justice even though he was an Arian. His tolerance went beyond Christianity, too, for he protected the Jews of his realm.

Under Theodoric, Italy emitted a few last feeble rays of Roman scholarship.

The chief Italian scholar of Theodoric's time was Anicius Manlius Severinus Boethius. Born in 480, Boethius was the last of the ancient philosophers. He served as consul in 510, and his two sons served as consuls together in 522. The feeling that Rome was still what it had been was so strong that Boethius felt he had reached the summit of happiness at seeing his sons

achieve the eminence of a title which was, in truth, quite meaningless except for the honor it conferred.

Boethius translated some of the works of Aristotle into Latin
and wrote commentaries on Cicero, Euclid, and others of the
ancients. It was his works, rather than the originals — his
translation of Aristotle's *Logic,* for instance — that survived
through the next six centuries.

Another Roman, Flavius Magnus Aurelius Cassiodorus, who
was born in 490 and survived to the patriarchal age of ninety-
five, served as treasurer under Theodoric and his successors.
He devoted his life to the acquisition of learning, and hoped to
found a Christian University in Rome to reverse the gradual
decay of education. The times were not suitable, however, and
there was no way in which secular society could support such
an educational institution. He had to turn to religion. He
founded two monasteries, granting them support in return for
their assurance that they would gather worthwhile books of all
sorts and copy them.

It was Cassiodorus who established the connection between
monks and the copying of manuscripts. This was crucial in
keeping lit, however dimly, the lamp of learning in the harsh
centuries that were on their way.

Cassiodorus wrote voluminously in the fields of history, theology, and grammar. Theodoric had him write a history of the
Goths which was intended to serve as pro-Gothic propaganda
and present them in a favorable light to the Roman populace.
This book is, unfortunately, lost, but from later references, we
gather that Cassiodorus identified the Goths with the ancient
Scythians and claimed that since the Scythians had adopted
Graeco-Roman culture long before, the Goths ought not be
considered barbarians.

This is quite wrong, of course. The Scythians lived north of
the Black Sea about 350 B.C. and the Ostrogoths lived there
about A.D. 350, but there is no other connection. The Scythians

were utterly gone five centuries before the Ostrogoths appeared on the scene.

If we pause, then, in the year 500, it might seem that the ancient world was even yet not lost. The Eastern Empire was intact and the better part of the Western Empire made up two enlightened Gothic kingdoms. Almost all of Spain and half of Gaul were under Alaric II the Visigoth. Italy and the upper Danube were under the control of Theodoric I the Ostrogoth. Both were enlightened and civilized monarchs and both had the interests of all their subjects, Roman as well as Gothic, at heart. Both were tolerant in religion as well.

What went wrong?

Well, one can't stop history. The German invasions were not yet over.

3

THE DARKNESS COMES

CLOVIS

Through all the troubles that had begun with the westward
outpouring of the Huns, the name of the Franks has hardly
been mentioned. They had been foremost in invading Gaul in
Julian's time in 355, but for more than a century afterward they
had been rather tame, as though their defeat at Julian's hand
had been a salutary and long-remembered lesson.

Indeed, throughout that century, they had acted, for the
most part, as loyal allies of Rome and as defenders of the Empire against their fellow Germans. It was to a Frank, Arbogast,
that Theodosius had entrusted the care of the Western Empire
(although that trust had been betrayed). When the Sueves
and Vandals broke into Gaul after Stilicho's defeat of Alaric,
the Franks fought on the Roman side.

To be sure, the Franks had finally been forced to invade Gaul
themselves in their attempt to flee the advance of Attila the

Hun, but once there they fought loyally with Aëtius against the Huns at the Battle of the Catalaunian Plains.

After the Huns were gone, certain Franks found themselves in possession of the northeastern section of Gaul. They were a group known as the Salian Franks because in Roman times they had lived along the Sala River, one of the streams making up the Rhine Delta. (It is now known as the Ijssel River and flows north through the central Netherlands.) Their ruler, Childeric I, acted always as a Roman ally and established his capital, with Roman permission formally but helplessly granted, in what is now Tournai. This is in modern Belgium, near the French border, 120 miles southwest of the Rhine.

Childeric was the son of Merovech (or, in Latin, Merovaeus) and for that reason he and his descendants represent the "Merovingian dynasty." The whole line was characterized by the possession of long hair as a symbol of royalty. If a king was deposed, his hair was cut as a sign of deposition.

In 481, when Odoacer was ruling over Italy and Euric over the Visigoths, Childeric died and his fifteen-year-old son succeeded. The son's name was Chlodovech, but he is better known to us by the simplified version of his name, Clovis. (Actually, he should be called Clovis I.)

Clovis was one of those men who, on succeeding to a throne, can think of nothing but war and aggrandizement. His driving obsession was to expand his holdings as far as he could, and he began to cast about for the best place to begin.

To anyone lacking Clovis's drive, the case would have seemed hopeless. He had a narrow realm with no record of an-cestral derring-do. There were other Frankish tribes, notably the Ripuarian Franks, who lived along the Rhine River, east of Clovis's territories, and who might grow peevish if Clovis at-tempted too much.

To Clovis, however, a way out suggested itself. There was a section of northern Gaul which was under the control of a Ro-man named Syagrius. He did not rule in the name of a nonexistent imperial court in Italy, but entirely on his own. His capital was at the city of Soissons, eighty-five miles south of Tournai, and his dominions are therefore referred to as the Kingdom of Soissons.

The Kingdom of Soissons represented the only stretch of land in what had once been the Western Empire which was not ruled by a German warrior band. Against Syagrius, Clovis could appeal to the national pride of the other Frankish tribes. He could march against Syagrius as the head of an army of allies or, at the very least, with the other tribes neutral and unthreatening in his rear.

In 486, Clovis beat Syagrius in one quick battle and the last bit of Roman territory in the West fell to the Germans. Clovis annexed it all and his realm was suddenly tripled in size so that he found himself a "great power." What's more, his prestige was enormously enhanced and the other Frankish tribes who had been willing to help found that they had helped themselves to a master.

Syagrius fled to Alaric II, the Visigoth, and Clovis further enhanced his standing in the eyes of his warriors by fearlessly demanding his defeated enemy of the powerful Visigoth, and getting him, too. Alaric, young, newly crowned, and not anxious for war, was unheroic enough to yield to Clovis's loud threats. He gave up the fugitive, whom Clovis promptly executed.

Clovis made his own capital at Soissons and spent ten years in making sure that the fruits of his victory were secure and that all the Franks would follow where he led.

Once he was confident of that, he had to decide where next to strike. To his south were three German kingdoms. Reading from west to east, they were the Visigoths, the Burgundians, and those Alemanni left in place after the Sueves among them had crossed the Rhine a century before and ended in Spain. Beyond the Alemanni was the newly established kingdom of the Ostrogoths.

The Alemanni, Clovis judged, were the weakest of the three and therefore the logical next victim. In attacking a series of enemies one at a time, though, it is always best to form alliances with the group slated for the number two position on the menu, while number one is being disposed of — if that can be arranged.

Clovis, therefore, wishing to assure the neutrality (if not the help) of the Burgundians, married Clotilda, a princess of that nation, in 493.

To Clovis this was only an item of power politics, but it turned out to be of world consequence, for Clovis was a pagan and Clotilda was a Christian. Clotilda was more than that. The Burgundians, like all the rest of the German tribes within what had once been the Western Empire, were Arians, but Clotilda (and what an important "but") was a Catholic.

Constantly, she importuned her fierce husband to abandon paganism and become a Christian — a Catholic Christian, of course. Clovis held firmly to his paganism but weakened to the extent of allowing his first son to be baptized a Catholic. When the child died almost at once, he frowned and allowed the second to be baptized only after considerable argument. The second son sickened, and when Clovis jeered angrily at the wickedness of baptism, Clotilda prayed fervently and the child recovered. Clovis could not help but be impressed.

In external affairs, things went well. He was ready to pick a fight with the Alemanni, but they saved him the trouble. They were being pushed from the southeast by the expanding kingdom of the Ostrogoths. Of their own accord, then, they turned northward in 496 to attack Clovis, who was thus granted the privilege of fighting in self-righteous self-defense.

Joyfully, Clovis joined battle, but the war was a hard one, for the Alemanni were as fierce as the Franks. There is a story that at the height of the crucial battle, when it seemed that the Alemanni might win, Clovis remembered his wife's constant nagging and struck a bargain with heaven. If his wife's God

would give him the victory, he said, then not only would he
turn Christian, but he would see to it that his entire army
would be suddenly overcome with Christian piety and that
they, too, would be baptized.

The tide of battle turned and Clovis kept his promise. He
and three thousand of his followers were baptized before the
year 496 was over in an impressive religious ceremony at
Reims, twenty-five miles southeast of Soissons.

The conversion was a matter of prime importance. For the
first time, an important group of Germans had become not only
Christians, but Catholic Christians. It meant that in any war
between the Franks and any other group of Germans (Arians
all), the sympathies of the Roman subjects, led by the priesthood, would be on the side of the Franks. It might well make
all the difference and certainly it was an important factor in the
train of events that led to the ultimate victory of the Franks,
and to the fact that it was the Catholic Franks and not the
Arian Goths who were the real inheritors of the mantle of the
Western Empire.

There are some who suspect that Clovis may have foreseen
all this and that he underwent conversion to Catholicism as still
another exercise in shrewd politics and not out of some sudden
inspiration in battle. There is no way of telling.

THE CATHOLIC CONQUEROR

The Burgundians were next on Clovis's menu. One might
suppose that since his wife was a Burgundian princess, the
Frank would find it difficult to fight with them. Not necessarily; relationships among royalty have never prevented war, and
have often encouraged it. This was never truer than in the case

of the Germans who were squabbling over the decaying pieces of the Roman Empire.

As a matter of fact, Clovis did not need to have any qualms of conscience at all (assuming he ever had any, which he probably didn't) at fighting the Burgundians. Conditions were such as to make it possible for him to present himself as a loyal husband avenging the mistreatment of his wife, Clotilda.

The old king of Burgundy, Clotilda's grandfather, had died in 473, while Clovis was still a child, and had left his kingdom to four sons, dividing it up so that each might have a piece.

This was often done by the Germanic kings of the era, who viewed their realms as personal estates to be disposed of at will. When more than one able-bodied son existed, it was customary to give each a section of the kingdom, supposing that they would rule in brotherly amity and unite against a common foe. The fact that this almost never happened did not stop the custom. In almost every case, civil wars would break out and brother would fight brother far more fiercely than either would fight a stranger.

There was, indeed, ruthless fighting among the Burgundian brothers. The oldest brother, Gundobad, whose capital was Lyon, managed to capture and murder the third brother, Chilperic. Clotilda, who was Chilperic's daughter, was just a child at the time, but she would undoubtedly have been killed if she had been caught. She and her sister managed to find refuge with the second brother, Godegesil, whose capital was at Geneva.

When, therefore, it was time for Clovis to turn against the Burgundians, it was logical for him to make a secret pact of friendship with the good brother at Geneva, who had once protected Clovis's queen, and to make ruthless war on the wicked brother at Lyon, who would have killed her.

In 500, Franks and Burgundians met in battle near Dijon, 170 miles southeast of Soissons. Gundobad, unaware of his brother's treaty with Clovis, fully expected fraternal reinforcements

from Geneva. They never came. Gundobad was defeated and
fled. He was pursued, caught, and finally forced to agree to pay
a healthy tribute. The various Burgundian kingdoms became
Frankish puppets and were never to be entirely free again.
Still, they kept their royal family and a certain national identity for a while.

All the land north of the Loire River, from beyond the Rhine
to the Atlantic, now lay under the sway of Clovis. Through his
Burgundian puppets, he controlled southeastern Gaul as well.

But there were still the Goths. South of the Loire lay the
kingdom of the Visigoths under Alaric II. East of the Alps lay
the kingdom of the Ostrogoths under Theodoric I.

Clovis had no trouble deciding which to choose. The Visigoths were nearer at hand and indeed their border lay at points
within 150 miles of Clovis's capital at Soissons. He therefore
prepared for war against the Visigoths.

For all Clovis's victories it might be thought that here at last
he was attempting too much. The Visigoths had been steadily
victorious in war for a century now. Their present king, Alaric
II, mild and just, might have expected the enthusiastic support
of his people against a conqueror who had shown himself over
and over again to be barbarically cruel and brutal.

But there was the factor of religion to consider. Here at last
Clovis could use his own Catholicism to the full. He was
marching against Alaric II, he announced, on behalf of the
Catholic faith, and his war was against heresy.

This meant that the Frankish army, marching into Visigothic
territory, could count on the aid of the population of the land,
while the Visigoths themselves would be fighting in their
own — yet hostile — countryside. The importance of this is
made plain when it is considered that though the Arian Visigoths dominated the land, they were outnumbered four to one
by Catholics.

In 507, the two armies met at Vouille, eighty miles south of
the Loire. Here Clovis won the greatest of all his victories,

smashing the Visigoths and pursuing them far southward. Alaric was killed in the course of the flight, and the story went round that he fell before Clovis's own sword.

That one battle sufficed to hurl the Visigoths out of Gaul altogether, except for a small section of the Mediterranean coast, and to confine their kingdom to Spain.

As for Clovis, he promptly moved his capital south to Paris, which, thanks to the extension of his realm, was now more centrally located than Soissons had been. Paris was not always to remain the capital of the Frankish realm, but Clovis's stay there gave it its first chance to play the role of capital, a role that would one day make it one of the great cultural centers of the world.

Now there remained Theodoric the Ostrogoth.

Theodoric was a man of peace and his efforts were to mediate. In particular, he had tried to prevent war between Alaric and Clovis, and he might have felt some optimism here, for he was related by marriage to both men. Alaric was married to Theodoric's daughter, while Theodoric was married to Clovis's sister. Mediation failed, though, for Clovis was intent on war.

Mistakenly, Theodoric refrained from actually joining his Visigothic son-in-law in the crucial battle against his Frankish brother-in-law. Perhaps he thought that Alaric would win, or that the battle would be indecisive and that he would then have another chance to mediate. If so, the actual event must have cruelly disappointed him. Clovis, he now realized, had grown entirely too strong and must be stopped by war. Nothing else would do.

He made a firm alliance with Gesalric, the illegitimate son of Alaric II, who had now succeeded to rule over the Visigoths. With that done, he led a combined Gothic army into southern Gaul.

There he found an allied army of Franks and Burgundians laying siege to Arles, a Visigothic city in southern Gaul, only forty miles northwest of Marseilles. A battle was fought in 508 and the Franks were defeated. We don't have the details, for we know of Clovis through the histories of a Frankish chronicler who preferred not to speak overmuch of Frankish defeats.

Clovis, stopped at last, was forced to turn on his allies. The Ripuarian Franks had stood loyally by his side through twenty years of conquests, but they still retained their independence under their own chieftain, Sigebert.

According to the tale, Clovis managed to adjust this situation by means of a trick that was diabolical even by his own standards. He managed to persuade Sigebert's own son to kill his father while out hunting, then arranged to have the murderer denounced and executed. That removed both father and son, and it was easy, in 509, for Clovis to have himself elected to fill the vacant position. The Frankish realm, stretching over almost all of Gaul and much of the Rhine Valley, was now completely consolidated.

Although most of Clovis's reign was spent in war and intrigue, in eliminating rivals and smashing armies, he did have time to take care of internal matters, too. He had the Frankish law code edited and recorded in Latin. This, named for Clovis's tribe, is the Salic Law.

The Salic Law was not the first of the Germanic codes to be reduced to writing. Both the Burgundians and the Visigoths had beaten the Franks to that particular punch. The earlier law codes, however, had shown strong Christian and Roman influence. The Salic Law was more purely German and is interesting to historians for that reason. Its most important section was an almost casual comment to the effect that women could not inherit land. This was later to have an important influence on decisions as to which member of a royal house might or might not become king and eventually led to mighty wars that are not, however, part of the subject matter of this book.

Clovis also brought together a church council at Orléans in 511, the first such council that could be considered as bringing together bishops from all of what had once been Gaul.

To say "what had once been Gaul" is to point out that this geographical name, famous since the early days of Roman history, was losing its meaning. The Frankish conquests, unlike those of other Germanic tribes, had been adjacent to their original lands. Because the source of their population was always in reach, they alone of all the Germans could colonize at least some of their conquered land intensively. This was all the easier since Catholic Franks could melt together with the earlier population of Catholic Romans whereas the Arian Goths and Vandals could not.

The Kingdom of Soissons, Clovis's first conquest, became thoroughly Frankish in population. The Franks called it Neustria ("new land") while they referred to the original Frankish territory east of Neustria as Austrasia ("east land").

The southern portion of Gaul, which Clovis took from the Visigoths, remained largely Roman in population, rather than Frankish. It can be referred to as Aquitaine, which is derived from its name as a Roman province. The cultural difference between Frankish Neustria in the north and Roman Aquitaine in the south remained a forceful fact for centuries, and was frequently translated into political separation as well. Even the languages were different, though both (even in the Frankish portion) were descended from Latin. The term "Gaul" then fell out of use, for it no longer signified any clearly defined geographic or cultural unit.

THE ARIAN KING

To Theodoric the Ostrogoth, the victory over Clovis in 508 must have brought only limited satisfaction. To defeat the Frank was better than to be beaten by him, but events were closing in about Theodoric in ways that armies could not help.

He found his greatest difficulty in the fact that the Franks were Catholics. That was something he could not settle with spears. For one thing, it gave the Eastern Empire an opportunity to turn against him.

For nearly twenty years, Theodoric had kept the faith with Constantinople but that did not help him. As soon as Clovis had beaten the Visigoths, Anastasius, the Eastern Emperor, recognized with joy a Catholic champion he could oppose to Theodoric, who might be loyal but who was too strong for the Emperor's taste and, besides, a heretic.

Anastasius sent the news to Clovis that he was being granted the titles of patrician and consul, and the Frankish monarch was transported with joy at the news.

One might think that Clovis was being childish, that he was clapping his hands at empty titles — but not at all. The imperial titles granted him a legitimacy that would count a great deal with his Roman subjects. Furthermore, they made it impossible for Theodoric to claim that Clovis was in illegal possession of the land he had conquered, for the land really belonged to the Empire — as was admitted by all — and the Empire had granted Clovis the imperial titles that left him in charge.

Theodoric understood this well and was not at all blind to the manner in which he had been knifed by his imperial ally. He did what he could to improve the situation militarily by annexing the southern portion of Burgundy. In this way he took over the Mediterranean shores all the way westward to where the Visigoths still held sway. The Franks were thus barred from the southern sea by a solid Gothic phalanx.

Theodoric must have greeted with grim joy the news of the death of Clovis in 511. The Frank, after all, might have lived considerably longer, for he was only forty-five, a dozen years younger than Theodoric.

Clovis's death changed matters drastically, moreover. In his life he had striven to unite the Franks and build for them, and for himself, as extensive a realm as possible. Then, in his will, he followed the usual Frankish custom of dividing the inheritance of the kingdom as though it had been a herd of cattle.

He had four grown sons and each was granted a portion of the realm. At once, as in the earlier case of the four brothers of Burgundy, they began the bloody game of fighting each other. (Their mother, Clotilda, whose Catholic zeal had changed the face of Europe, retired to a monastery, occupied herself in religious works, and was eventually sainted.)

While the Frankish kingdom, divided into four mutually hostile parts, no longer served as a danger to anyone but itself (at least for a while), Theodoric strove to unite the Goths.

In the same year that Clovis died, the Visigothic king died, too, leaving only a younger brother, Amalaric, to succeed. Amalaric was too young to rule by himself in these hard times. He was, however, the grandson of Theodoric, who therefore exercised the right of guardianship, taking over the rule of both great branches of the Gothic nation.

Even this could not have made Theodoric feel really secure. He was a sincere Arian, even if not a bigoted one, and he must have been intelligent enough to see that there was no future for Arianism.

For a century now, the Arian Goths and Vandals had ruled over various provinces of the Western Empire without ever making serious inroads into Catholicism. They gained few, if any, converts.

What's more, the Arian minority, completely dependent on their German kings for safety, was dominated by those kings. The Arians in Spain, Italy, and Africa were separate "national churches" and felt little common bond among themselves. The Catholics, however, were Roman, and, remembering the Empire, never lost the feeling that they represented a universal body that rose above regional boundaries. Catholic unity gave it additional strength.

With each decade, then, the Catholics grew stronger and the

Arians weaker, and now that the Franks had become Catholic, the Arian Goths and Vandals were encircled. There were the Catholic Eastern Empire to the east, the Catholic Franks to the north, and the Catholic subjects below.

Theodoric, for all the enlightenment of his rule, must have felt the ground stirring under him. The Catholic majority among his subjects could scarcely have been overjoyed at his victory over a Catholic enemy. This was all the more true since Rome was the center of Western Catholicism.

In the early centuries of Christianity, the bishop of Rome had had a certain prestige because he ruled over the Christian community resident in the very center and capital of the Empire. This was heightened by the fact that, according to tradition, the Apostle Peter had been the first bishop of Rome and had been martyred in that city. It was considered that Jesus had appointed Peter head of the Church, and later bishops of Rome claimed to have inherited this leadership.

While the Roman Empire lasted, this claim was not taken very seriously. The large majority of the Christian population was in the East and so, after the time of Diocletian, was the imperial capital.

But then, when imperial authority began to collapse in the West after Alaric's raid through Italy, the bishop of Rome was able to step in as the only strong authority in the city itself.

This fact became dramatically evident when Attila the Hun was ravaging his way toward Rome. The Western Emperor was only a shadow, but the bishop of Rome was the forceful Leo I. Holding office from 440 to 461, he was a strong and dominating individual who hunted down heresies with vigor and worked tirelessly to improve the educational and moral level of the clergy.

Papa (meaning "father") was a common way of addressing priests in Italy, and in the time of Leo, it became customary to speak of him as *the* priest, the *Papa* with a capital P. In English this becomes "the Pope."

Leo I is sometimes called the Father of the Papacy, in the sense that he was the first to claim leadership of the Church effectively. Other Western provinces, under the rule of Arian foreigners, turned to the Pope as their only refuge. Although his actual power was confined to Italy, Leo's influence thus spread over all the West.

It was Leo who went to meet Attila when no one else would have dared to and it was Leo who labored to ease the effects of the sack of Rome by Gaiseric the Vandal.

After the Western Empire crumbled in 476, and no Emperor reigned in Italy, successive Popes recognized their only important rival within the Church to be the bishop of Constantinople. (This bishop was commonly called a patriarch, meaning "chief father," and hence a term quite analogous to that of Pope.) And behind the Patriarch of Constantinople was the Eastern Emperor.

In 492, Gelasius I became Pope. He met the problem of the Empire boldly, and insisted that Church and State were independent. The view that the Emperor could not interfere with the Church had been maintained by strong bishops earlier. Gelasius, however, demonstrated his belief in a particularly dramatic fashion. There was heresy in Constantinople, and Gelasius, as punishment for tolerating this, excommunicated the Patriarch; that is, he declared him to be no longer a member of the Church and therefore incapable of participating in its rites.

Naturally, the excommunication was disregarded in Constantinople, but Gelasius had nevertheless shown that the Pope considered himself superior to the Patriarch and could behave so without being punished.

The Pope's immunity came about because Theodoric was just at this time establishing his rule over Italy. Though Theodoric was an Arian who didn't recognize the Pope as head of the Church, he was nevertheless bound to back the Pope since Theodoric didn't want imperial interference in Italy any more than Gelasius did.

And so matters remained throughout the first half of Theodoric's reign, and an uneasy alliance was set up between Arian king and Catholic Pope that depended on the tolerant principles of the former and the practical politics of the latter. The coming of the Catholic Franks shook but did not destroy the alliance.

In 518, however, the Eastern Emperor, Anastasius, died and Justin I succeeded to the throne in Constantinople. Justin was a rough and uneducated soldier who had the help of his brilliant young nephew, Justinian.

Justin suppressed the heresies that had flourished under Anastasius and moved to accept the Roman view on various disputed points. As a result, there was a slow warming of relations between Pope and Emperor, with Theodoric finding himself increasingly isolated.

Justin also initiated stringent anti-Arian policies that Theodoric found disturbing. In 525, Theodoric sent Pope John I to Constantinople to negotiate an easing of imperial bigotry. Instead, the evidence was quite strong (and was conclusive to Theodoric) that Pope and Emperor were conspiring against the old king.

When John I returned empty-handed, Theodoric threw him into prison. Theodoric was desperate by now. He was about seventy and death was at hand. He had no grown son to succeed him and Catholicism was victorious on every side.

He had begun to see conspiracies even beyond what was justified. As a result, the last years of his reign closed in blood and ruined the record of a man justly called Theodoric the Great.

The most important victim of Theodoric's purges was Boethius, who, so short a time before, had been in ecstasy over the sight of both his sons as consuls at the same time.

Boethius was arrested on suspicion of correspondence with the Emperor, underwent torture and, in 524, was executed. While waiting for torture and execution, he wrote his greatest work, *On the Consolation of Philosophy*. If he was in agony of

mind at the time, it never shows in his calm style. Nor does any
clear sign of Christianity appear in it. He chose to write in the
fashion of the pagan philosophers.

Theodoric himself died in 526, having reigned thirty-seven
years in peace and prosperity and yet ending in failure.

He lived on, however, in legend, in a curiously distorted
form. In various German epic poems, in versions dating back to
the thirteenth century (seven hundred years after Theodoric's
death), he appears as Dietrich von Bern. In these poems, Dietrich von Bern is pictured as being driven away by Ermanaric,
king of Bern (Verona) in northern Italy. Dietrich seeks refuge
among the Huns and eventually returns at the head of a Hunnish army to defeat and kill Ermanaric.

Through this can dimly be seen the history of the Ostrogoths
as a whole. A Hunnish army did indeed defeat Ermanaric and
bring about his death, but that had been in the far-off land
north of the Black Sea. The Ostrogoths had (like Dietrich von
Bern) been with the Huns afterward, as subjects, and had
fought in their armies. And eventually, the Ostrogoths, again
like Dietrich von Bern, and under the leadership of Theodoric
(the real Dietrich) had come to Italy.

THE IMPERIAL GENERAL

One thing Theodoric could not possibly have foreseen was
the fact that the Eastern Empire, rather than the Franks, was to
prove the undoing of the Ostrogoths.

The Eastern Empire had held firm through all the terrible
century and a quarter after the death of Theodosius, but it had
done no more than that. Through force, diplomacy, intrigue,
bribery and good fortune, it had kept its borders intact. The
Visigoths, the Huns and the Ostrogoths had each in its turn
penetrated the Danubian border while the Persians had maintained a constant pressure from the east. The Empire had,

nevertheless, weathered every storm and its territory was as extensive when Theodoric the Ostrogoth died as when Alaric the Visigoth had begun his march.

Yet the Empire had never been able to regain the West or to carry the fight into the enemy's territory. It had throughout the fifth century been governed by Emperors who, at best, were well-meaning second-raters, and they had not had a single first-class general.

Then, in 527, the year after Theodoric's death, everything changed. Justin I died and his nephew Justinian came to the throne. He had served his uncle as a kind of prime minister and, particularly toward the end of Justin's reign, had been the real ruler. When he succeeded to the throne, then, he had already had considerable training in the business of emperorship.

Justinian, already in his middle years at the time of his accession (he was forty-four), had a vaulting ambition in every field, and succeeded in most. He ran the Church with an iron hand, built a spectacular cathedral, established a law code that rang famously down the centuries, reorganized and strengthened the government, and saw his realm achieve a material and cultural revival.

His dreams included nothing less than the complete restoration of the Roman Empire to a reality. He wanted to win back all the lost provinces of the West.

There was one difficulty involved, however, in accomplishing the western conquest. He himself, for all his intelligence, industry, and very real ability, had not an ounce of military talent. If he were going to be a conqueror, he would have to find the general of first-rate ability that the Eastern Empire had so long lacked. What is more, he had to find one who could be trusted not to take the throne by a military coup once he had become successful. (Justinian's own uncle had taken the throne in that manner.)

It was Justinian's great good fortune to find just such a general. In the war against Persia which had been proceeding, on and off, for centuries, a twenty-five-year-old warrior, Belisarius, won an astonishing victory over the enemy in 530.

Then, in 532, he proved his worth even more directly. When a dangerous riot in Constantinople nearly drove Justinian from the throne. Belisarius, with a mere handful of men, managed to calm the city.

Justinian was grateful and impressed. He had his man.

Next, in order to begin his western conquest, he needed an excuse. It is an odd fact that anyone who wishes to start a war must always make it appear that he is fighting in a just cause even if the real motive is naked aggression. Fortunately for the would-be aggressor, a "just cause" is very easy to find.

Justinian's first target was the Vandal kingdom of Africa. It was a logical choice, for the Vandal kingdom was not as extensive as the Gothic and Frankish kingdoms. It was confined to a thin rim of the African coast about Carthage, together with a tenuous hold over the islands of the western Mediterranean. The sea separated it from possible help from the Goths and had kept it so secure for fifty years that it had not felt the pressure that would have served to keep it in fighting trim.

In 477, Gaiseric, the founder of the kingdom, had died. He had been a man of first-rate caliber, but those who followed were completely unworthy of him.

Like Gaiseric, his successors were Arians. In 523, however, Hilderic, a grandson of Gaiseric, came to the throne, and showed a distinct sympathy toward Catholicism.

The Arian clergy among the Vandal aristocrats were promptly outraged at this. Matters grew steadily more turbulent until finally, in 531, an army coup succeeded in overthrowing Hilderic. The deposed monarch was imprisoned and a safely Arian cousin, Gelimer, was made king.

Here was Justinian's excuse: a monarch sympathetic to Catholicism who was unjustly dethroned and imprisoned by a heretic. To attack the Vandals now was to strike a blow in the cause of religion and justice. Justinian was a pious Catholic and was surely sincere in thinking so, and the people of the Empire were behind him.

In 533, Belisarius was therefore placed in command of a fleet of some five hundred ships, carrying thirty-five thousand soldiers and sailors, five thousand horses and all the needed supplies. Westward toward Carthage sailed the fleet.

Ordinarily, one would not expect such an expeditionary force, large but certainly not overwhelming, to succeed against an entrenched hard-fighting foe on the foe's own grounds. But to make up for the smallness of the imperial army and for the difficulty of fighting far from home with the sea at one's back, Belisarius counted heavily on one imponderable. The Catholic population was surely going to welcome his troops as liberators from the oppression of an alien and heretic aristocracy.

With this in mind, Belisarius was farsighted enough to prevent any careless looting by his troops. He wanted nothing to happen that might turn the general population against him. Fully able, then, to keep himself supplied by the willing help of the people, Belisarius marched on Carthage after landing on the North African shores.

Gelimer was in a quandary. The fortifications of Carthage had been destroyed when the Vandals had conquered the city almost a century before and there had never been any occasion or need to rebuild the walls. He could not, therefore, wear out Belisarius by forcing him into a protracted siege, but had to meet him in the field. And that was made hard by the fact that the best Vandal troops were unluckily off on the island of Sardinia, fighting what now must have seemed to Gelimer to be useless battles against the natives.

The inevitable battle was finally fought ten miles from Carthage. Belisarius, through his own skill and the Vandals' lack of skill, was able to prevent different parts of the enemy from uniting. He defeated first one part of the army and then the other.

With that done, Belisarius marched into Carthage, still keeping his men under firm discipline. The Carthaginian Catholic populace cheered loudly.

The Vandal army in Sardinia hastily returned home. They gathered their forces and tried a second battle with Belisarius but were routed again. Gelimer fled and was taken prisoner.

The entire Vandal kingdom fell to the Eastern Empire, including the west Mediterranean islands Sardinia, Corsica and the Balearics. Arianism was suppressed and disappeared permanently from Africa. The cause of Empire and Church was triumphant, and the Vandals, like the Huns before them, lost their national identity and vanished from history. All that remains of them is the common word "vandal," which does them an injustice, and the section of southern Spain called Andalusia which (having lost the initial V) commemorates the twenty years from 409 to 429 when the Vandals controlled that section.

Belisarius returned to Constantinople in triumph, with the deposed Vandal king in his train as a captive. Justinian could not help but be pleased at a success that was greater than even the most optimistic would have expected. Yet, being a practical politician before he was anything else, he could not help being aware that the enormous popularity that Belisarius had earned was dangerous. He could not keep him in Constantinople but would have to send him on another expedition.

It was easy to do so. The Ostrogothic kingdom was the logical next candidate for destruction. It was the nearest of the remaining German kingdoms; it was in political chaos; and it had just given him a perfect excuse for attack.

THE RUIN OF ITALY

Theodoric left behind him an intelligent and capable offspring but it was the misfortune of the Ostrogoths that she was of the wrong sex. She was a daughter, Amalasuntha. Her nine-year-old son Athalaric succeeded to the throne and she served as regent.

Amalasuntha realized that her position was not secure among a turbulent Gothic aristocracy who resented having to take orders from a woman. She cast about for methods of strengthening herself, and one device was to favor the Roman population. This, of course, further estranged the aristocracy.

Amalasuntha therefore did her best to establish good relations with the Eastern Empire. She even came to a secret understanding with Justinian that would enable her to flee to Constantinople if her position in Italy was seriously threatened.

She remained safe as long as her son was king, but life was short and uncertain in those days and Athalaric died of disease in 534, when he was only sixteen.

Amalasuntha could not possibly reign by herself and she therefore arranged to have Theodahad, her first cousin, serve with her as a joint sovereign. Theodahad's only merit was that he was a male of the royal family. He had no sooner achieved the rank of co-ruler when he did an amazingly stupid thing. He had Amalasuntha imprisoned and then assassinated.

The news reached Justinian even as Belisarius was celebrating his triumph over the Vandals and the Emperor could not possibly have asked for a more suitable situation to serve his ends. Once again, he had a wicked usurper on his hands, an assassin and an Arian heretic — Theodahad. Justinian could march to war on behalf of a poor murdered queen, who had had an alliance with himself and sympathy for Catholics. And he could get Belisarius out of the city.

In 535, Belisarius led his fleet to Sicily where the Gothic positions were thinly manned and was able to take the large island almost without a fight. Once again a Catholic populace welcomed him enthusiastically against their own rulers. He then crossed over into Italy itself and reached Naples before encountering significant resistance. He took that city after a siege of less than a month.

Theodahad, the Ostrogothic king, was clearly not suited for warfare with so determined and skillful an adversary. With Naples lost, he gave up and asked for surrender terms. This, however, the more determined among his own warriors would not allow. They murdered him, and a general named Witiges was elected king in 536. Thus, the line of Theodoric the Great came to an inglorious end only ten years after his death.

Belisarius had time to march into Rome itself against virtually no resistance before Witiges could organize his forces for the counterattack. Witiges then led the full strength of the Ostrogothic army to the outskirts of Rome and there he laid siege to Belisarius, who held his ground firmly and skillfully.

Justinian managed to send occasional reinforcements — but never really enough. After all, Justinian's many projects were a terrible drain on the Empire's resources and there was a limit to how much he could pour into Italy. It is also quite possible he was none too anxious to give Belisarius much help. With a large army at his back, the general might be as dangerous to Justinian as to the Ostrogoths.

What reinforcements did come, however, were put to good use by Belisarius and he made sure that the besieging host bled steadily as a result of skillfully led forays from the city. Finally, after a full year, Witiges and his Ostrogothic army were forced to raise the siege and retreat to the safety of impregnable Ravenna.

The Huns themselves had not threatened Ravenna and Theodoric had been able to take it only by treachery, forty years before. No doubt the Ostrogoths felt that from Ravenna they could keep up the fight indefinitely and finally wear out the Imperials. Justinian must have felt the same, for he signed a treaty of peace over his general's head, agreeing to divide Italy with the Ostrogoths and leave them the northern half.

Belisarius refused to accept the treaty, pressed the siege of Ravenna, cutting off every avenue of approach and, apparently against the advice of his own officers, insisted on letting famine do its work.

He succeeded. The Ostrogoths, hungry (but, even more than that, disheartened), surrendered the city. There is a story that they did so only on condition that Belisarius rule over them as king and not turn Italy over to the Empire. Belisarius, it is said, agreed to the condition but had no intention of keeping it, so that it might be said that Ravenna was taken by treachery once again.

Belisarius may have expected Justinian to be pleased with all this, but if so, he did not understand human nature. The general was entirely too successful and, what was worse, he had pressed for victory and won where Justinian had given up. He had made Justinian seem a man lacking in faith and resolution.

Justinian instantly recalled Belisarius from Italy and gave him a most chilly reception despite the fact that he brought a second captive German king (Witiges) with him. The tale that the Ostrogoths had offered to make Belisarius king was uncovered (or possibly invented by the general's enemies) and Justinian felt he could trust him no more.

The imperial generals left in control of Italy made a mess of it, however. They lacked Belisarius' ability and humanity. The imperial soldiers, out of control, made it clear to the populace that a Catholic army could be as harsh and as dangerous as an Arian one, and the best weapon the Romans had, the goodwill of the people, was lost.

Slowly, the Ostrogoths recovered from the shock of defeat; slowly they gathered their numbers together and found they still outnumbered the thin imperial garrisons. Finally, in 541, a capable general, Totila, was elected king. Under Totila's vigorous leadership, the Ostrogoths took city after city until they laid siege to Rome itself in 544.

Justinian was forced to act. Gritting his teeth with frustration, no doubt, he found he had to send Belisarius back to Italy, to avoid the disgrace of losing it. Perhaps it occurred to him that it might not be so bad to lose Italy if the disgrace could be transferred to Belisarius. This might explain why he sent the general to Italy with a ridiculously inadequate army and that he never sent him the quantity of reinforcements needed for victory.

Belisarius did not have the troops with which to drive Totila from Rome, and in 546 the Ostrogothic army once again took the city.

The city of Rome had had a century and a quarter of crises but until now it had almost miraculously survived with scarcely a scratch. Alaric the Visigoth had occupied it but done it no harm. Attila the Hun had approached it but had left without touching it. Gaiseric the Vandal had looted it but done it no real damage. Odoacer and Theodoric had each in turn established his rule over Italy without hurting Rome.

But now after two Ostrogothic sieges, the first unsuccessful and the second successful, the city met its disaster at last. Its walls were battered down and its aqueducts broken. The running water and drainage that had been the pride of the city vanished. The higher regions were without water, the lower regions became malaria-ridden marshes.

Totila, in a fit of exasperation, seems even to have played with the notion of leveling the city altogether after he had taken it. A plea from Belisarius, reminding the Ostrogoth of the glorious history of the fallen city, is supposed to have saved it.

But Rome did not recover. It is the year 546 that marks the true end of the ancient city.

Belisarius kept on fighting, marching into ruined Rome the next year and being forced out again. In 549, Belisarius was recalled by a satisfied Emperor. The general had acquitted himself loyally and capably, but he could point to no spectacular victory (something the Emperor had made sure of by giving him nothing to fight with) and the magic of his name was dimmed.

So the darkness came. Italy, the most cultured and prosperous province of the West, the beneficiary of the enlightened rule of Theodoric, was left a shattered ruin at last. The Imperials and Ostrogoths, who wrenched the peninsula back and forth, found themselves with nothing but a wreck on their hands.

And what was left beyond Italy? Africa receded into the imperial structure and was never to return to the West. Visigothic Spain sank into isolation and decay — the only remnant of Arianism left in a totally Catholic Mediterranean.

Only the Franks remained vigorous, and of all the German tribes of that day, they were the most barbaric. If the hopes of Western civilization were to rest on their muscular shoulders, those hopes had to be dim indeed.

4

THE MEROVINGIANS

JUSTINIAN AT THE PEAK

Now that Belisarius was taken care of, Justinian was not actually ready to give up Italy. The thing to do, as he saw it, was to send a second capable general who, for one reason or another, wouldn't be a threat to the Emperor under any circumstance.

As it happened, he had the perfect candidate. (Things always seemed to break right for Justinian.) There was an Armenian named Narses, who had been part of Justinian's immediate entourage and who had proved himself a most capable and intelligent man, one on whom the Emperor found he could thoroughly rely. He also showed himself knowledgeable in military matters.

In 538, he had been sent to Italy, ostensibly to help Belisarius, but probably to keep an eye on him for Justinian. Naturally, the two men did not get along and Justinian had to recall Narses. Now with Belisarius permanently out of Italy, Justinian sent Narses back in 551, this time as commander-in-chief of the imperial forces there.

He was a commander-in-chief after Justinian's heart, for he was a wizened little man over seventy years old and someone who was not calculated to win the overwhelming enthusiasm of his troops. If appearance were not enough, Narses was a eunuch, and it was absolutely inconceivable that a eunuch could ever be accepted as a serious rival for the imperial throne.

Justinian was served even better than he could have expected, for it turned out that the old eunuch was not only a good general, but almost as capable a general as Belisarius had been.

Narses, once in Italy, realized that a decision would have to be sought rapidly, for any delay would thin and weaken his forces and make it necessary for him to wait for further reinforcements which might or might not come. He therefore moved to press Totila to a battle, which the Ostrogoth was eager to accept. Totila, after all, had had years of victory even against Belisarius and he was now faced only with an aged eunuch.

In 552, they met at Taginae, about a hundred miles north of Rome. Totila hastened to attack in an attempt to catch the imperial forces off guard. His cavalry rushed in without proper infantry support and found Narses thoroughly prepared. The Ostrogothic cavalry was trapped and knocked out, and after that the fight was heavily in favor of the Imperials. Totila himself was killed.

This was the end for the Ostrogoths. They were never again able to bring a full army into the field. They were reduced instead to a harassing kind of guerrilla warfare, which Narses patiently countered, taking cities here, knocking out war bands there.

By 553, the Ostrogoths passed from history, only sixty years after Theodoric had established himself in Ravenna. They had lost their Italian kingdom as once they had lost their Ukrainian kingdom — and a third chance they were never to have.

While Narses was clearing up Italy, Justinian was looking toward the other lost provinces. Spain under the Visigoths was clearly going through a period of decay.

Theodoric the Ostrogoth had been the real ruler of Spain as well as of Italy, but after his death, the two nations separated. Theodoric's grandson and ward, Amalaric, was now old enough to rule on his own and he set up his capital in Seville — the first Visigothic capital within the confines of Spain itself.

The Franks were still the great enemy, all the more so now that the strong arm of Theodoric was removed. To be sure, Clovis was long dead and his sons were squabbling among themselves, but Amalaric thought, nevertheless, that it would be a prudent act to request a daughter of Clovis in marriage. The request was granted but it proved a bad idea.

Amalaric was an Arian and his new queen was a Catholic. Each tried to convert the other and each failed. The result was that Childebert I, one of Clovis's sons, felt it was time for another holy war against the heretics. In a battle inside Spain, the Visigoths were defeated a second time and Amalaric was killed. The Franks marched away with the rescued queen and much booty.

The death of Amalaric brought to an end the line of Alaric, a century and a quarter after that ancestral Visigoth had taken Rome.

A series of undistinguished kings followed Amalaric. They managed to hold off the divided Franks, but followed each other to destruction in a welter of palace intrigue and civil war.

Justinian used one of these civil wars as the necessary excuse for his aggression. One of the competing would-be kings, Athanagild, asked for Justinian's help. Before the eager Justinian could send it, Athanagild won on his own and canceled his request. It was too late. Justinian insisted on sending his forces anyway. The southern third of Spain was quickly reduced and the Visigothic dominions were squeezed into a corridor through central Spain between the imperial forces on the south and the Sueves in the north.

By 555, then, Justinian's power had reached its peak. His reign had lasted nearly thirty years and during its course he had brought back to imperial control all of Africa and Italy, wiping out the Vandals and Ostrogoths. He had taken much of Spain, and left the Visigoths impotent. Only the Franks (and the Saxons in distant Britain) remained untouched.

But Justinian could do no more. Having reached the peak, there was nowhere to go but down. The western wars, however successful they seemed to be, were costing the imperial treasury a great deal. Combine the endless wars in the West with the endless wars with Persia in the East, and it was quite clear that the throne at Constantinople was succeeding itself right into bankruptcy.

Indeed, the real beneficiaries of the imperial campaigns under Justinian had been the Merovingian rulers of the Franks — the sons of Clovis. These sons, while mutually hostile and never pausing in their drive to seize as much of one another's inheritance as possible, still managed to recognize the need for a common front against outsiders. They conquered the Thuringian tribes in central Germany and gradually deprived the Burgundians of what independence Clovis had left them.

Once the imperial invasion of Italy began, the Franks quickly seized the opportunity to press southward. Justinian himself encouraged them to do so and offered them an alliance. The result was that the Frankish borders were pushed to the line of the Alps.

By the conclusion of the warfare in Italy, two of Clovis's sons had died, and in 558 a third son died. The fourth and youngest son, Clotaire I, had been steadily annexing section after section, ignoring the claims of various nephews, and now he had the

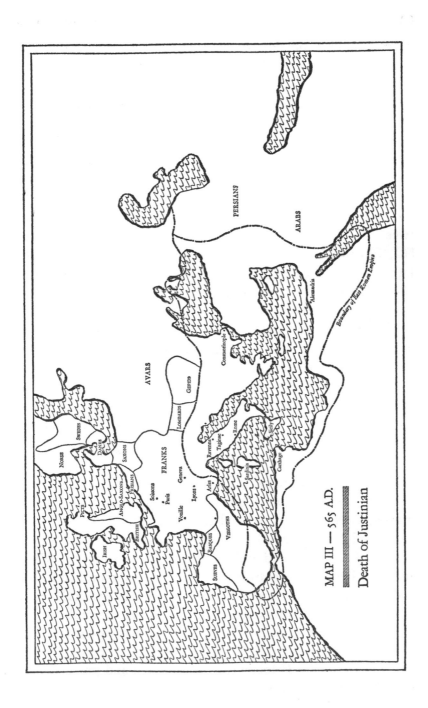

MAP III — 565 A.D.

▨▨▨▨▨ Death of Justinian

PERSIANS

ARABS

Boundary of East Roman Empire

Alexandria

Constantinople

AVARS

GEPIDS

LOMBARDS

FRANKS

Ravenna

Taginae

Rome

Sicily

Carthage

Sardinia

Arles

Lyons

Genoa

Paris

Soissons

Vouillé

Basques

VISIGOTHS

SUEVES

NORSE

SWEDES

DANES

SAXONS

FRISIANS

ANGLO-SAXONS

BRITISH

PICTS

IRISH

entire Frankish kingdom in his sole control. What's more, it was a kingdom nearly twice as large in extent as that which Clovis had left.

If, then, the power of the Eastern Empire had been greatly extended (at least judging by the map), so had the power of the one great remaining Germanic kingdom, that of the Franks. And if the Frankish kingdom was not nearly as wealthy and cultured as was the Empire, its lands were more compact and its armies fiercer.

The stage was now set for a seemingly inevitable clash between the Franks and the Imperials, but fate intervened. In 561, Clotaire I died after a reign of fifty years. He, like his father Clovis, left four grown sons. These sons, like the sons of Clovis, divided the kingdom into four parts and each received one share selected by lot (!).

The Frankish kingdom, united for a bare three years, was once again in fragments and imperial Italy remained safe after all — at least from the Franks.

THE LAST OF THE ARIANS

Narses continued to rule all Italy from Ravenna for fourteen years, growing ever older but never less forceful. By 565, he was eighty-seven years old and still going strong. His rule was harsh and taxes were high. Italian emissaries carried strong complaints to Constantinople demanding his removal. While Justinian lived, this went for nothing, but Justinian died in 565 and was succeeded by a nephew, who reigned as Justin II.

Any strong ruler who reigns for a long time accumulates displeasure and unpopularity. It is often the first care of his successor to begin by courting popularity through reversing all the old policies. Justin II followed this principle and proceeded to get rid of Narses, who seemed to be immortal.

There is a very well-known story that the dismissal of Narses was carried through with incredible brutality. The new Empress is supposed to have sent a message to the aged general to leave warfare to men and, as a eunuch, to join the palace maidens and confine himself to spinning.

Narses is reported to have answered, "I will spin her such a thread as she shall not easily unravel." And, before leaving, he invited a new group of Germanic tribesmen to invade Italy.

This story was first told a couple of centuries after the event and, while dramatic, is probably not true. The new wave of Germanic invaders did not have to be invited. It was pushed in — and in the same manner that the earlier wave had been pushed west and south two centuries before.

It was a case of invaders from Asia again.

A new set of horsemen, the Avars, came thundering out of the east during the reign of Justinian and quickly established their domination over the Slavic peasants of eastern Europe. (The poor Slavs had by now been ruled, lorded over, and mistreated by one war band after another: Gothic, Hunnish and Avaric. So helplessly downtrodden were they that the very word "slave" is supposed to have been derived from "Slav.")

By the time of Justinian's death, the Avar realm was a somewhat smaller version of what Attila's had been a century before. The Avars ruled from the Don River to the Elbe River, their borders coming up hard against the northern edge of the Eastern Empire and the eastern edge of the Frankish kingdom.

Lying just north of Italy were two Germanic tribes who were exposed to the full force of the Avar advance. These were the Lombards and the Gepids. (The word "Lombard" is a corruption of the Germanic "Langobards," which means either "long beards" or, perhaps more likely, "long axes.")

The Lombards and the Gepids were continuing a long-established feud when the Avars appeared on the horizon. Each tribe sought the help of the invaders against the other and it was the Lombards who gained that help.

In 565, the same year in which Justinian died and Narses was recalled, Alboin became king of the Lombards. With the help of the Avars, he defeated the Gepids in a final battle in 567. He killed the Gepid king Cunimund, and then united the two tribes by marrying his dead enemy's daughter Rosamund. (Any son they might have, you see, would be of both royal houses.) According to the old chroniclers, Alboin kept the skull of Cunimund and fashioned a drinking cup out of it.

Once the Gepids were defeated, the Lombards could scarcely have felt comfortable with their new neighbors, the Avars. In all likelihood, the Lombards discovered that the Avar alliance merely gave them the privilege of being the last to be swallowed. A couple of decades earlier, they had sent mercenary contingents to the aid of Belisarius so they were familiar with the faded wealth of Italy. It was an easy decision to exchange the hardships of Avaric oppression for the role of conquerors in Italy.

In 568, therefore, the entire nation, men, women and children, together with contingents of other tribes who thought they would like to join the adventure, crossed the Alps and poured down into northern Italy. The Lombards were Arians, so once more — and for the last time — an Arian war band poured over a Catholic land.

It is these Lombards that Narses was supposed to have invited into Italy, but the unlikelihood of that is obvious. Narses left Italy three years before the Lombards came; and the Avar pressure was quite enough to push the Lombards into Italy without any invitation at all.

The invasion of these last of the Arians was a particularly easy one. Italy had gone through a whole generation of marches and countermarches, of imperial devastation followed by Gothic counter-devastation followed by imperial counter-counter-devastation. As a land it was worn out and its people had settled into a kind of mute acquiescence to any rulers. All they asked was to be left alone, if that were at all possible.

It was only the fact that the Lombard numbers were so small that kept them from occupying more of the land than they did. As it was, they occupied the northern third of Italy. This included the city of Pavia (on the upper Po, about twenty-five miles south of Milan) which fell in 572 and which eventually became the capital of their kingdom. They also occupied the interior of the southern part of the peninsula, about the city of Benevento, forty miles east of Naples.

Alboin did not long survive his easy conquest but died soon after he had captured Pavia. Legend embroidered his end with a rather horrid tale. In the course of the drunken brawl that celebrated the fall of Pavia, Alboin made his wife drink from the cup fashioned out of her father's skull, whereupon she arranged his assassination.

THE BEGINNING

OF THE MIDDLE AGES

The peninsula of Italy had been unified under the single rule of the Romans about 220 B.C. For seven centuries it had remained so. With the coming of the Lombards and their incomplete conquest, however, Italy was divided. It was to stay divided for thirteen centuries.

To begin with, the invasion produced two Italies, one Lombard, and one imperial, each in two portions. The Eastern Empire retained the far southern portion of the peninsula, including the "toe" and "heel," as well as the islands of Sicily, Sardinia and Corsica. In addition, the Imperials controlled a fat strip of land, north and south, across the center of the peninsula from Rome to Venice, including the capital at Ravenna.

The imperial forces had lacked the numbers to oppose the Lombards everywhere but they held on grimly where they could. Imperial Italy was reorganized in 584 as the Exarchate of Ravenna (an exarchate is an outer province).

In Lombard Italy, the clock seemed to have been turned back a generation to Ostrogothic times. Once again, there was a Germanic Arian aristocracy and a Roman Catholic peasantry. Once again, there was a double system of law and of religion.

The division of Italy was a boon to papal power, for that could grow best when secular power in the peninsula was weak or divided. While imperial forces had controlled all of Italy under Narses, for instance, the Pope had been reduced to a puppet. In 552, Pope Vigilius I was imprisoned at the orders of Justinian with as little ceremony as Pope John I had been imprisoned by Theodoric. Now, however, with a new period of secular weakness, the Papacy had another chance, and the man to exploit that chance was fortunately on the scene.

He was Gregory, a man of patrician Roman family. He had been prefect (that is, mayor) of Rome while still a young man of about thirty. This was in 573, when the Lombards were pouring southward. The ominous character of the times and his own yearning for the contemplative life led him to resign. He assigned his property to churchly use, founded six monasteries in Sicily and one in Rome, and entered the Roman one himself.

His monasteries followed the Benedictine rule set up some forty years earlier by Benedict of Nursia (a town some ninety miles north of Rome). Monks, living alone or in communities, engaging in prayer or in self-discipline, were a well-established part of Eastern Christianity. It was Benedict, however, who first introduced into the West a successful, rational and workable system for running a monastery.

He established his retreat on Monte Cassino, about seventy miles southeast of Rome, shortly after the death of Theodoric ushered in a generation of troubles, and the monastery there became a model for all the West. He bound the monks over whom he ruled to obedience, poverty and chastity but discouraged useless asceticism. He did not want his monks to be beggars, vagabonds or masochists. He insisted, rather, that they labor, either manually in the fields or intellectually at the writing desk. Activity followed an unvarying routine. Discipline was firm and the abbot in charge was elected for life and had absolute authority. Each monastery was to be self-sustaining and a haven, in a troubled world, for industry and learning.

Benedict died in 543, but his system lived on triumphantly after him. The Benedictine monasteries served as virtually the sole educational institutions in the West from 550 to 1150 (the "Benedictine centuries"). Fully ninety percent of all literate Westerners were trained in them. What spark of learning was kept alive in those hard times was kept alive by the Benedictines.

After Benedict himself, the first great Benedictine was Gregory. He proselytized industriously and initiated the slow spread of the order outside Italy.

In addition to his monkish duties, Gregory served as papal ambassador to Constantinople, wrote a commentary on the book of Job and produced other writings which earned him the title of the last of the Four Fathers of the Western Church. Indeed, he was the first great interpreter of religious thought in the West since the coming of the Germans, though he was more a popularizer than a bold innovator himself.

In 590, Pope Pelagius II (an Ostrogoth by descent) died, and Gregory's quiet life came to an end. Much against his will, he was elected to the papal throne. The story is that Gregory went so far as to write to the Emperor at Constantinople, begging him to refuse to ratify the election, but the letter was intercepted, and Gregory himself was dragged out of hiding and virtually forced to assume the papal dignity.

Once Pope, though, he went about the task vigorously and proved himself the first strong Pope since Gelasius I a century before. He reorganized the Church ritual and may even have regulated the manner of chanting. (At least, one still speaks of the "Gregorian chant.")

He carried through reforms in matters of morals, encouraging celibacy among the priests (partly in order to minimize the chance of corruption arising from the desire to pass office to one's children) and supervising elections strictly.

His connection with the Benedictines led him to give great influence to monks as opposed to bishops. Gregory placed emphasis on learning, but on Christian learning. There are tales (perhaps exaggerated) of his rooting out and destroying pagan books in his effort to wipe out the last feeble lingering traces of paganism in Italy.

In any case, if the last bit of ancient Italy ended with Belisarius and Narses, the first bit of medieval Italy began with Gregory. Gregory's own writing helped spread the kind of theology one associates with the Middle Ages — it deals with angels and demons, with penance and purgatory, with miracles, relics and all the rest.

(The term "Middle Ages" was not used in the Middle Ages, of course. The men of the period naturally felt their age to be that of "modern times." Centuries after Gregory, however, the classics of Greece and Rome were rediscovered and scholars began to feel there was a renaissance, or renewal, of learning. Those scholars then began to sneer at the thousand-year gap between ancient learning and the revival of ancient learning and to speak of the Middle Ages between. The early centuries of that period, the centuries dealt with in this book, are sometimes called the Dark Ages because learning had fallen to so low an ebb during them.)

Gregory strove earnestly to spread Christianity among the pagans. In fact, the best-known tale of him (at least to English-speaking people) is that he once saw a group of fair-haired youngsters being sold as slaves. Struck with their appearance, he asked of what nation they were.

"They are Angles," he was told (these being one of the tribes who had invaded Britain a century and a half before and who had eventually given the land its new name of England). Gregory replied with a Latin pun that survives translation: "Not Angles, but angels." He then set about sending missionaries to the land of the Angles in order that so beautiful a race might not be lost to God.

But Gregory's most important practical task was to contain the Lombards and see to the physical safety of the Church. He could not rely on the imperial forces for help. The Exarchate of Ravenna was always short of funds and the imperial soldiers were not being paid. This would inevitably have driven them to revolt and even, perhaps, to join the Lombards.

But if the Exarchate was poor, the Papacy was rich. Estates had been willed to the Church by the pious for many years and these had accumulated until the Church was by far the largest landowner in Italy. Gregory organized these widespread holdings and placed them under his firm control, instituting a rational system of collecting revenues. He was then able to pay the imperial troops and, moreover, to use the grain harvested on these holdings to feed the Roman populace.

Naturally, he who pays the soldiers and feeds the populace controls both, and Gregory became the real ruler of Rome and its surroundings, offering only lip service to the representative of the Emperor at Ravenna.

Yet Gregory did not use the army to begin warfare with the Lombards. Rather he labored to convert them from Arianism. The strongest Lombard leader at the time was Agilulf, and Gregory talked peace to him even though the Exarch at Ravenna urged war.

Agilulf, impressed (and softened, too, by a discreet gift of money) grew friendly, first to the Pope and then to Catholicism. Between the Pope's urgings and those of his Catholic queen, he allowed the heir to the throne to be baptized a Catholic and then followed suit himself. Conversion spread rapidly

among the Lombards thereafter. Conversion softened them
and they accepted the language and laws of their subjects.

By 600, then, the brief generation of Arianism which had returned to northern Italy was gone — forever. Indeed, the Visigoths of Spain were converted to Catholicism at about this
time, too, and Arianism thus came to a final end after an existence of three fateful centuries.

Gregory was not blind to the fact that the Lombards were a
danger even though Catholic. Cheek by jowl with the Papacy
as they were, there was bound to be friction. The Lombards
had an army and it was clear that the Papacy had to have an
army too.

Gregory was the first Pope, therefore, to cast his eyes specu-
latively toward the Franks beyond the Alps. He wrote friendly,
even deferential letters to Childebert II of Austrasia (the eastern part of the Frankish realm). Not much came of it at the
time, but a precedent was set which was to bring about important events in the future.

In all, Gregory had virtually established a third power in
Italy, that of the Papacy. Because of his accomplishments, he
is widely known as Gregory the Great, and since he was canon-
ized soon after his death in 604, he may fairly be called St.
Gregory, too.

Gregory's establishment of the independent power of the
Church was carried over to the bishoprics, since Gregory insisted that each bishop be as independent of the secular power
as the Papacy was. Every sizable town had its bishop, which
meant that the separate towns were very nearly independent
and only the countryside was under Lombard rule.

In northern Italy, especially, the cities were thereby
strengthened and their population grew as individuals fled the
comparatively harsh arm of the Lombard king for the relative
freedom of the city.

While city life decayed and dwindled almost everywhere
under the Germanic rulers, it held on to some of its vitality in

northern Italy in consequence and the foundation was laid for a
revival of Western culture centuries later.

THE GRANDSONS OF CLOVIS

The Lombard invasion of Italy and the confusion that followed in that land might well have drawn down the Franks
from the north — but the Franks were tied down by internal
problems.

Of the four sons of Clotaire I (the last surviving son of Clovis), the eldest soon died and the youngest, Chilperic, seized
the vacated territory. That left the Frankish realm divided into
three parts.

Sigebert I, Clotaire's third son, with his capital at Metz, about
180 miles east of Paris, ruled Austrasia, the eastern section of
the Frankish realm. Most of it had never been part of the Roman Empire and in it Roman influences were weakest.

Chilperic, Clotaire's fourth and youngest son, ruled from Soissons over Neustria, while Gontram, the second son, with his
capital at Orléans, ruled over Burgundy. Neustria, taking up
the north of what was once Gaul, and Burgundy, the southeast,
still had the Roman tradition left and were distinctly different,
even in language, from Austrasia.

It is perhaps reasonable that there might be steady warfare
between Austrasia and Neustria, considering that they were
neighboring lands of different culture (the difference steadily
growing more marked) and that their kings were brothers each
of whom thought he might easily rule the other's kingdom as
well as his own.

Sigebert had one advantage he couldn't possibly have realized. He had made a monk named Gregory the bishop of Tours,

and this Gregory became the historian of the Franks. His history survives to this day and remains our principal source of knowledge of Clovis and his immediate descendants. Because Gregory was under Austrasian rule, the picture we get from him is distinctly anti-Neustrian. Sigebert and the Austrasian side, generally, come down to future ages perhaps a little better than they deserve.

Sigebert, occupied by the Avar wars on his eastern frontier and a little concerned about the sudden increase in Chilperic's power, decided to find an ally by way of matrimony. In the same year that his oldest brother died and Chilperic grew powerful, Sigebert married a Visigothic princess. Her name was Brunehilde and she was the daughter of Athanagild, the same Athanagild who, thirteen years earlier, had had the poor judgment to enter into alliance with Justinian and so brought imperial forces into Spain.

The marriage was a carefully calculated one. While the Visigothic realm had lost considerable territory to the Imperials, it had regained some internal stability during Athanagild's comparatively long reign. The position, then, was that if Visigothic friendship could be counted on, Sigebert would, in case of any war with Chilperic, have an army which could fall on the Neustrian rear. As it happened, the marriage even seemed to be happy and Brunehilde, who was an Arian to begin with, allowed herself to be converted to Catholicism without trouble.

Chilperic of Neustria must have felt uneasy at his brother's new Visigothic connection. He had a wife of his own, but that was scarcely anything to worry about. He managed to get the Church to approve a divorce and then married Galswintha, another daughter of Athanagild. Both Frankish kings had the same Visigothic father-in-law and Sigebert's move had been neatly countered.

In fact, both brothers outsmarted themselves in a way, for their careful moves and countermoves came to nothing when Athanagild died in the very same year that both marriages were made. The Visigothic kings who succeeded, with a fairly rapid turnover, were far too occupied with internal coups to be able to make their weight felt in external wars. If the two Frankish kings were going to fight, it would have to be without Visigothic help either way.

Chilperic was the more vexed of the two, for Galswintha was not to his liking personally. His real love was a woman called Fredegund, who had attracted his attention when she was merely a servant in the castle. (The ancient historians may well have been more horrified by her "low birth" than by anything else.)

Fredegund had undoubtedly been delighted when Chilperic divorced his first wife, hoping (or perhaps even expecting) that he was going to marry her. She must have been absolutely furious when, for reasons of state, he married a Visigothic princess instead. Then, when the reasons of state collapsed with Athanagild's death, Fredegund managed to arrange the assassination of the new queen. Chilperic could not have been very displeased at this, for he then married Fredegund and made her his third queen.

It is quite clear that neither Chilperic nor Fredegund were admirable characters, and Gregory of Tours speaks of Chilperic with detestation as "the Nero and Herod of his time." Still, it is probable that Chilperic was but a fair sampling of the Merovingian kings of the century and that, evil as he was, he was not very much more evil than the times.

THE GREAT FEUD

Fredegund had achieved the height of her ambition when she became queen of Neustria, but in doing so she had made a

fierce enemy. In killing Galswintha, she had killed and replaced the sister of Brunehilde, the Austrasian queen, and
Brunehilde was not the kind to forgive even a much lighter in-
jury. Nor did the savage Fredegund hesitate to accept the consequences of her deed. A deadly feud began!

Sigebert's war against the Avars was going poorly and he
even spent some time as a prisoner of war. He was not entirely
unwilling, then, when Brunehilde urged him vehemently to
switch wars and send his armies west against his brother.

Accordingly, in 573, Sigebert demanded that Chilperic give
up the dowry he had received with his murdered queen (certainly a reasonable demand). Chilperic refused and war broke
out between the two Frankish powers.

Sigebert carried all before him, driving to Paris and beyond.
Chilperic seemed totally defeated and in 575, Sigebert, count-
ing the victory his, was being raised on the shields of his warriors as a sign that he was now the victorious king of Austrasia
and Neustria, when Fredegund intervened. She had her particular weapons and she used them now. Two hired assassins
were on the scene; their knives found their mark and Sigebert
fell dead. At once the demoralized Austrasians retreated.

Brunehilde was taken captive and it is remarkable that she
wasn't executed out of hand at Fredegund's orders. Apparently, she found favor in the eyes of Merovech, a son of Chilperic by his first wife. He arranged her escape; the two married
and fled to Tours, where they remained for a while under the
guardianship of Gregory, the historian-bishop.

It was a union of two people with a common enemy. Merovech, as the son of Chilperic's first wife, could scarcely feel safe
while Fredegund was surely intent on seeing that the inheritance would fall to her own children.

This new marriage saved Brunehilde, for although Chilperic
had it annulled, he allowed the queen to return to Austrasia.
There she proclaimed her young son, by Sigebert, as King
Childebert II, and ruled both him and the kingdom, finding

enough strength and spirit to assert her domination over the fractious Austrasian nobility.

For Merovech, the marriage was fatal. Fredegund undoubtedly had him on her list in any case, but his temporary marriage to his stepmother's deadly enemy made the end come the sooner. She therefore procured his assassination and the assassination of two other sons of Chilperic. That left only Chilperic himself and in 584 he died under mysterious circumstances. Naturally, the early chroniclers assumed Fredegund had had him assassinated, too, and perhaps that was so.

Fredegund promptly had her own baby son crowned as Clotaire II, king of Neustria. This was not a popular move, for there were many of the Neustrian nobility who objected to having the baby son of a low-born queen as their ruler.

The one remaining son of Clotaire I, Gontram of Burgundy, openly expressed doubts as to the baby's legitimacy. In order to set that doubt at rest, Fredegund had to stoop to the indignity of producing bishops and nobles to swear that her child was Chilperic's son. To make sure there would be no trouble in this, she had her chief Neustrian opponent, the bishop of Rouen, cut down in the usual way — by a hired assassin!

She tried, as a kind return for Gontram's inconvenient doubts, to have him assassinated, too, but somehow he escaped her henchmen long enough to die a natural death in 593, leaving no child to inherit, but directing in his will that his kingdom go to Austrasia.

The question now was: To whom would Burgundy fall? To Childebert II of Austrasia, son of Brunehilde, or to Clotaire II of Neustria, son of Fredegund? It was not a question to be answered by sweet reason where those queens were concerned.

The matter seemed to be settled when Childebert of Austrasia moved more quickly and seized Burgundy. Since he was Gontram's legal heir, this seemed justified.

But then, in 596, Childebert died. Some said it was by poison administered at the orders of you-know-who, but one can't help but wonder if all the supposed poisonings of early times were really poisonings. Disease was sudden and deadly in those days; young men might die without warning even in the absence of poison.

One of Childebert's sons, Theudebert II, aged ten, inherited Austrasia; the other, aged nine, inherited Burgundy. Attempting to be the real ruler of each land was their aged grandmother, Brunehilde. Still her enemy, was that other aged woman, Fredegund. The war continued till, in 597, Fredegund died in her Parisian palace.

Clotaire II of Neustria, freed of his domineering mother and attaining his majority, kept the pot boiling, however. He fought on with a merciless cruelty that showed that whether he was Chilperic's son or not, he was certainly Fredegund's. In the end he was completely victorious, capturing Brunehilde and her young great-grandchildren in 613. He killed the children (though he is supposed to have saved one out of pity, a rare emotion indeed among the Merovingians).

Brunehilde was now an old woman of about eighty. Nearly a half century had passed since her sister had been killed and her feud with Fredegund had begun. Now she was in the power of Fredegund's son and he did not fail his mother's ghost. The old woman was mercilessly humiliated and tortured, and was finally killed (according to the story) by being tied to the tail of a wild horse and dragged to death.

The tale of this feud lived on in very distorted fashion in a medieval German epic poem, written about 1200. It is the *Nibelungenlied* ("song of the Nibelungs"), in which the Nibelungs are an alternate name for the Burgundians.

In it, Siegfried, a German hero, comes to woo the princess Kriemhild, daughter of Gunther, king of Burgundy, then ruling at Worms on the Rhine river. Later, with Siegfried's help, Gunther woos and wins a warrior princess named Brunhild. The two queens quarrel and in the feud that follows, Siegfried is killed by treachery. Kriemhild then marries Etzel, king of the Huns, to get revenge on those who killed her husband. In the process the Burgundian kingdom is destroyed.

Part of the story was undoubtedly inspired by the fall of the early Bungundian kingdom on the Rhine to the Huns in 437, for Etzel is clearly Attila. The tale of the feud of the queens must hark back to the later events that involved, in part at least, the later kingdom of Burgundy southwest of the Rhine. Even the names are similar. Brunhild is the historic Brunehilde, while Gunther is Gontram, king of Burgundy. And both the legendary Siegfried and the historical Sigebert meet their ends at the treacherous knives of assassins.

Once the long feud was over, it seemed that the Frankish realm might settle down to peace. Clotaire II was now, like his grandfather Clotaire I, king over a united land. He ruled from 613 to the time of his death in 623, and his son Dagobert I continued to rule over the entire realm till his death in 639.

But the feud of Brunehilde and Fredegund, and the long and ferocious civil wars it had inspired, ruined the Frankish realm as the wars of Justinian had ruined Italy.

The peasant population, harried by contending armies, could barely feed themselves. Very little food was left over for the cities and what there was could scarcely be transported into town as the old Roman roads fell into disrepair and were scarcely usable.

The land fell into a kind of village economy, in which each little tract was forced to be as self-sufficient as possible, and the city population dropped to not more than three percent of the whole. The aqueducts were broken down too, and as the supply of reasonably clean water diminished and life grew more miserable, disease flourished.

So the darkness grew deeper.

5

THE MAYORS OF THE PALACE

SPAIN UNITED

While the Franks were consuming themselves with civil war and while their land was falling into utter barbarism, the Visigoths seemed — temporarily, at least — to recover some of their past power. Partly, of course, this followed naturally, since their Frankish enemies were too self-absorbed to bother them.

In 568, soon after the death of Athanagild (the father of those fateful sister-queens, Galswintha and Brunehilde), a man named Leuvigild became the Visigothic king.

For nearly twenty years he fought, in the main successfully, to extend the boundaries of the kingdom. In 584, he completed the conquest of the Sueves. These had worked their way into Italy in the very earliest years of the German invasions nearly two centuries before. They had maintained themselves as an independent power (though at times just barely) ever since. Now, worn-out, they yielded at last to the Visigoths and vanished from history.

Southward, too, the Visigoths spread. Foot by reluctant foot, the imperial forces fell back until they retained only a few stretches of the immediate coast. The Visigoths were now supreme over all the peninsula except for some of the coastal region and for a section of mountainous territory in the north.

Internally, the religious question was raised. Leuvigild was an ardent Arian in a world in which Arianism was slowly dying. Only the Visigoths and Lombards remained Arian and the Lombards were wavering and were soon to give in.

Arianism in Spain reached the beginning of the end when Leuvigild arranged a marriage between his son and a daughter of the famous Brunehilde of the Frankish feud. Brunehilde, who had been Visigothic and Arian to begin with, had turned Catholic for the sake of her Frankish marriage. Her daughter, who was Catholic, would not, however, turn Arian for her Visigothic marriage. (It was the essence of the Catholic victory that Arians frequently turned Catholic while Catholics almost never turned Arian.)

Leuvigild's new daughter-in-law brought a fervid Catholicism to the palace and ended by converting her husband. Now a religious war opened between father and son. The father won and the son was captured and executed.

This was, however, no victory for Arianism, for when Leuvigild died in 586, another son, Recared I, succeeded, and he turned Catholic. What's more, he saw to it that the Visigoths generally shared in his conversion and then thoroughly rooted out all evidence of Arianism in Spain. He did it so thoroughly and well that not a book or scrap of writing in Visigothic remains to be seen — which, from a historical standpoint, is deplorable, whatever religious justification Recared may have thought he had.

The disappearance of Arianism in Spain was different from

its disappearance elsewhere. In Spain, it seemed to leave a heritage of guilt among the rulers. In the case of the Vandals and the Ostrogoths, the ruling Germans lost their national identity along with their religion and no one was left feeling guilty. In the case of the Lombards, their short history of Arianism seemed to have left them unmarked.

The Visigoths, however, had been Arians for two centuries and now that they were Catholics they still remained Visigoths. It seemed as though the now-Catholic Visigoths had to do penance for the sins of their heretic ancestors and be more Catholic than the Catholics. The extremism they developed remained, somehow, a Spanish heritage right down into modern times.

A new intolerance swept over Spain. Until then, the West had seen a general policy of religious toleration, the deliberate policy of most of the Arian monarchs of the Germanic kingdoms. The reason was not that these Arian monarchs were so much nobler and kinder than Catholic monarchs might have been, but that the Arians were everywhere in a minority. An Arian king who tried to repress Catholicism by force would have faced a massive revolt that he might not have survived, particularly since he would have had to face a Frankish invasion on top of it.

The religious tolerance, once established, was usually extended to the Jews as well. These, few in number and isolated in religion, were no true danger to anyone.

Once the Visigothic kingdom went Catholic, however, the kings had to prove their orthodoxy by taking stern action against non-Catholics. This might have meant the Arians, but they all vanished as conversion spread. That left the Jews. The later Visigothic kings therefore initiated a policy of brutal anti-Semitism, which has stained Christian Europe ever since.

Again, apparently as a consequence of guilt, the king and the aristocracy (which remained Visigothic for a century and a quarter after the conversion) became remarkably subservient to the Catholic clergy, who were of Roman Catholic descent.

Spanish churchmen insisted on crowning the Visigothic kings and presenting the crown as a gift of the Church, which could be withdrawn at any time. They discouraged the succession of sons to make the monarchy more nearly elective. This kept the monarchy weak and the aristocracy divided and turbulent, something which, in the end, was the ruin of Visigothic Spain.

For a while, though, the coming ruin was not apparent. The Visigothic kings who followed Recared I continued to expand southward at the expense of the Eastern Empire. They were aided by a series of disasters, soon to be described, that were befalling the Empire at home. Under the Visigothic king, Suintila, the last of Constantinople's possessions in Spain fell in 625. The imperial presence in Spain following Justinian's reconquest had thus lasted but three-quarters of a century.

This same Suintila managed to subdue the last of the northern mountain strongholds. These were inhabited by a people known as the Basques, a strange people whose language is unrelated to any other known language on earth. From their blood types, it would seem that they represent a European population that preceded the tribes who populated the continent in historic times.

The Celts who flooded western Europe in the days when Rome was a small, unregarded Italian village supplanted and perhaps destroyed an earlier group of inhabitants in Gaul and Spain. These survived only in the hidden valleys of the western Pyrenees and we know them as the Basques.

Since then, the Basques had maintained their identity through the period of the Celtic and Roman domination of Spain. After the fall of the Western Empire, they fought off Sueves, Vandals and Visigoths with unwearied resistance. Even when bending to Visigothic domination at last, they waited stubbornly for the chance to break loose again.

In Suintila's reign, the Visigothic kingdom was at a new height, judging by geographical extent. It controlled the entire Spanish peninsula and a bit of the Mediterranean coast of Gaul.

Spain could even, at this time, manage to contribute an important personage to early medieval culture. This was Isidore, a scholar of an old Roman family of North African origin. In 600, he became bishop of Seville and is therefore universally known as Isidore of Seville.

Isidore made it his lifework to bring together all the knowledge that was available to him. Much of what he collected came from books written by other men who had gathered information similarly from still earlier books. With each step in the process, unavoidable distortions crept in, legends were accepted as reality, superstitions as truth. Isidore's work is therefore largely worthless as a scholarly report. Nevertheless, it was extremely popular during the Middle Ages and may even have helped the cause of learning indirectly by making knowledge (however false and distorted) seem interesting.

Suintila's reign ended in failure however. He made an effort to see to it that his son would succeed him, which pleased neither the aristocracy nor the churchmen. The aristocrats elected another king and the Church supported them. In 633, a synod gathered in Toledo, under Isidore of Seville himself, and excommunicated and deposed Suintila.

After Suintila, there was a series of kings who were careful to be subservient to the clergy, impeccable in their Catholicism, and heartless toward the Jews. One of these, more spirited than some, was Wamba, who came to the throne in 672. With a strong hand, he put down rebellions and banished all those Jews who would not accept baptism. His reign came to an end, however, in a peculiar manner.

In 680, he seemed to have had some sort of cataleptic fit, and while he was paralyzed and apparently dying, his servants shaved his head and wrapped him in a monk's cloak. He was, in other words, made into a churchman in order to improve his chances of Heaven. When he snapped out of his fit, it was too late. He was irrevocably a monk and could no longer be a king.

There were stories afterward that Wamba's fit was not a natural one, but had been the result of a narcotic given him at the instigation of the man who later became king in Wamba's place. The servants who shaved the king knew very well (according to this view) what they were about. Perhaps so! The kings of Western Europe had an exciting life of it in the Dark Ages and few, if any, were not the subject of all kinds of conspiracies.

In any case, Wamba was the last Visigothic king of any account. The temporary recovery was over, and the final decline to destruction was about to begin.

THE EMPIRE DISRUPTED

While the early seventh century saw the Visigoths painfully struggling upward and the Franks frantically trying to keep from sinking downward, the Eastern Empire, which had seemed such a colossus a century earlier under Justinian, met with disaster. It was as though the mighty effort it had made under that Emperor had left it utterly exhausted.

Justinian had not been dead for more than twenty years when his far less capable successors found enemies closing in on every side. In Europe the Avars thundered across the Danube and eventually reached the very walls of Constantinople. Slavic tribes began to infiltrate the Balkan peninsula more quietly but more permanently and to settle there.

In the East, Persia, under Chosroes II, a king of great ambitions, began the last and greatest of the many wars between Persia and the Empire. With almost ridiculous ease, the Persians invaded and occupied Syria, Egypt and Asia Minor.

By 626, when Clotaire II, son of Fredegund, was on the

Frankish throne and Suintila was the Visigothic king, the East
Roman dominions were reduced to no more than the city of
Constantinople itself plus what remained of Justinian's con-
quests in the West.

Somehow, Constantinople found the man for the time. Heraclius, from the province of Carthage, sailed to Constantinople
to assume the burden of Empire. After long preparation and
heroic efforts he managed to save the Empire from what had
seemed certain destruction.* He beat off the Avars and the
Persians and restored the lost provinces in full. The Empire
had, however, in the turmoil lost its last footholds in Spain and
those it could not regain.

Nor, as it turned out, was this eastern recovery more than
temporary, for a new enemy was arising in the East, one far
more terrible to Constantinople than any enemy it had yet met
and one that was to plunge even the West into desperate peril.

About 570, when Leuvigild, ruler of the Visigoths, made his
last despairing attempt to save Arianism; when the Lombards
were beginning their sweep into Italy; and when Brunehilde
and Fredegund were starting their deadly feud, a child was
born in the depths of Arabia. His name was Mohammed and in
middle life he devised a new religion which was based on Juda-
ism and Christianity, plus some Arabic refinements of his own.
The religion was Islam ("submission" — to the will of God,
that is). Those who practiced it were Moslems ("those who
submitted").

While the Eastern Empire was beating off the Persians, Mohammed succeeded in imposing his belief on all of Arabia and
in welding the Arabic tribes into an inspired army. They were
ready to fight for Islam and ready to die if necessary, for they
were convinced that death in battle against the infidel meant
instant transportation to paradise.

---

* For some detail on this supremely dramatic story, which lies outside the scope of this book, see my *The Near East* (Houghton
Mifflin, 1968).

Mohammed died in 632 and a united Arabia was now ready to explode outward. Only six years had passed since the Empire and Persia had made peace. Neither had yet recovered from the unexampled exertions of their great war. Both were exhausted.

Consequently, when the Arabic armies dashed northward, they had less trouble than they might otherwise have had in taking and occupying all of vast Persia and in taking Syria and Egypt from the Eastern Empire.

Heraclius, having expended enormous efforts in beating off the Persians, now saw Syria and Egypt wrenched away a second time and lacked the force or the will to try to regain them again. The provinces were permanently lost, not only to the Empire, but to Christianity.

Yet this time, the Empire held on desperately to Asia Minor. This, together with the Balkan peninsula in Europe, served as a nucleus that persisted for another eight centuries. This shrunken Empire is known to historians as the Byzantine Empire, though the people of the realm thought of themselves as the Roman Empire to the very, very end.

With great difficulty but unfading resolution, the Byzantine forces held the line along the eastern boundary of Asia Minor. Nor did they voluntarily loosen their grip on a single foot of what remained of their western possessions.

The Germanic kingdoms of the West were eventually to be threatened, too, by this eruption out of Arabia, but not for some decades. For a long time, the Byzantine Empire absorbed and muffled the entire shock of that first explosion.

For more than half a century after the death of Mohammed, the West must have heard of the Arabic advance only distantly if at all. To them it consisted of battles being waged on the other side of the world, far beyond their horizon. To be sure, the Arabs struck westward from Egypt, but for over a generation, the Byzantines held on to Carthage grimly, and as long as Carthage stood, the West was protected.

THE MEROVINGIAN DECAY

At the time of Mohammed's death, Dagobert I was king of the Franks. A century and a half had passed since Clovis had come to the throne and the Franks had begun their rise to power, and still their kingdom seemed to be expanding. The Avars, defeated by the forces of the Eastern Empire, were suddenly shrinking in power and were no longer the great menace they had been a half century before, when the great Brunehilde-Fredegund feud had started. As evidence of their weakness, Dagobert carried on successful campaigns against them on the upper Danube.

But appearances were deceptive. The Merovingian kings were in greater and greater trouble — trouble of a kind that doesn't show on the map. Communications had so decayed in the realm that it was difficult, even impossible, to get from place to place rapidly enough for any but the most forceful king to keep a firm grip on affairs.

More and more the king had to delegate authority, by appointing governors to care for this region or that. These governors were responsible for regions small enough to control. Though they were theoretically responsible to the king, they gradually grew more and more independent.

This was particularly so because financial control slipped from the king's fingers. For a while, the Merovingians had attempted to maintain the old system of administration dating from Roman times, but this required a body of civil servants that could no longer be supplied by a realm in which education and learning had nearly died. By 600, the system had broken down altogether and taxes could only be collected on a smaller scale by the king's delegates.

The king's governors, who pillaged the people as long as they worked for the king, gradually came to exercise complete control over their regions. The titles "duke" and "count," which originally denoted the military representative of the king and the civil representative, respectively, became titles of nobility.

The kings depended on their delegates to carry on the civil wars of the Brunehilde-Fredegund era. In return for military and financial help, they were forced to grant the delegates greater and greater independence — an independence that could no longer be withdrawn once the emergency was passed. The delegates became landed magnates of great power.

Once they controlled regions which were their own rather than the king's — once they were "in business for themselves" so to speak — their government became milder and more efficient. The people, therefore, preferred the new situation and upheld the process of decentralization.

The situation was more extreme in Austrasia than in Neustria, for in the former region there was no trace of Roman heritage to act as even the dimmest reminder of a onetime state of efficient government.

But then a new factor appeared on the scene . . .

When a king was primarily engaged in warfare and in long, arduous campaigns on the borders of the kingdom, he could not properly attend to the handling of internal affairs. It became necessary to choose someone to whom such responsibility could be delegated.

This official would remain behind in the palace while the king was on campaign, and would supervise matters there. He was the *major domus,* that is, "the great one in the palace." (We still use the term "majordomo," derived from the Spanish form of the phrase, to refer to the chief servant of a household.) In English the phrase is partially translated to "mayor of the palace."

Originally, the mayor of the palace was only a servant of the king, a kind of clerk who took care of paper work and carried

messages. Gradually, as the kingdom's administration broke
down, he had to take more and more duties under his wing
until he was virtually what we would today call a prime minister.

The power of the office was such that the great landowners
— the lords — competed for it and would suffer only someone
of their own number to fill it. Indeed, the mayor of the palace
could very well be considered the greatest of the lords.

The first important mayor of the palace made his appearance
under Clotaire II, the son of Fredegund. He was an Austrasian
named Pepin I of Landen. (Landen was the name of one of his
estates, located about fifty miles north of Metz, the Austrasian
capital.)

When Dagobert succeeded to the throne, however, he could
still exert the royal power (and was the last Merovingian of
whom this could be said). Displeased with Pepin, he summarily removed him, and kept him out of office for the rest of his
reign. In 638, however, Dagobert died and Pepin of Landen
came back to power for the brief period that remained to him.
Pepin died in 640.

But the situation had changed with Dagobert's death. The
Frankish realm was split once more between Dagobert's two
young sons. One, Sigebert III, ruled over Austrasia and the
other, Clovis II, over Neustria. Both were too young to wield
power at first and were forced to depend entirely on the mayors
of the palace. By the time they were old enough to govern,
disintegration had proceeded so far that they could not become
kings in fact, even if they would. They and their descendants
were the prisoners of the great lords, who alone possessed the
money and men with which to fight.

So obvious did it become that the Merovingian kings were
powerless and the mayors of the palace were kings in
everything but name, that it was inevitable for some mayor
eventually to begin wondering if he might not gain the name as
well.

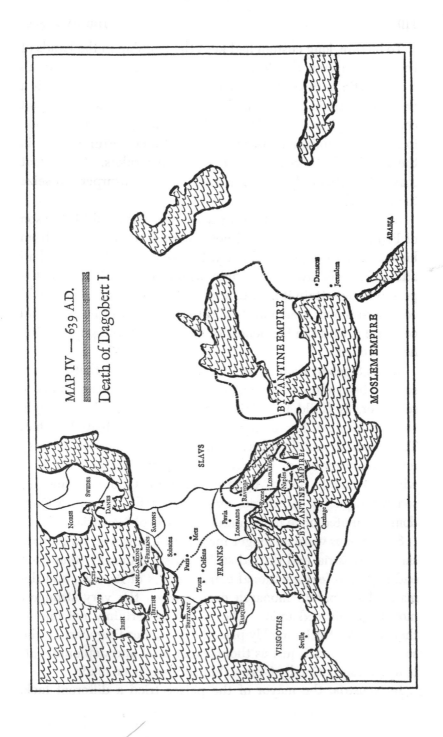

MAP IV — 639 A.D.

Death of Dagobert I

SWEDES

SLAVS

NORSE

DANES

FRISIANS

PICTS

SCOTS

ANGLO-SAXONS

IRISH

BRITISH

SAXONS

Soissons

Metz

Paris

BRITTANY

Tours

Orléans

FRANKS

LOMBARDS

Pavia

BASQUES

VISIGOTHS

Seville

Ravenna

Rome

LOMBARDS

Naples

BYZANTINE EMPIRE

Carthage

BYZANTINE EMPIRE

Damascus

Jerusalem

ARABIA

MOSLEM EMPIRE

To be sure, long custom had kept the kingship in the hands of the Merovingians, the descendants of Clovis. There was an almost mystic faith on the part of the Franks that only such a descendant could possibly be king; that only such a descendant could be "legitimate." (This feeling for legitimacy is common in all long-established monarchies and is a powerful weapon in the hands of otherwise feeble or vicious rulers. It is what makes it particularly hard for even an able "usurper" to seize the throne.)

In this case, the would-be "usurper" was Grimwald I, the son of Pepin of Landen. He had not inherited the mayoralty from his father, for the post had not yet become hereditary. He had attained it only after a long fight with other candidates for the position. But attain it he did, and once that was done, he could consider his own great efforts and the great power he held, and compare it with the feebleness of Sigebert III, the puppet king he controlled.

When Sigebert died in 656, Grimwald gave out that his own son had been adopted by the dead king and proclaimed him the successor, as Childebert III. He found out quickly, though, that the magic of legitimacy was not as easily defeated as that. The Frankish nobility was willing to serve (more or less) under descendants of the great Clovis, but not under a king who was merely one of themselves. Both Grimwald and his son were quickly murdered, and for a while the entire kingdom was united once more under Clovis II of Neustria.

Such unions were no longer meaningful, however, for Austrasia and Neustria had drifted so far apart, culturally, that each had begun to feel a national consciousness of its own, and demanded a separate monarch except when the very strongest monarchs enforced union. Clovis II was certainly not one of these and Austrasia quickly placed itself under Dagobert II, the son of Sigebert III, just as though that brief and deplorable attempt at usurpation by Grimwald had never been made.

In Neustria, the mayor of the palace tried a different tack.

His name was Ebroin, and he came to power in 664, when Clotaire III, son of Clovis II, was reigning. In Neustria, the old tradition of strong central government was stronger than in Austrasia, and Ebroin tried to make himself the expression of that tradition. He realized that the only way to bring some sort of stability to the land was to repress the turbulent lords. To do that, against their strong hostility (naturally) he had to work under the mantle of legitimacy and see to it that all was done in the name of Clotaire III.

A point of danger arose in 670 when Clotaire died. Who would control the new king? Ebroin tried to secure himself, not by displacing the Merovingian line as Grimwald had tried to do, but by handpicking the successor. He chose the late king's younger surviving brother, as the easier to handle, and set him on the throne as Theuderich III. He refrained from taking any chances of having the nobility and clergy veto this, by carefully omitting to consult them.

This was too much. The Neustrians rose in revolt and put the older brother, Childerich II, on the throne. The older brother died, though, in 672, and the younger brother succeeded again — but without Ebroin, whom the Neustrian lords were determined not to tolerate.

The resourceful Ebroin escaped to Austrasia and managed to put up still another puppet Merovingian, Clovis III, a son of Theuderich. Behind this new puppet he could return to power over the angry protests of the lords. Indeed, when Dagobert II of Austrasia died in 678, Ebroin attempted to extend his power over that portion of the realm as well.

In Austrasia, still another mayor of the palace arose from the old family of Pepin of Landen. The murdered Grimwald had had an older sister, whose son survived the massacre of his uncle and cousin. He was another Pepin, Pepin II of Heristal, so-named after the town in which he was born, a town in what is now eastern Belgium.

Pepin of Heristal represented the interests of the lords as op-

posed to the centralizing tendency of Ebroin. The two mayors
went to war as though they were sovereigns. No one paid any
attention to the Merovingians who were nominally kings. They
were merely names to be used in order to invoke the mystique
of legitimacy.

In the initial stages of the war, Pepin let himself be surprised
by Ebroin, was defeated and had to flee. Pepin's chief associate, Martin, fled to sanctuary and was lured out of it in a manner rather typical of the times.

Ebroin sent a couple of bishops to the church in which Martin
was hiding (and from which he could not be taken by force
without the committing of a serious sacrilege) and asked him
to come with them. They insisted he would not be hurt and
swore to this on a chest containing holy relics. At least, Martin
thought it contained the bones of saints. Actually it was empty,
and when Martin reached Ebroin he was forthwith executed.
No one seemed to think there was anything wrong with such a
trick.

Pepin got away cleanly and, in 681, Ebroin was assassinated
in the course of a private feud. Thus vanished the last small
chance for an effective Merovingian monarchy. Slowly, Pepin
gathered another army and the war began again against a new
Neustrian mayor. In 687, Pepin won completely and was
mayor over all the Frankish realm, though Theuderich III, and
later his successors, remained as kings.

The Merovingians who followed Dagobert I were helpless
creatures, who were encouraged to occupy themselves with
women and wine, whose education was neglected, and who
usually died young. They remained in their palaces and were
displayed, with their long hair, on state occasions when they
said and did what they were told to say and do.

In the age that succeeded the days of the Merovingian monarchs, these last kings were sneered at as the *rois fainéants* or
"do-nothing kings." But then what *could* they do under the
circumstances? Their situation was rather like that of King

Victor Emmanuel III of Italy during the 1920's and 1930's, who played at being king while the real power was held by the dictator Mussolini.

THE LAST OF THE GOTHS

While the Frankish kingdom was disintegrating, the menace to the south, still distant, was gathering momentum. The advancing Arabs were converting the people in the conquered provinces to Islam and their religion was marching even faster than their armies.

While the fading Byzantine garrisons hung on to strong points in North Africa, the population all about them swung over to Islam. In part, this was a national reaction to the Byzantines. The natives resented the Imperials who governed them and therefore favored the Arabs and the new religion.

The Byzantines, in consequence, had not only to repel attack after attack from the Arabs, but had to do it against the gathering hostility of the people of the land. In 698, the wearied grip let go. The land that Belisarius had reconquered for the Eastern Empire a century and a half before was now lost forever both to the Empire and to Christianity. (To the diminished Empire, all that was left of Justinian's great surge were parts of Italy.)

The conquering Arabs swept across all of what was left of North Africa and turned the entire south shore of the Mediterranean Sea into Moslem territory — which it still is today.

This was a greater loss than might appear to us today, when we are used to thinking of North Africa as something apart from Europe. Throughout ancient times, the Mediterranean Sea was a unifying force, for sea travel in its inland waters was easier than land travel. Under the Roman Empire, all the shores of the Mediterranean shared a common culture and the North African province about Carthage was as Roman and as Latin-speaking as Gaul.

North Africa was part of the western branch of Christianity and contributed important writers to the early Church, men such as Tertullian and St. Augustine. The latter, in fact, was probably the most influential theologian since the time of the Apostle Paul.

Now North Africa was gone, fading forever beyond the Christian horizon. The Mediterranean Sea became what it has been ever since, a division between two cultures that were usually at bitter enmity with one another. Trade decayed and the cities on the southern coast of western Europe, which had managed to survive so far, now began to deteriorate.

But the worst for Europe and for western Christianity still loomed ahead.

The victorious Moslems had not yet met a serious check and were in no mood to call a halt to expansion. The Mediterranean narrowed to a mere dozen or so miles at its western end and across that narrow stretch of water was Visigothic Spain — and Europe. The vista was an attractive one and within Spain there was, unfortunately for its people, chaos.

Wamba, the last effective king of the Visigoths, had tried to establish a navy a generation earlier, while the Byzantines still held off the Moslem menace beyond Carthage. His successors had allowed that effort to fade and now there was nothing with which to guard the vulnerable coast.

In 709, the Visigothic king Witiza had died and in the face of a great and victorious army just across the strait, the nobles began the usual squabbling over the succession. It is all very dim, for the chronicles of the time are confusing and uncertain. Apparently, though, a Visigothic nobleman named Roderic seized the throne and wangled the necessary clerical approval.

Left behind, angry and determined to change the situation, were the sons of Witiza, who gathered partisans about themselves and prepared for civil war. In their anger and frustration, they apparently yielded to the temptation of turning for help to the army on the other side of the strait.

The later Spaniards tell a most dramatic tale of this fatal moment. Roderic, they said, was in love with a girl called Florinda, who was the daughter of one Count Julian. Julian was, in his turn, the governor of Ceuta, a town just across the strait from Spain. When Florinda refused Roderic's advances, he forced her. The indignant Count Julian therefore invited the Moslem army into Spain, joining and guiding them.

This story is ridiculous on the face of it. It isn't found in any of the chronicles until four centuries after the time when it was all supposed to have happened. Nor did the Visigoths rule in Ceuta then or at any time. Rather, it was Byzantine territory before the Moslems came, the last scrap of such territory in Africa.

It may well have been that Count Julian was the Byzantine governor of Ceuta, who, seeing that Islam was unstoppable, at least at that moment, joined it. It is much more likely, though, that the impetus to cross into Spain came not from him but from the anti-Roderic nobles among the Visigoths.

The enemy now gathered south of the strait was not really an Arab army. The Islamic Empire by this time stretched some five thousand miles east and west and it could not possibly be held by Arabs alone. The army in Africa consisted mostly of Berbers; that is, of North African natives. The portion of North Africa nearest Spain had, in Roman times, been called Mauretania and an inhabitant of the region was termed a Maurus. To the Spaniards the word became Moros and to ourselves, Moors.

The commander of the Moorish forces in North Africa was Musa ibn-Nusair and he undertook the Spanish invasion most cautiously. First, he conducted a preliminary raid with a small number of men, and when the results proved satisfactory, he sent off some seven thousand Moors under Tariq ibn-Zayyid. The troops landed on a promontory on Spain's southern coast.

The Moors named the promontory Gebel al-Tariq (meaning "Mount Tariq"). This was corrupted later to Gibraltar, the name it still bears. The strip of water separating Spain from Africa became the Strait of Gibraltar.

The Moorish army, later reinforced to twelve thousand, met a much larger army of Visigoths near Cádiz on July 19, 711. The Visigoths might have been expected to win but they were riddled with dissension and treason. At a crucial point in the battle, sizable sections of the Gothic army broke away, their leaders hoping that a defeat would put Roderic out of business and would lead to one of their own becoming king. They miscalculated disastrously, for the entire army crumbled and the defeat was total.

Roderic was last seen in wild flight and is supposed to have drowned while trying to cross the nearby river. The Visigoths, like the Ostrogoths before them, now disappear from history and Roderic is commonly known as "the last of the Goths."

It had been about 260 that the Goths had reached the Black Sea and had begun to make their power felt on the borders of the Roman Empire. In 711 the end came. They had wound their way through four and a half centuries of turbulent history and left behind one great name, Theodoric the Ostrogoth.

Spain fell rapidly before Tariq's men. The great victory had completely demoralized the Visigoths, while the peasantry was helpless. Moreover, wherever the Moors went they could count on the aid of the Jews, to whom a century of the cruelest persecution by the Christians of the peninsula had shown that no change could be for the worse.

Musa, Tariq's superior, hastened across the Strait of Gibraltar with more men in order that the glory of the conquest should not be assigned entirely to Tariq. With both on the scene, the conquest of virtually the entire Visigothic kingdom was completed by 714. Only in the northern mountains, among the Basques in particular, was the conquest not final.

Christian guerrillas remained there to form the nucleus of

small Christian kingdoms that, over the course of seven centuries, were to retake the peninsula for Christendom. But that was for the future, and for the while, Spain slipped out of the main stream of Western history.

CHARLES MARTEL

At the moment of the Moorish conquest of Spain, with the Franks now face to face with a monstrously strong enemy, Pepin of Heristal lay dying. He had been a strong mayor of the palace and his loss would have been bad enough. Worse yet, a deadly quarrel was already beginning, in the very face of the enemy, to determine his successor.

Pepin himself tried to insure peace by willing his office to his son Grimwald II, but there was an all-too-easy way of canceling that bequest. The nobles in opposition to Pepin arranged to have Grimwald assassinated. Since Pepin himself was clearly close to the grave, it seemed that this deed could be carried out with impunity.

Pepin roused himself, however, and staved off death by a supreme effort of will; in a last fight he defeated the opposition — and died in December of 714.

But the damage was done. With Grimwald dead, civil war continued while the Moors watched from the Pyrenees.

Pepin's legitimate sons were all dead, but his queen tried to control the land in the name of her grandchildren, the sons of the assassinated Grimwald. Government by a queen and by infants was not very attractive however, and the Neustrians were in any case unenthusiastic with the notion of being ruled by Austrasians. They rose in rebellion. (Of course, there was a Merovingian king, Dagobert III, who at the time ruled over both Neustria and Austrasia, but no one cared about that.)

There was, however, one more person in the field. Pepin of

Heristal had had an additional son, an illegitimate one, who was twenty-six years old at the time of his father's death. The young man's name was Karl and that name has an interesting history. It stems from an old Teutonic word for the lowest class of freeman and it came to be degraded even farther and applied to serfs. The English word "churl" originates from the same source.

Its application to Pepin's son may have been a father's fond pet name indicating that the young boy was of low birth. Nevertheless, Karl eventually covered himself with such glory (and so, even more so, did his grandson and namesake) that the name, originating in the stables, so to speak, became a favorite among the royalty of Western Europe. It has been borne by kings in Austria, Great Britain, France, Germany, Hungary, Italy, Spain and Sweden. And of them all, Karl, son of Pepin of Heristal, was the first. The Latin form of the name is Carolus, and the descendants of Karl are therefore "Carolingians."

To be sure, the Germanic name Karl is better known to us in its French form, Charles. Because Karl, in later life, delivered hammerlike military strokes, he is best known in English-language histories as Charles Martel (Karl the Hammer).

Pepin's queen had imprisoned Charles Martel immediately upon Pepin's death, since she realized he would be a great danger to the rule of her grandchildren. Her power was broken, however, when the Neustrians defeated her in battle. Charles, escaping, took over the demoralized Austrasian forces and beat the Neustrians twice. He forced Pepin's queen to recognize him as lord of Austrasia, then advanced into Neustria to win again.

Ten years and more Charles Martel was fighting to consolidate the Frankish realm under his rule as it had been under his father's, and all that time the Moors were growing more threatening.

South of Neustria, between the Loire and the Pyrenees, was

Aquitaine, the land which once, as the Kingdom of Toulouse, had been the first of the Germanic kingdoms on Roman soil.

Clovis I had taken Aquitaine from the Visigoth Alaric II over two centuries before, in his last and greatest conquest, but it had never been a firm part of the Frankish kingdom. It retained a certain semi-independence under its own line of dukes, and a culture that was much more Roman and civilized than that of the Frankified land of Neustria (let alone the purely German Austrasia).

When the Moors conquered Spain, Aquitaine was under a duke named Eudes (yood). Eudes attempted to use the civil wars that followed the death of Pepin of Heristal as a means of establishing his own complete independence, and he might have succeeded if it had not been for the Moorish menace.

Eudes had to face about after making peace with the embattled Charles Martel, and defend himself against Moorish raiding parties. He managed to defeat one Moorish army at the gates of his capital, Toulouse, in 721, and thus bought a few years of peace. Then he tried to extend that period by encouraging dissension among the Moorish generals. (There is a story that one Moorish general, Othman, fell in love with the daughter of Eudes, and married her. After that the general favored Eudes against his own superior, Abd-er-Rahman. It is hard, however, to tell how far to trust chroniclers when they start breathing love and romance.)

Still, Abd-er-Rahman must have grown impatient at Eudes's intrigues and decided to take the tough way out. In 732, the Moors organized an expeditionary force and marched into Aquitaine. Eudes found himself unable to stop them and was forced to call upon Charles Martel.

Charles Martel was not blind to the danger, of course. He had drawn up his army on the Loire River, near the city of Tours, at the northern limits of the Aquitanian duchy. In order to face the Moors, who relied heavily on their excellent light cavalry, mounted on nimble Arabian horses, Charles required a cavalry of his own. To suit the Frankish manner of fighting, he needed large horses and developed a heavy cavalry. It was the first such fighting force to appear on European soil and it was the kind that eventually gave us our notion of the medieval knights and of their appearance at jousts and tourneys.*

To prepare his cavalry, Charles had to have money and he had no choice but to get it from the Church. The Church had accumulated land over the centuries and now possessed nearly one-third of all the land in the Frankish realm. Some of it was under the control of bishops who had fought on the Neustrian side against him and who might be judged to have forfeited their rights.

In any case, Charles had assigned valuable estates to his warriors, estates that could enable them to get and support the horses and equipment necessary to form the heavy cavalry he needed. Since this was all intended to fight the Moorish infidels, one would suppose the Church would agree, and indeed there was no open censure at the time. In later centuries, though, priestly chroniclers were much incensed with Charles and spread the story that after his death he was carried off to hell by a demon.

The crucial year 732 saw Charles's heavy cavalry crossing the Loire River at Eudes's invitation and advancing southward toward Poitiers, sixty miles away. The two armies met at a site which has not been located exactly, and the resulting battle is therefore variously called the Battle of Tours and the Battle of Poitiers.

The Moorish cavalry charges broke again and again against the heavier weight on the Frankish side and the cost of the at-

---

* We associate this with King Arthur and his knights, but King Arthur, or the legends on which he is based, date back at least two centuries before this time, so the armored knight of the Round Table, as usually pictured, is a complete anachronism.

tack grew unbearably great for the Moors. When night fell on the battlefield, the Moorish commanders had to decide whether to renew the battle the next day against the monstrous Frankish horsemen. They decided on the better part of valor and when dawn broke they were gone. They had retreated during the night and Charles Martel's heavy cavalry had won a great battle.

It is fashionable to think of this battle as one of the turning points in history, as the place where the great forward surge of Islam was stopped exactly one hundred years after the death of Mohammed. If the battle had not been won by the Franks, goes the usual argument, all of Europe might have fallen to the Moslems.

It is possible to doubt this, however. The Moors might not have been so formidable an enemy north of the Pyrenees as is usually pictured. The Moors in Spain had their troubles. There were the guerrilla forces in the northern mountains and much dissension among their own leaders. They could scarcely have spared a great force, and the army Charles Martel had defeated may well have been only a raiding party of not more than moderate size. So, even if Charles Martel had lost the battle, it is quite doubtful that the Moors could have gone much further. The weight of the huge Moslem Empire was already breaking down its structure.

In fact, if one must seek a particular battle that stopped the forward surge of Islam, one should look to Constantinople, which in 717 and 718 (while the conquest of Spain was proceeding) withstood a great Arabic siege and inflicted a tremendous defeat upon the enemy. The defeat of the main Islamic forces at the very heart and center of the strongest and richest Christian power of the time was of much more importance than a skirmish in the wilderness of the Frankish realm.

Nevertheless, historians are self-centered. We derive our culture from the ancient world by way of the western Franks,

not by way of the eastern Byzantines, and it is the battle with
the Franks and not with the Byzantines that will always seem
important to us.

There is no question, though, that whatever the real signifi-
cance of the victory, it succeeded in enhancing Charles's prestige and helped him in his project of unifying the Frankish
realm.

Yet he recognized his limits and remained always and merely
mayor of the palace, while one or another of the Merovingians
remained king. Dagobert III, who was on the throne when
Charles Martel began his career, was succeeded first by a
cousin, Chilperic II, then by a son, Theuderich IV. In 737,
Theuderich died and Charles allowed the throne to remain
empty. It is a good measure of the state of the Merovingian
dynasty that the emptiness of the throne affected nothing. Perhaps nobody even noticed that it was empty.

And yet Charles did not attempt to make himself king or to
establish a kingship for his son. The magic of legitimacy still
held, and he must have remembered what had happened to his
grandmother's brother Grimwald.

6

FROM MAYOR TO KING

CRISES IN ROME

After the death of Pope Gregory the Great in 604, the Papacy was left with the task of juggling the two secular powers which shared Italy. There was the imperial Exarch at Ravenna and the Lombard duchies, with their most powerful ruler at Pavia.

Both were dangerous in that both possessed armed power that could, under certain conditions, dominate Rome and threaten to make the Pope a puppet once more. What saved the situation for the Papacy, at least on a short-term basis, was that the Lombard nobility was divided among themselves and the Empire faced first the Persians and then the Moslems in a series of great and disastrous crises.

When the danger came, then, it was not brought by the spears of armed men, but on the wings of thought. When Heraclius was Emperor, he could not help but realize that the Per-

sians had taken Syria and Egypt as easily as they had because
the Syrians and Egyptians were at odds with the theological
doctrines upheld at Constantinople. Such was the mutual bit-
terness that the Syrians and Egyptians virtually welcomed the
Persians as liberators.

Heraclius therefore set about proposing a compromise between the orthodoxy of Constantinople and the heresy of Egypt
and Syria. This compromise was known as monotheletism. It
was a monumental failure. The Egyptians and Syrians would
not accept it and capitulated as easily to the Islamic armies as
they had earlier given in to the Persians. The orthodox, on the
other hand, were also dissatisfied and the Popes, in particular,
were absolutely horrified.

The religious dispute reached its climax soon after 649, when
Martin I, just elected to the Papacy, called a council to de-
nounce monotheletism and then tried to organize the Western
Church into unified resistance. The Byzantine Empire, however, though badly shattered by the Moslem advance, was still
strong in Italy. The Exarch arrested Martin in 653. He was
sent to Constantinople where he was tried, threatened with
death, and finally sent into exile to the Crimea (the "Siberia" of
the Byzantine Empire). He died there in 655.

But it was Constantinople that was forced to give in. With
Syria and Egypt apparently gone past all hope of recovery,
there was no point in trying to conciliate the heretics there.
Furthermore, Constantinople's security had further weakened. The Moslems had laid siege to the capital city itself and,
though driven off, were clearly intending to come back some-
day with overwhelming forces. The Empire could no longer
carry off matters with a high hand and needed friends wherever
it could find them.

In 680, therefore, a council of bishops met at Constantinople
and dropped the monotheletist compromise altogether. In 692,
the Patriarch of Constantinople was even willing to concede
equal status to the Pope.

But if the Papacy could feel relief at the recession of the theological danger, that relief had to vanish as the more mundane secular danger suddenly increased. In 712, a new and vigorous monarch, Liutprand, succeeded to the Lombard throne in Pavia and set about at once bending the fractious aristocracy to his will. The danger was that if he could unify the Lombards the Pope would be nearly helpless before them.

It is odd to think that Liutprand, a capable monarch, should be so entirely occupied with his own Lombard affairs in 712 and the years immediately following. To anyone who was capable of looking at Europe as a whole in that time, absolute disaster threatened at both sides simultaneously. On the west, Spain was overrun and soon Moslem raids were pushing north of the Pyrenees. On the east, Moslem forces were infiltrating Asia Minor and the huge offensive against Constantinople itself was finally under way.

Was it not time for Christian Europe to bury its local feuds and stand shoulder to shoulder against the Moslem menace?

Unfortunately, the Europe of 712 could not possibly have done so. It was too far gone in distintegration. Communications were so battered, transportation so nearly impossible, all sense of unity so lost, that a pinch at the nerve endings in the Pyrenees simply could not be felt in the Alps, three hundred miles away.

If Christian Europe was to survive, it would have to be saved by independent armies, working separately and without coordination. Fortunately, that turned out to be enough.

The Byzantine Empire, faced in 717 with a huge land and sea siege of Constantinople by the Arabs, found for itself a new and vigorous Emperor, Leo III. Resolutely he organized Byzantine defenses and then went over onto the offensive, making skillful use of "Greek fire" (a mixture of chemicals, probably including a petroleum fraction that burned hotly on contact with water) to fire and drive off the Arab fleet.

With the Moslem sea power beaten, Constantinople could be

supplied with food and arms and could no longer possibly be taken. A counteroffensive against the disheartened Moslem army in Asia Minor was successful, and in 718 the completely beaten survivors of the great expedition had to scuttle back home ignominiously.

It was this victory, as I said before, that turned the tide of the first flood of Arab conquest. The victory of Charles Martel fifteen years later was only a minor incident in comparison.

As viewed from Rome, the Byzantine victory offered a way out against the growing Lombard menace. It might well have seemed sensible for the Pope to form an alliance with the Exarch against the increasing power of Liutprand.

Unfortunately, the revival of Byzantine self-confidence extended to matters theological as well, and their eagerness to appease the Pope died. Leo III himself aspired to become a religious reformer. To his mind, the Christian Church was riddled with superstitious practices of all sorts. In particular, statues and images were popular with the people and were the objects of worship.

The official view of the Church was that the images, or "icons," merely served to focus the thoughts of the worshiper on the historical personage represented by them. Leo and his party, however, insisted that the images themselves were, in ignorance, worshiped and that Christianity was in danger of becoming an entirely idolatrous religion.

Leo ordered the images broken and thus began the period of iconoclasm (image-breaking). Leo and his successors supported iconoclasm for over half a century, and during all that time were opposed by the Western Church, with the Pope himself leading that opposition.

So great was papal horror at this Constantinopolitan line of action, that Gregory II (who was then Pope) felt it was necessary to make the best arrangement possible with Liutprand. Better the Lombard spears than the imperial heresy.

Liutprand welcomed an alliance with the Pope. At the moment, he felt his immediate enemy to be the Exarch. Once the imperial dominions were neutralized and absorbed, time enough for the Pope. He therefore attacked the imperial forces and began to drive them back bit by bit. In 728, he even took Ravenna itself temporarily.

And now Gregory II began to have second thoughts. He could see quite clearly that if the imperial forces were driven out of Italy altogether, he would be absolutely helpless before the Lombards unless help could be sought elsewhere.

The first Gregory had already looked toward the Franks, comfortably distant and traditionally Catholic. Gregory the Great had written to a Merovingian king but of course there was no point in doing that anymore.

The new Gregory, Gregory II, turned to the mayor of the palace and appealed to Charles Martel for help. Charles Martel, however, sent back a polite refusal. He had his hands full, and more than full, at home, fighting his own nobles, and the Battle of Tours had not yet taken place. (Nevertheless, this hesitancy on the part of Charles to come to the aid of the Pope was another point held against him by the priestly chroniclers who later consigned his soul to the devil.)

In 731, Gregory II died and was succeeded by Gregory III. This still newer Gregory was an even fiercer opponent of iconoclasm than his predecessor and went so far as to excommunicate Emperor Leo III. The excommunication did not, however, lessen the Lombard menace at home, and in 739 the new Pope had to repeat the appeal to Charles Martel.

The situation had now changed. For one thing, the Battle of Tours had now been fought and Charles's prestige was sky-high. He could afford greater risks. What's more, since the Emperor was excommunicated, the Pope (in his own view) succeeded to the imperial powers and felt he had the ability to grant imperial titles. He offered to make Charles a consul of Rome if Charles would but come to his aid.

If Charles had been a younger man, he might well have taken

the bait, but he was fifty now and he was war-worn. So he
hesitated and debated with himself while ambassadors continued to trudge back and forth between the Pope and the mayor.
And while the hesitation continued, the old cast of characters
was swept off the board. Emperor Leo III died in 740 and both
Charles Martel and Gregory III died in 741.

The new cast kept up the game, however. Leo's successor
was his son Constantine V, a forceful man who was even more
committed to iconoclasm than his father had been. And the
new Pope, Zacharias, remained as utterly opposed to iconoclasm as his predecessor.

In fact, Zacharias' election saw a significant step taken in the
development of the Papacy. Since the Emperor was excommunicated, Zacharias saw no necessity, or even fitness, in seeking
the usual imperial approval of the election. He took the tiara of
the Papacy without referring to Ravenna, an innovation that
was to remain permanently.

Liutprand died not long after, in 744, but the Lombard menace remained. The papal dilemma was not yet resolved. But a
new Frankish mayor of the palace was now on the scene who
would resolve it — at a price.

PEPIN'S PRICE

Charles Martel had two sons among whom he divided the
Frankish kingdom, acting, in this fashion, as though he were its
monarch. And, to be sure, there was no other monarch, for no
Merovingian was on the throne, nor had there been one for four
years.

The older son, Carloman, ruled as mayor of the palace over
Austrasia, while the younger son, Pepin, held the same office
over Neustria. To distinguish this Pepin from the earlier ones,

Pepin of Landen and Pepin of Heristal, he is usually known as
Pepin III the Short, presumably because he was short of stature.
He was not, however, short of ability, for he managed well in
the inevitable civil wars that accompanied the succession. He
made good use of psychological warfare, too.

Charles Martel, toward the end of his rule, had been secure
enough and renowned enough to make do without a Merovingian monarch, but his sons were by no means that secure to
begin with.

In 742, the young monarchs found a prince of the Merovingian line, the son of one who had reigned for a time twenty
years before. They crowned him as Childeric III and from then
on all their acts would bear the mark of Merovingian legitimacy. Their rivals could not say the same and were corre-
spondingly weakened.

To be sure the new king is known in history as Childeric the
Stupid, which may be an accurate measure of his abilities, but
those abilities didn't matter. The mantle of legitimacy was an
abstraction that took no account of actual personalities.

Together, the brothers, backed by Merovingian legitimacy,
won out over the opposition. Then, in 747, Carloman retired to
a monastery. Apparently, this was the result of a sincere dedi-
cation to the religious life, but Pepin's whole career shows great
political skill and he may perhaps have maneuvered his brother's retirement somehow. In any case, Pepin the Short now
ruled, unopposed and unchallenged, over the entire Frankish
realm, and suddenly he must have felt that he needed the
Merovingian puppet no longer. It must have proved completely irritating to the energetic and capable mayor that a
cloudy-witted nonentity was king, while he himself was only
the first of the king's subjects.

Yet what was he to do? Charles Martel had done without a
monarch by waiting for the old one to die and then not enthron-
ing a new one. In his own case, Childeric III was alive and
showed no signs of dying. He might be killed or forcibly de-

posed but Pepin, the politician, realized this would be the perfect excuse for renewed civil war.

He needed some other way out and it occurred to him that
any ordinary law or custom could be avoided if it conflicted
with God's will. And who interpreted God's will? In Western
Christendom at least, it was the Pope who interpreted that will,
and Pepin's eye began to wander over the Alps to Italy. Surely
something could be arranged there. After all, twice in his father's time had the Popes sent humble pleas for help and certainly such help ought to carry a price tag.

The situation in Italy seemed made to order for Pepin. After
Liutprand's death in 744, the Lombard pressure on the Pope
had lightened while there was the inevitable squabble for the
succession. But then, in 749, one Aistulf (who was not of Liutprand's line) became king and adopted a strong aggressive foreign policy at once. It was clear that the Pope would soon be in
trouble again.

Initially, Aistulf bent his efforts against the imperial forces in
Italy and all went his way. In 751, he drove the Exarch out of
Ravenna as Liutprand had done a couple of decades earlier.
This time, though, the Byzantine loss was permanent and the
Exarchate of Ravenna came to an end.

For three and a half centuries, Ravenna had been a capital
city. It had become the seat of the Western Emperor in the
days when Alaric and his Visigoths had marched into central
Italy. Odoacer had ruled there, so had Theodoric the Ostrogoth. When Justinian reconquered Italy, Narses had ruled
there, and so had the Exarchs who had succeeded Narses. But
now Ravenna's days of glory came to an end forever, and the
realm that still called itself the Roman Empire was driven from
central Italy for the last time.

Yet not all the conquests of Belisarius were gone. The extreme south of Italy, the toe and heel, as well as the island of
Sicily, still remained Byzantine and still owned the overlordship of the Emperor at Constantinople. The cities of Venice

and Naples also found it expedient to recognize imperial overlordship. Most of the rest of the peninsula, however, was now
entirely Lombard.

Zacharias could view Aistulf's advance only with the gravest
misgivings. He began to think of the Franks again; he had to.

With Pepin thinking of the Pope, and the Pope thinking of
Pepin, all that was needed was some means of communication
and that means was right at hand. Carloman, Pepin's brother
and ex-king, was at the Benedictine monastery at Monte Cassino. He was the perfect intermediary between Pepin and the
Pope, and he was indeed received by the Pope. The groundwork was laid for an important agreement.

After all, it was possible for each party to the agreement to
help the other enormously. The Merovingian monarch Childeric III would no longer be legitimate if the Pope said he
wasn't. The Lombards would no longer be a menace if struck
from the rear by an overwhelming Frankish force. It was perfectly plain that one move hinged on the other. Agreement
having been reached in private, it was now only necessary to go
through the motions, solemnly, in public.

In 751, therefore, with Aistulf about to take Ravenna, a
stately embassy traveled from Pepin's capital to Rome with a
question: Was it right that a person with no authority should
be called king? Or should the title go to the person who actually ruled in fact?

The Pope replied, with all suitable ceremony, that the person
who filled the role of king should, by right, also bear the title.

This message was brought back, and Childeric, a ninth-
generation descendant of Clovis, was deprived of his throne.
His long hair — the inevitable badge of the Merovingian king
— was ceremoniously shorn and he was retired into a monastery, where he eventually died, little noticed or mourned. Thus
ended the line of the Merovingians, two hundred and seventy
years after the accession of Clovis. The dynasty that had begun
with such a bang, ended with a long-drawn-out whimper.

In January, 752, the Frankish nobility met at Soissons and went through the formality of electing Pepin as king of the Franks, the first of the Carolingian dynasty. But if Pepin had his price, he had to pay one, too. The clamor of the nobles and the raising of Pepin on his shield was not all there was to the ceremony. The priesthood was present, and the eventual coronation was a religious ceremony, with Pepin being content to be called king "by the grace of God."

In other words, Pepin had acknowledged the right of the Pope to say who was a legitimate sovereign and who was not. Once acknowledged, such a right was hard to withdraw and there were yet to be centuries of dispute in later European history over just this point.

THE STATES OF THE CHURCH

Pepin, in return for his kingly title, had made a commitment. He had to use his army against the Lombards to protect the Pope. And the occasion was upon Pepin almost at once.

Within two months of Pepin's coronation, Zacharias died. There followed some momentary confusion. His elected successor, Stephen, died in three days, before he could be consecrated, and another candidate, also named Stephen, was made Pope. There is no settled agreement as to whether to count the earlier Stephen in the list of Popes. The one who actually assumed the office is sometimes called Stephen III and sometimes Stephen II. I shall call him Stephen III.

Even as Stephen III became Pope, however, he found himself facing Aistulf and his Lombards at what seemed a moment of truth. The Lombards had taken Ravenna, cleaned out the Imperials, and were now camping before the gates of Rome trying to force the surrender of the Pope.

Everything, for both sides, depended on the Franks. Stephen III realized he would have to surrender if he could not obtain help from Pepin. Desperately he played for time, offering costly bribes and attempting to involve the Lombards in protracted negotiations — anything to give himself time to get Pepin to honor his commitment.

On the other hand, Aistulf was in a quandary himself. He could not retreat from Rome without losing face to the point where his own nobles might overthrow him. On the other hand, he was intent on doing nothing that would force Pepin to march into Italy. An actual attack on Rome might do so.

Aistulf might well have reasoned that Pepin, having received the royal title and achieved his aim, would not be willing to risk an Italian war if he could decently avoid it. A peaceful and undramatic surrender on the part of the Pope might be quietly accepted by Pepin.

So there was an impasse and the question mark was Pepin.

As it turned out, Pepin, that consummate politician, was indeed ready to help, but on his own terms. He was quite ready to turn the screw another notch and coin more benefits for himself out of the Pope's necessity.

For instance, Pepin must have been conscious of the fact that he had become king only through the Pope's permission. He could easily have fancied this cast some sort of shadow over the dignity of his title. If the Pope wanted help, let him, then, come to Pepin, personally, and ask for that help, humbly. The vision of the Pope at the king's feet as a suppliant would help restore the dignity of the kingly title in full.

Besides, it may well have been in Pepin's shrewd mind, that the actual vision of king and Pope together would further reinforce the legitimacy of the new dynasty. It would be all the more effective, too, if the meeting took place in Neustria where Pepin, descended as he was of an Austrasian family, had something of the look of a foreigner.

Pepin therefore sent ambassadors to the Lombard court to

demand (and receive) a promise of safeguard for the Pope, in order that he might travel through the Lombard dominions and even through Pavia itself, on his way to the Franks.

It was clearly to Aistulf's disadvantage to allow such a trip and yet he dared not refuse for then the irritated Pepin might go to war at once. All he could do was to try to persuade Stephen by efforts short of force to return to Rome.

As for Stephen, he was willing to pass through Pavia and see Aistulf. Perhaps he hoped he might persuade Aistulf to relent and save himself the long trip and the humiliation of the appeal to Pepin.

Aistulf would not give in. He preferred to gamble, apparently, on the possibility that Stephen and Pepin would not come to an agreement, that one side or the other would demand too much.

Stephen had to move on, therefore, and was the first Pope in history to travel beyond the Alps during his term of office.

As 754 opened, Stephen approached Châlons, where Pepin was residing at the time (and near where Attila and his Huns had been stopped by Aëtius three centuries before). Coming to meet him was Pepin's twelve-year-old son Charles (later to be the famous Charlemagne).

Pope and monarch remained together for months that were filled with pageantry. The occasion was used to the full by the propaganda-conscious Pepin. He had himself anointed and crowned again by the very hand of the Pope. He had the Pope anoint his two sons as well, the aforementioned Charles and his younger brother, the three-year-old Carloman. He persuaded the Pope to make an official declaration that the Franks were to choose kings only from Pepin's family throughout all future ages.

In addition, the Pope gave Pepin the title of "Roman Patrician," the same title that Clovis had once held, as still another sign that all was transferred from the Merovingians to the new dynasty.

It was enough. Pepin had all he wanted; indeed, all he could think of. Everything had been done to establish the legitimacy of his title that could be done.

Now it was his turn. He sent a message to Aistulf, demanding imperiously that the Lombard monarch disgorge all conquered territory that had formerly been part of the Exarchate of Ravenna. Aistulf refused and offered only to grant Stephen safe-conduct back to Rome.

Pepin must have answered that he himself would supply the safe-conduct, and when the Pope turned his steps back toward Italy in 755, it was with a large Frankish army as escort.

Aistulf tried to hold the passes of the Alps against Pepin, but was defeated badly. The Franks poured into northern Italy and settled down for a siege of Pavia.

Aistulf promptly promised to restore his conquests and the promise was quickly accepted. Pepin was not overly anxious to be drawn into a long and tedious siege so far from home.

But the acceptance of the promise was too quick. Aistulf had not, as yet, really been hurt and he was ready for another gamble. He may have reasoned that Pepin had come to the Pope's help and had paid his debt, had gained successes and prestige, and had returned home. He had done it for a huge price which he had received in full.

Would he now be ready to go through the whole thing a second time, risking the loss of all he had gained? In 756, therefore, the Lombards placed Rome under siege again.

Aistulf's gamble nearly paid off. Pepin was indeed most reluctant to move again and some of his nobles were loud in their opposition to a second Italian adventure. Stephen had to send a long letter, pleading, threatening, calling on every possible resource of eloquence, to persuade Pepin to come a second time. In the end, Pepin decided he would have to, and for a second time in little over a year, a Frankish army moved into Italy.

Once again, Pepin overcame all Lombard resistance and

once again, Pavia was placed under siege. Again the chagrined Aistulf was forced to offer to give up his conquests and this time Pepin insisted on stronger oaths, more hostages and a much larger payment in money.

While Pepin yet remained in the neighborhood of Pavia, envoys from the Emperor at Constantinople reached him. The territory of the Exarchate of Ravenna, which Aistulf was now giving up, had been taken from the Empire. The emissaries haughtily demanded that Pepin give that territory back.

It was in Pepin's power to go along with this request, but he would have been a great fool to do so, and no one was less a fool than Pepin. Neither the friendship nor enmity of the distant Empire was of much interest to him, whereas the friendship of the Papacy could be of the greatest possible importance. Pepin therefore granted the territory that had once been part of the Exarchate (including Rome itself, of course) to the Pope.

The Pope thus became a temporal sovereign, a ruler of land just as Pepin himself was, and Pepin acknowledged this new status of the Pope by ceremoniously leading his horse a few paces and playing the role of servant as one monarch does for another out of courtesy.

This is the famous "Donation of Pepin," which turned a broad strip of central Italy into a kind of elective theocracy. The Papacy maintained its control over this section of Italy (which came to be known as the States of the Church or the Papal States) for over eleven centuries. It was a moderately sizable realm, too, by later medieval standards. At its peak, it had an area of some sixteen thousand square miles, or twice the size of the state of Massachusetts.

Nevertheless, it must have chafed the Pope to have to depend entirely on the free gift of the Frankish monarch for the right to rule over central Italy (just as it must have chafed Pepin to owe his legitimacy to the Pope). What the monarch gave, after all, the monarch could take away.

Yet there was a legend that seemed to show the Pope had a

prior claim not only to a piece of Italy, but to all of it, and even to all the western half of what had once been the Roman Empire. Gregory of Tours, the historian of the Franks, mentioned this legend and it went something like this:

About 330 the Roman Emperor Constantine I was suddenly stricken with an attack of leprosy. He consulted his pagan priests who advised him to bathe in the blood of babies. This the humane Emperor refused, with horror, to do. Then in a dream he was instructed to see Pope Sylvester I.

The Pope baptized Constantine and at once the leprosy disappeared. The grateful Emperor promptly gave the Pope title to the western half of the Empire and the supremacy over all bishops. Then, in order not to dispute the rule over the West with the Pope, he himself retired to a new capital in the East, Constantinople.

The story is, of course, completely unhistorical and is nothing but someone's pious invention. Taken by itself, the mere existence of the legend could never have convinced any hard-headed monarch that the Pope was his ruler or even that the Pope had any legal right to any part of Italy.

Somehow, though, a document came into existence that purported to be the actual deed made out by Constantine to Sylvester. If this deed were authentic, then the Pope's right to his territory would far antedate the very existence of the Frankish monarchy and Pepin would only be giving the Pope what was his to begin with.

Clearly, since the legend on which the deed is based was pure fable, the deed could not be genuine. Indeed, from its language alone it could be shown that it could not possibly date back to Constantine's time.

Historians are not certain when and where this "Donation of Constantine" was first composed. Some think it was originally prepared in Rome at the time of the Lombard crisis in order that Stephen III might take it along to show Pepin, so that the Frankish king might imagine that ancient law was on his side in his fight for the Pope and against the Lombard. It seems more likely, though, that it was prepared somewhere close to Paris at least fifty years after the Lombard crisis, for there are signs of Frankish rather than Roman authorship. It may have been intended primarily to defeat persistent Byzantine claims to dominion over Italy — something on which the Frankish king and the Pope could see eye to eye.

It was not till 1440 that doubts concerning the authenticity of the Donation of Constantine were openly raised, and although many Catholic authorities fought a rear-guard defense of it, it was finally admitted to be a forgery by everyone. Nevertheless, during the centuries in which it had been accepted as authentic, it had done its great part in the establishment of the powerful Papacy of the later Middle Ages.

THE CAROLINGIAN KING

Pepin's second invasion of Italy did indeed seem to settle matters there. Aistulf died, during a hunt, toward the end of 756. One of his generals, Desiderius, became the new Lombard king but showed no inclination whatever to renew the drive against Rome. Rather, he humbly asked for papal support, offering to grant the Pope additional strips of territory and to make gifts of money as well. Stephen accepted with considerable gratification.

With Italy taken care of, Pepin could turn his attention to his own dominions.

He was king, thoroughly king. Yet though none questioned his legitimacy, there were sections of Pepin's dominions that wanted their independence and chafed under the rule of an outsider, however legitimate.

Chief of these was Aquitaine, where there lingered remnants

of the Roman tradition. The Aquitanians were most conscious of what seemed in their eyes to be a definite superiority of themselves over the barbarous people to the north and east. (This view, with some justification, was to endure for centuries.)

To be sure, it had been to the northern barbarians under Charles Martel that the Aquitanians had been forced to turn for help against the Moors and the Aquitanian duke had had to acknowledge Charles's overlordship — but that had been a generation before.

Since then, the dukes had done their best to keep their ties to the Frankish kingdom as loose as possible. In this they were helped by the fact that the Moors in Spain were showing no disposition to renew their attacks north of the Pyrenees. Even the Moors who occupied the Mediterranean coast east of the Pyrenees (land that had long formed part of the old Visigothic kingdom) were making no trouble, so the Aquitanians had no cause to seek a Frankish alliance. Aquitaine's push for independence was also aided by Pepin's preoccupation with Italy.

What resulted then was a kind of anarchic border warfare along the line where Aquitaine and Neustria met. When Aquitanian raiders looted Neustrian territory, the Neustrian men-at-arms were not slow to return the compliment, and vice versa.

Pepin, who after his return from Italy had to spend some time securing his eastern frontiers against neighboring, still-independent German tribes, was forced at last to turn to the southwest.

In 759, he began a series of yearly campaigns that managed to make their weight felt against stubborn Aquitanian resistance. By 766, Aquitaine was forced to submit. The duke had been killed and northern officials were sent down to administer the duchy. The Moors on the Mediterranean coast were driven beyond the Pyrenees and, for the first time, Frankish dominion was brought down to the Mediterranean shore all the way from the Alps to the Pyrenees.

When Pepin died in 768, he had the satisfaction of knowing that the Frankish kingdom, which had had its start with Clovis three centuries before, now for the first time included all of what had once been Gaul from the English Channel to the Mediterranean and from the Atlantic Ocean to the Rhine River. Extensive territories east of the Rhine were also part of the kingdom.

(The only flaw to the picture was the peninsula of Brittany in the northwestern corner of the kingdom. To the Romans, it had been Armorica, but in the last days of the Western Empire, when Saxons were flooding into Britain, numerous Britons fled across the Channel and established themselves in Armorica, which then came to be called Brittany. It had maintained a precarious independence ever since, stubbornly preventing the Franks from taking over completely. Even under Pepin, the Bretons clung to self-rule.)

Pepin the Short, then, had ruled twenty-seven years and his reign had witnessed unvarying success. He had consolidated his power over rebellious lords. He had arranged to have himself elected king and had made the new dignity stick. He had invaded Italy twice, defeated the Lombards, and established the warmest relations with the Papacy. He had secured his borders and put down rebellion, and when he died, the Frankish kingdom, ruled by himself alone, was larger and stronger than it had ever been before.

One might well suppose that his reign would be considered a landmark and that Pepin himself would be remembered as a most remarkable man and even, perhaps, have been granted the title of "the Great."

Not so. Pepin is one of the not-very-many examples of a monarch of the first magnitude who is completely overshadowed by his successor. The successor, in this case, was Pepin's older son Charles, who, as a boy, had galloped forth to meet Pope Stephen when the latter was coming to beg the help of the Frankish king.

7

CHARLEMAGNE

THE LAST OF THE LOMBARDS

Charles was twenty-six years old at the time of his accession. He and his seventeen-year-old brother Carloman had both been anointed by Pope Stephen when they were children. According to the foolish old Frankish custom, which Pepin faithfully followed, both inherited a portion of the realm, so that the Frankish kingdom was split once more.

Charles received the coastal regions along the Atlantic and the Channel. The shape of his lands was like a clutching hand grasping the more compact realm of his brother, who ruled over the districts north and west of the Alps.

Charles was every inch a king. He was over six feet tall and large-boned. (The length of his foot was supposed to have set the standard for the measure of length which we now call the foot.) He was robust and enjoyed excellent health. A contemporary who wrote a biography of him that survives lists his physical shortcomings (in later life) as including a thick neck, the possession of a potbelly, and a high-pitched voice. He ate heartily (hence, no doubt, the potbelly) but was abstemious in his drinking, something most unusual for a Frank.

Carloman did not, apparently, like or trust his overpowering older brother and was not disposed to cooperate with him. When the Aquitanians seized the opportunity of Pepin's death to revolt, Charles (in whose territory Aquitaine was included) had to deal with it himself. Carloman made no move to help.

To be sure, Aquitaine, weakened as a result of its long and unsuccessful resistance to Pepin, was in no real condition to fight a prolonged war. Rather, she made her move at the time of the accession of a new king in the clear hope that the new king might prove incompetent or might become involved in civil war.

Neither chance took place. The Aquitanians had completely misjudged their man, for Charles fell upon them like a thunderbolt, forced them to surrender almost at once, and placed them under harsher rule than before.

It was the first warlike move of a career that was to see many, and all successful. His deeds were to bring Charles the title of "Great," so that he is Karl der Grosse in German and Carolus Magnus in Latin. In French, however, the epithet is made an integral part of his name, a unique situation, so that he is Charlemagne to the French, and it is that combined name that is adopted in English, too (we pronounce it as shahr'luh-mayn).

When Charlemagne subdued that initial revolt and felt himself firmly seated on his throne, he established his capital at Aachen (located at what is now the German border, just where the boundaries of Belgium and the Netherlands meet). It was probably the city of his birth, and it was also an Austrasian city. Charlemagne much affected Frankish costume such as furred jackets and gartered legs, together with the old Frankish ways, so he may well have deliberately shunned the too-Romanized Neustrian cities that had so often served as Frankish capitals.

Outside the Frankish dominions, watching anxiously, was the Lombard king, Desiderius, at Pavia. Adjoining his kingdom were the lands of Carloman, which served as a buffer between himself and the energetic Charlemagne.

Desiderius had begun his reign with a policy of conciliation toward the Pope, but had gradually shifted to a more aggressive policy as Pepin spent the last years of his reign in stubborn fighting in Aquitaine. Now he wondered if he could not make capital out of the split in the Frankish kingdom under the sons of Pepin.

He cultivated the friendship of Carloman, the younger and weaker of the two, flattering him and feeding his jealousy of his brother. He arranged a marital alliance in which one of his daughters married Carloman.

In this policy, the Lombard king seems to have been aided and abetted by Pepin's widow, the mother of the two Frankish monarchs. Her name was Bertrada, but she was known to later legend as Bertha of the Big Feet. (Perhaps Charlemagne inherited his size from his mother; he could not have done so from Pepin the Short.)

Bertrada, apparently anxious to keep the peace between her sons, persuaded Charlemagne to marry another of Desiderius' daughters. Surely there would now be friendship between the Franks and between both and the Lombard.

But not even the best devices can fend off the vicissitudes of circumstance. In 771, Carloman, still only twenty, died, leaving behind his Lombard widow and a couple of infant sons. Charlemagne decided quickly that he could not leave half the Frankish realm in the hands of infants, when the real ruler would surely be the Lombard grandfather, Desiderius. He swooped down with the thunderbolt speed that was characteristic of him and made the entire kingdom of Pepin his own. Carloman's widow had to flee to Pavia with her children and with a burning and indignant hate of Charlemagne. In Pavia, she engaged in dinning that hate into her father's ears and urging him to take some sort of action.

Charlemagne, aware that he had made an enemy of Desiderius, realized also that his own Lombard marriage was now politically inadvisable. He needed a free hand against the Lombards and couldn't accept the discomfort of a Lombard wife. We are probably safe to suppose that he didn't like her much, personally. In any case, he discarded her and sent her back to Pavia, too, and now he had another enemy there.

Desiderius could scarcely believe that he could win in any straightforward fight between himself and the Franks, but are fights always straightforward? He had the right on his side, for Charlemagne had discarded his lawful wife, appropriated the lands of his brother illegally, and driven out his brother's wife and children.

Surely such a righteous cause as his own would inspire any of the disaffected lords in a holy war against Charlemagne. (Not that the lords were themselves much given to righteousness, but even the most unprincipled can always fight better if a cause can be presented as righteous.)

What Desiderius chiefly needed to make all this stick was papal recognition of the rights of the young children, and this recognition could surely come if a little pressure were applied. The Papacy was at the moment in the usual state of confusion that accompanied the election of a new pope, and in 772, Desiderius seized the opportunity to invade the Papal States and place an army about Rome to inspire the new Pope to make the correct decision.

The new Pope, Adrian I, promptly appealed for help to Charlemagne, and not long after, Desiderius saw he had made a rather dreadful mistake. The Frankish lords showed no signs of any disposition to rise against Charlemagne, and that monarch, less hesitant about foreign adventures than his father, rapidly moved a large army over the Alps. In 773, there began a third Frankish invasion of northern Italy.

For the third time Pavia was placed under siege, but Charlemagne was not his father. Twice Pepin had let Pavia off the hook in return for promises; Charlemagne would accept no promises. Pavia remained under siege for nine months, and when Desiderius gave in, it was by way of unconditional surrender. He was forced to abandon the throne of the Lombards, and thus the kingdom came to an end two centuries after the Lombard invasion of Italy. Desiderius, who might be considered the Last of the Lombards, was carried to Frankish territory, there to end his days in genteel imprisonment.

All were gone now of those tribes that had ripped the Western Empire apart since the time of Alaric. Gone were the Visigoths, the Vandals, the Sueves, the Alemanni, the Ostrogoths, the Lombards. All had vanished from the pages of history — all but the Franks. They alone survived.

There remained, to be sure, a nominally Lombard duchy south of the Papal States, the duchy of Benevento, so called after its capital. It had generally maintained its independence of Pavia, although accepting the domination of particularly strong kings such as Liutprand. Now it remained outside the Frankish realm and continued to do so for a century. Its Lombard nature was excessively faint, however. The Lombards there had lost their national identity; they were Italians.

Nor was the Lombard name forgotten in the north. The kingdom remained as a name on the map and Charlemagne himself took on the title of King of the Lombards. To give the region an appearance of autonomy and encourage its quiet, he let his young son Pepin be his deputy there, thus avoiding a too blatant personal rule. (Indeed, Lombardy is still the name of a rich province of north central Italy.)

Whatever the pretense, though, northern Italy had become an integral part of the Frankish Empire, and this had important consequences for the future. The monarchs who succeeded Charlemagne never forgot that their great predecessor had ruled in Italy and they maintained a hold on the land for a thousand years, to Italy's great torment and to their own as well, for often they sacrificed their home interests in grasping at the Italian will-o'-the-wisp.

Charlemagne's victory removed the Lombard threat forever from the Papacy. The Frankish monarch reaffirmed the Donation of Pepin and established a close relationship with Pope Adrian. Charlemagne was earnestly pious, attended all church services unfailingly, and always showed the deepest respect for the Pope. He visited Rome in 780 and in 785 (the first Frankish sovereign to do so) and his attitude toward Adrian was a model of what it should be.

However, even the piety of a strong monarch can be dangerous to the Church. Charlemagne was anxious to improve and elevate the Church but he did it by impatiently playing the role of Pope himself, as strong monarchs are usually tempted to do — as Justinian had done, and Constantine before him. Thus, he encouraged liturgical reform and called together councils to combat heresy, but he made it plain what his wishes were in these respects and saw to it that they were carried out.

The Pope could only be patient.

CONVERSION BY THE SWORD

Charlemagne's piety and his youthful eagerness for martial glory led him on to what would, in future centuries, be called crusades. We might say he embarked on the first crusade in history, the first war of Christians against non-Christians in which at least part of the motivation was the conversion of the non-Christians to Christianity — by force, if necessary.

Charlemagne's object was the German tribes who in the past three centuries of German adventurism had remained at home, and had remained pagan, too. A line of such pagan tribes rimmed the eastern border of Austrasia during Merovingian times. From south to north, they were the Bavarians, Thuringians, Saxons, and Frisians.*

Thuringia was brought under Frankish control as early as 531 by the sons of Clovis. The other tribes maintained a precarious independence despite occasional campaigns against them by Charles Martel and Pepin the Short and despite pressure on the east from the Avars.

They were under attack spiritually as well, a war that was carried on not by armies but by the will of a single man from the island of Britain. That this was possible at all was the result of the decision by Gregory the Great to send missionaries to the island, a result that Gregory could scarcely have foreseen.

While German tribes were ripping up the Western Empire, the island of Britain, deserted by its Roman garrison, had been invaded by a group of German tribes moving westward across the North Sea. These included the Angles, the Saxons, and the Jutes. The Celtic Britons were driven out before them and were replaced by "Anglo-Saxons." Most of the island became "Angle-land" or England.

The Anglo-Saxons were pagans, but their Celtic predecessors had been Christian and this Christianity had spread to Ireland, which had never been part of the Roman Empire. In Merovingian times, Ireland experienced a period of enlightenment. Its monks spread Christianity among the Anglo-Saxons and established monasteries far and wide on the continent. These Irish monasteries, however, did not follow the Benedictine rule and

---

* There are regions in modern Europe still called Bavaria, Thuringia, and Frisia at the site where these tribes existed in Frankish times. There is also a region called Saxony but, for a variety of historical reasons, it is located to the southeast of the place of the early tribes.

their ritual differed in important respects from Roman orthodoxy.

Gregory's missionaries brought not only Christianity, but Roman Christianity to England. By 664, the Roman version had
won out over the Celtic and, eventually, even Ireland itself
turned toward the Roman version.

Eight years after England had self-consciously chosen to be
Roman Catholic, a child was born who was named Winfrid. By
the age of seven, he took the road to monkhood and the name
Boniface. After reaching manhood, he devoted his life to the
conversion of the still-pagan German tribes.

It was because of Gregory's action, then, that Winfrid, or
Boniface, in converting the Germans brought them to Roman
Christianity and not Celtic Christianity. In this way, the
Church was spared a new dose of German heresy, like the Ari-
anism it had had to fight centuries before.

In 716, Boniface made his first proselytizing endeavor by
crossing the Strait of Dover into Frisia (on what is now the
Dutch coast). He was promptly expelled from that land by its
ruler, Radbod.

He traveled to Rome, received papal permission to continue
his work among the Germans, and then spent years in Bavaria
and Thuringia, accepting conversions, building churches, and
destroying idols when he could. When he heard that Radbod
of Frisia had died, he returned there and experienced additional success. Always he had the advantage that, being not so
far removed from Saxon ancestry himself, he spoke the tribal
languages, understood their ways, and could make use of Ulfilas's old Gothic Bible.

Furthermore, Charles Martel, who ruled over the Franks at
the time, served as Boniface's secular protector. Armed with
Charles's safe conduct, Boniface could move freely through the
east, for the tribes were rather reluctant to earn the ferocious
anger of the Hammer by harming someone he chose to protect.

After Charles's death, Boniface, who had by then returned to

Frankish territory, supported Pepin and Carloman in their struggles to establish themselves. He labored to reform the Frankish church and may have had a hand in convincing Carloman to adopt the monkish life. He also served as one of the intermediaries between Pepin and the Pope in the negotiations that led to the crowning of Pepin and it may have been Boniface's hand that performed the anointing ritual the first time.

In return, Pepin, like his father before him, supported Boniface's missionary endeavors wholeheartedly. Even if it had not been a question of gratitude, Pepin's shrewd foresight must have made it plain that Christian Germans would be easier to absorb into the Frankish kingdoms than pagan Germans would be.

Boniface lived long enough to see Christianity established firmly and permanently among almost all the tribes east of the Frankish realm. Finally, he found martyrdom in 755 (even as his patron, Pepin, was settling affairs with the Lombards) at the hands of a band of heathen Frisians.

Pepin's estimate of the situation was right. Charlemagne found it not at all difficult to absorb the Bavarians and Frisians into his kingdom, for they were largely Christian.

Boniface, however, had had no success at all with the Saxons, and with the passing of time, they became increasingly intransigent. They saw that Christianization meant Frankification, and they clung to their paganism as their only means of insuring their freedom. Having repelled attempts by the earlier Carolingians to invade their territory, they now stood ready to do the same for any attempts on the part of Charlemagne.

Charlemagne, for his part, felt a war against pagans to be a holy one, and a God-given opportunity besides, to extend the limits of his kingdom. As early as 772, when he was sole master of the realm after Carloman's death, and even before he had settled matters with Desiderius in Pavia, he was already sending his soldiers into Saxony.

The Saxons faded before them and the Franks had their own

way. Vigorously, Charlemagne's soldiers went about establishing Christianity, fully convinced that only their own religion had any validity and that the Saxons had no religious rights of their own that had to be respected.

Thus, the invading Franks came across a huge tree trunk called Irminsul, an object of particular veneration by the Saxons, who viewed it as a symbol of the tree that, in Nordic mythology, supported the world. Without flinching, the Frankish priests ordered its destruction as a detestable idol, and down it came.

But such desecration of Saxon belief succeeded in hardening Saxon hearts. Saxony was not Lombardy; it was no settled area, with an apathetic population and a large capital city waiting to be put under siege. It was, instead, a trackless wilderness with small settlements that could be destroyed one by one without affecting the heart and will of the fighting Saxons.

There began a guerrilla warfare, then, that was infinitely frustrating for the Franks. If a Frankish army marched against the Saxons, the latter retreated hastily, accepted conversion if asked to do so (with a sword at the throat in case they thoughtlessly refused the kindly request), swore oaths, gave hostages. Then, when warfare elsewhere caused the Franks to march out again, after establishing outposts and building churches, the Saxons would rise in instant revolt. They would burn the churches, kill those among them who insisted on being Christian, overpower the outposts, and yell defiance at the Franks.

Always, Charlemagne would send back his army. Each time they marched deeper into Saxony, killed Saxons with greater fervor than before, took greater numbers of hostages, and made the oaths more fearsome. Always the Saxons gave in and surrendered, only to repeat what they had done before at the first opportunity.

In 778, the Saxons found a leader named Widukind, who sharply escalated the horrors of the endless war. Charlemagne was at this time engaged in warfare in Spain — at the other side of the world as far as the Saxons were concerned — and he might, for all any Saxon knew, be already defeated or killed. Widukind had no trouble, therefore, in rousing the Saxons and carrying through reprisals that put everything before into the shade. He had every Christian priest and layman in Saxony killed, and carried raids into Austrasia itself, penetrating to the Rhine.

Charlemagne had to escalate his own responses (or give up the war, which he refused to do). At one point, he is supposed to have ordered the decapitation of forty-five hundred Saxons in a single day. It was not until 785 that Widukind gave in and accepted conversion himself. Even then, there remained frequent Saxon uprisings on a smaller scale. As late as 804, there was a revolt strong enough to call for an invasion and organized punitive action. The Saxon war may thus be said to have lasted over thirty years.

When it ended, though, Charlemagne was left the master of all the German-dominated land on the continent that was of any consequence. (To be sure, England and the Scandinavian countries, all independent, were sparsely occupied by men of Germanic speech, but they were separated from the Frankish heartland by water or, in the case of Denmark, by an uncomfortable distance. They might be safely ignored as beyond the horizon.)

NOT GERMANS ALONE

Yet Charlemagne had no particular feeling that some natural law restricted him to rule over the Germans only. Even before Saxony was subdued, he was looking eastward to the Slavic peoples beyond the Elbe.

The Slavs had not yet distinguished themselves in warfare against anyone. They had been the mute and patient victims of every band of conquerors from the Goths to the Avars, and they were not likely to oppose the Franks. Indeed, they viewed Charlemagne as a deliverer from the Avars.

The Avars, to be sure, had greatly weakened since the time, nearly two centuries before, when they had threatened Constantinople itself. They still held their central territory (in what is now Hungary), but to the east (in what is now Rumania) a related people had broken out of their grip and established a new kingdom of their own.

The new people called themselves Bulgars, a word which may have the same origin as the name of the Volga River. Indeed, in Charlemagne's time, a strong Bulgar kingdom existed along the Volga.

As for the Slavs, dominion by the Avars had not been all to the bad. Under the Avars' protection, they had managed to drift westward, infiltrating the lands from which German tribes (such as the Lombards) had fled before the Avars. As a result the land which is now Czechoslovakia, which had previously been German, became Slavic and has remained Slavic to this day. (The Slavic tide also crept west to the Elbe but from that river they were driven back by the Germans in later centuries.)

In Charlemagne's time, the Slavic tribes were beginning to dare assert their independence of the Avars. The Avars, bearded thus by their Slavic subjects and harried by their Bulgar brothers, now found themselves facing the hammerblows of the great Frankish monarch. In three successive campaigns, Charlemagne (with Bulgar help) smashed the Avars.

The last of them submitted by 804 and they vanished from history, with such suddenness that to this day the Russians use the simile "to vanish like the Avars." Actually, of course, they did not vanish; they merely lost their national consciousness, intermarried with their erstwhile subjects and faded into the general population.

The western Slavic lands, out to the great bend of the Danube River (where Budapest is now located), acknowledged Charlemagne's overlordship, though the Frankish hold was weak at those distances from Aachen.

Westward, too, Charlemagne's eyes turned. They looked toward Brittany, where the tough Bretons had maintained their independence even against Pepin. Against Charlemagne, however, they dared not stand. He did not have to send an invading army against them. Sullenly, they paid tribute and then maintained a cautious subservience.

Charlemagne's heart was set with greatest desire on the land to the southwest. He looked longingly toward the Pyrenees, where his realm touched the world of Islam — which, for a century and a half, had been pressing forcefully against Christianity on all sides.

Most of the Islamic world was now under a line of rulers called the Abbasids, whose capital was in Baghdad on the Tigris River. In Charlemagne's time, the Abbasid realm was at the peak of its power. Indeed, in 786, just when Charlemagne was reaching the climax of his Saxon war, Harun al-Rashid became caliph in Baghdad. It is this Harun al-Rashid who was idealized in the famous stories grouped together in the collection known as *The Thousand and One Nights* or *The Arabian Nights.*

Yet although the Abbasids ruled over much of western Asia and North Africa and were much the strongest single power in the world, there were Moslems who did not recognize the caliph in Baghdad.

The Abbasids, it seems, had seized power a generation before Harun's time, overthrowing the previous dynasty, the Omayyad. To avoid later trouble, the first Abbasid monarch coolly went about the business of killing every Omayyad he could find, so that not one would be left to claim the throne as rightfully his and to gather a following about him with which he could rouse a civil war.

The job was quite well done and, in fact, only one Omayyad escaped. He was Abdurrahman, a grandson of the Omayyad who had been caliph at the time of Charles Martel's victory at the Battle of Tours. After years of hairbreadth escapes, Abdurrahman managed to make his way across the full length of the Mediterranean from Syria to Spain. He landed in Spain in 756 and there, twenty-eight hundred miles from Baghdad, he made himself king of the land as Abdurrahman I, at about the time Pepin was making himself king of the Franks.

Abdurrahman established his capital at Cordova, and under him, Spain became a completely independent Moslem nation. He was an enlightened sovereign, who ruled for a generation over an increasingly prosperous land. His years as a hunted fugitive may have given him an insight into the kind of life a persecuted minority must lead, and he avoided persecuting his own. The Christians were allowed religious freedom on payment of a reasonable tax, while the Jews were treated with actual favor.

His greatest troubles, indeed, came neither from Christians nor Jews, but from his own turbulent Moorish nobles, who, in their quarrels with him, did not hesitate to turn to the Christian Franks for help.

It was to the interest of the Franks, first of Pepin, then of Charlemagne, to keep the Moorish nobility just as turbulent as possible, but there was a third party in the game, too — the Basques of the western Pyrenees.

The Basques were Christians, and fought fiercely and successfully in their wild mountain valleys against the Moorish flood. However, they were Basques even before they were Christians and to them the Franks, although Christian, were as alien as the Moors. When they went out raiding, it made little difference to them whether it was Franks or Moors whom they despoiled.

Charlemagne, stung by Basque incursions and invited to intervene in his neighbor's troubles by three Moorish emirs at war with the Cordovan monarch, decided to return the Moorish compliment of his grandfather's time and to invade Spain. As a side effect, he would take the Basques from the rear.

Charlemagne's plan was a good one on paper, but Abdurrahman I, while getting on in years, was still a vigorous and warlike monarch. And when the Christians actually invaded, the quarreling Moors found they had to stand firm against the common enemy after all.

Charlemagne's advance came up hard against the city of Saragossa, on the Ebro River, a hundred miles south of the Pyrenees. There he was forced into a siege. He was, however, too far from home to make the siege effective and couriers from Saxony brought news of Widukind's fierce uprising. Much against his will, he was forced to raise the siege and to retreat back across the Pyrenees. The Spanish adventure was a failure.

On Charlemagne's way back, another disaster took place, for the Basques saw the chance for a profitable stroke. The Frankish army filed through one of the western passes in the Pyrenees, at Roncesvalles, while Basque eyes watched (themselves unseen) from the mountain slopes. When the main body of the army had passed through, the Basques suddenly fell on the rear guard and destroyed it, gathering, no doubt, much loot. Among the fallen Franks was Charlemagne's viceroy in Brittany, who had come down to join the great crusade against the Moors. His name was Roland, and about him, as we shall see, a great story was eventually to rise.

Abdurrahman died in 788, and Spain was the weaker for his death. It was more foolhardy, too, for rather than leave well enough alone, it took advantage of Charlemagne's preoccupation with the Saxons to harry the Pyrenees frontier. In 793, a Moorish raiding party conducted a hit-and-run attack that penetrated to Narbonne, on the Mediterranean coast, sixty miles north of the Pyrenees.

Charlemagne was planning his campaign against the Avars but he could scarcely allow such an insult to pass. Once again, he turned on Spain. This time he attempted no quick, deep penetration but strove to establish a buffer zone south of the Pyrenees, one that would insulate the Frankish realm from Moorish attack and also quiet the Basques once and for all.

This was accomplished by 801, when Charlemagne captured Barcelona. The entire strip of territory south of the Pyrenees, to a width of some fifty miles was taken over. The western portion of the strip included the land of the Basques, which was now firmly in Charlemagne's hands, and received the name Navarre. The eastern portion was called the Spanish March.

The word "march" or "mark" is from an old German word meaning "boundary" and was a name given to any frontier land. There were other marches established under Charlemagne, strongly fortified areas under military rule, designed to keep an eye on the adjoining foreign power and to safeguard the heart of the kingdom.

The northeastern corner of the Frankish realm was the Danish Mark, a name eventually transferred to the land against which it guarded, which is now known as Denmark (or Danmark to its own population).

To the far east was Ostmark (the "Eastern March"), about where Austria is located now. In later centuries, when the region of Ostmark became a great independent power, it became Österreich ("eastern realm" or, in English, Austria). When the Nazis absorbed Austria in 1938, they restored the early name of Ostmark — until the land was freed again in 1945.

The man in command of a mark was a margrave, from the German "markgraf" ("count of the march"). In French, this became "marquis."

By 800 then, Charlemagne ruled over a truly enormous kingdom, if one considers the nature of the time and the difficulty of communication and transportation. Roughly rectangular in shape, but broadening to the east, it extended a thousand miles from west to east, from the Atlantic to the mid-Danube; and nine hundred miles from north to south, from Frisia to Rome.

The total area under Charlemagne's direct or indirect rule was about 700,000 square miles, over one-fifth the size of the United States.

This was the largest realm under a single powerful ruler that the West had seen since the days of the Roman Emperor Theodosius four centuries before.

EMPEROR IN SPITE OF HIMSELF

Through all this, Charlemagne remained on very good terms with the Pope. When he visited Rome in 781, he had Pope Adrian crown his son Pepin IV as king of the Lombards, and another son, Louis (or Ludwig, in German) as king of Aquitaine. In this way, he had the mantle of legitimacy thrown over those sons while he himself was yet alive, just as his father Pepin had done for Charlemagne himself and his younger brother.

In return, Adrian ceased to count the deeds of his pontificate by the years of reign of the heretic Eastern Emperor, but from the years of reign of Charlemagne, a most subtle but flattering compliment.

When Adrian died in 795, he had held the papal seat for nearly a quarter of a century, and in all that time he and Charlemagne had worked smoothly together. Indeed, they were a remarkably well-fitting pair, for Charlemagne's secular domination extended over all the lands in which the Pope could exert his spiritual domination. Even the small English and Spanish Christian principalities acknowledged a theoretical Carolingian overlordship to go along with their adherence to papal doctrine. It followed then that wherever Adrian was Pope, Charlemagne was king and vice versa. Never again in history was there to be so parallel a relationship between the dominion of king and Pope.

The new Pope, Leo III, hastened to make certain that the

powerful Charlemagne viewed him with as great a feeling of friendship as he had viewed the previous Pope. The announcement of the new election was, for the first time, not sent formally to the Eastern Emperor. It was sent to Charlemagne instead. Then, too, Adrian had granted Charlemagne the title of Roman Patrician and now Leo ostentatiously renewed the grant.

Part of Leo's intention here was to fortify himself against the turbulence at home. The Pope was a secular prince, as well as a spiritual leader, and princes had their difficulties. They had, for instance, an unruly nobility, who were sure to make demands of every new monarch in return for keeping the peace.

Leo had to face exactly this, and when he failed to give complete satisfaction, a conspiracy arose in 799 to seize and mutilate him, thus unfitting him for his position and forcing a new election.

It did not quite come to this, but the city was in an uproar and the local Frankish governor was either unwilling or unable to help. Leo was handled roughly by a Roman mob and had to flee the city. He sent a letter of supplication to Charlemagne but the monarch deliberately did not move. The Pope must come to him as an earlier Pope had come to his father. Leo had no choice. He had to cross the Alps as Stephen had done a half century before.

Charlemagne was in Saxony at the time and greeted Leo with the highest honors. Satisfied at having made the Pope come this long way, he agreed to escort Leo back to Rome with an army sufficient for the purpose.

But in Rome, further humiliation awaited the Pope. Those who had conspired against him naturally claimed they had done so out of a high regard for virtue and morality, since the Pope had been guilty (so they said) of a variety of heinous crimes. Charlemagne might have dismissed all this as poppycock, but he didn't. Instead, he seized upon these accusations to set up a solemn ritual in which he might sit in judgment upon the Pope. That would make it quite clear to the whole world that it was Charlemagne who was supreme.

On December 23, 800, he assembled a gathering of high Church officials, over which he himself presided. It was not exactly a trial, for there was no precedent for the trial of a Pope. Leo was, however, required to undergo the humiliation of having to declare under oath that he was innocent of all charges. Naturally such an oath was considered sufficient and Leo was put back on the papal throne.

Nevertheless, Charlemagne had been the judge and Leo had stood before him as though he were someone who could be condemned and punished at the king's will. Leo must have meditated on how to turn the tables and succeeded in an extraordinarily subtle way, one that must go down as one of the cleverest political thrusts of all time.

To see how it worked, let us turn to the Byzantine Empire.

After the last of the Western Emperors had been deposed in 476, the Eastern Emperor at Constantinople had been, in theory, ruler of the entire Roman Empire and, indeed, of all Christendom. This was recognized, in theory, even in the West, where the Emperor had no real power beyond such lands as his armies could capture and hold.

In the eighth century, the Emperors had fallen completely out of favor with the Pope because of their strongly iconoclastic position. The Popes excommunicated them and began to appropriate some of their rights, but even so, the magic about the word "emperor" remained. Whoever sat on the throne in Constantinople was still the successor of Augustus and Constantine, and no one could infringe on that.

In 780, however, the Emperor Leo IV had died and his son Constantine VI succeeded. He was a young boy, perhaps nine years old, and his mother, Irene, ruled as regent. Under her, in 787, the period of iconoclasm, which had lasted for sixty years, was brought to an end. The veneration of statues was permitted once more and the position of the Papacy had won out.

This did not lead to a reconciliation between Pope and Empire, however, for there were a number of other disagreements in viewpoint and ritual. The end of iconoclasm was, in fact, probably more of an inconvenience than anything else to the Pope, for it deprived him of the best possible excuse to deny his ancient dependence upon the Emperor.

Fortunately, the matter never came to a real issue, for as Constantine VI grew older, he began to chafe under the tutelage of his mother and attempted to establish a personal rule. His mother resisted, and in the struggle that followed, she won out. Callously she ordered her son killed and, in 797, she ruled alone in Constantinople as Empress.

Thus at the time that Charlemagne and Pope Leo were in Rome in 800, there was no Emperor in Constantinople! There was an Empress, yes, but to the Franks that scarcely counted. They did not recognize women as rulers and by the old Salic law even questioned whether rule could be inherited through a woman.

Perhaps from the moment Irene declared herself Empress, a certain thought went through Leo's mind whereby relations with Constantinople could be straightened out once and for all. And now, on December 25, 800, the perfect moment had arrived.

Two days had passed since Leo had stood an accused suppliant before the overpowering presence of Charlemagne. Now it was Christmas, and Pope and king knelt together at St. Peter's to worship on this holy day.

Leo had prepared an elaborate crown, and at the right time, when Charlemagne's eyes were, no doubt, devoutly closed, Leo rose, seized the crown, placed it on Charlemagne's head and declared him Emperor! The waiting crowd, led by individuals who had very likely been primed for the purpose, broke into loud cries of delight, hailing Charlemagne as Carolus Augustus.

Charlemagne had no choice but to go on. There was no way he could rationally refuse the honor. He was enthroned, anointed with holy oil, and put through an elaborate ritual. He was Emperor!

After more than three centuries, there was an Emperor again in the West! As the western Emperors after Charlemagne are often given numbers by historians, Charlemagne might be known as Charles I in his imperial role.

Yet Charlemagne must have known he had bought himself only trouble, in a variety of ways. The title brought him no additional power; indeed it weakened him. Two days before, the Pope had been at his feet. Now he was at the Pope's feet. Two days before, he had been king of the Franks by inheritance and by virtue of his own martial deeds. Now he was Emperor by the grace of the Pope, and what the Pope gave, the Pope could take away.

Furthermore, the acceptance of the title was bound to bring trouble with the Byzantine Empire and Charlemagne did not want that. He had been encroaching on Byzantine territory north of the Adriatic Sea and it would take little more to bring on a war. The title of Emperor was sure to do it and Charlemagne had enough trouble in Saxony, Spain, and among the Avars. He did not need a new war.

So although Charlemagne may well have daydreamed a little about being Emperor, and may have been flattered at the title, he could quite realistically regret the event. He said bitterly after it was all over that if he had known what Leo had intended, he would never have come to Rome. Surely that statement is not a modest avowal of unworthiness (which would have been completely unlike him) but a bald appreciation of having been outmaneuvered. What's more, he never called himself "Roman Emperor," directly challenging Constantinople. He called himself "Emperor, King of the Franks and Lombards," emphasizing the real dominions over which he ruled.

Naturally, from a purely secular standpoint, one could argue that the Pope had no right or precedent for the making of an

Emperor. Perhaps, then, it was not long after this that the Donation of Constantine was forged to show that the Pope was
both secular and spiritual master of the Western Empire, by
the will of Constantine, and that he could therefore, with full
right, give the secular power away and make an Emperor.

War with the Byzantines was indeed inevitable. While Irene
was Empress, she kept the peace, for she could scarcely lead
the armies, and as soon as some general did, he would overthrow her. As it was, though, she was deposed in 802 and a
government official, Nicephorus, became Emperor. Then the
war started.

It might be thought that with the powerful Frankish Empire
(as it may now be called) opposed to the waning and decadent
Byzantine Empire, only a Frankish victory could result. However, it wasn't quite that easy. Charlemagne was getting on in
years (he was over sixty) and even he was losing his early
vigor. The battlefield was far from the center of Frankish
power and the line of communications was thin and frayed.
And then the Byzantines were not all that decadent; they
might not have the Frankish delight in wild charges or in
swinging battle-axes, but their armies were much better organized. The war went on for years on fairly even terms.

But Charlemagne made an odd friend as a result of his acceptance of the imperial crown. There were now four great
powers rimming the Mediterranean Sea. Beginning with the
Frankish Empire and moving around the sea clockwise, they
were the Byzantine Empire, the Abbasid Caliphate, and Omayyad Spain. Each of these powers was at deadly enmity with its
two neighbors.

Both the Franks and the Abbasids were at war, separately,
with both the Byzantines and the Omayyads, again separately,
so that there were four wars (smoldering or active) in progress
about the Mediterranean.

Since the enemy of one's enemies is one's friend, Charlemagne and Harun al-Rashid, sharing enemies as they did, were

bound to be friends even though the former was the most powerful Christian monarch in the world and the latter the most powerful Moslem monarch. Embassies and presents moved back and forth between them, starting in 801. The two powers were too far apart for active cooperation in war, but the mere word of their friendship must have had a horrifying effect on the others.

Certainly, Nicephorus, facing an intensification of his war with the Abbasids, decided in 810 to make peace with Charlemagne on a compromise basis. He was willing to recognize Frankish ownership of what had once been the Exarchate of Ravenna, provided the Franks restored Venice and the Adriatic coast to Constantinople. Nicephorus' successor, Michael I, was even willing, in 812, to recognize Charlemagne as Western Emperor.

A BIT OF LIGHT

Most of what we know about Charlemagne and the monarchs that preceded him are the wars they fought. These were the dramatic events that interested the chroniclers of old. It never occurred to them to describe in great detail how ordinary people lived, what kind of clothes they wore, what kind of toys their children played with. If anyone had asked them why they did not, they would certainly have answered, "But everyone knows about that."

Yet certainly life went on in a very ordinary and day-to-day way. Through all the invasions and civil wars and religious disputes, ordinary people tended their farms, worked, slept, had children. And with each generation life in much of western Europe seemed to grow harder, poorer, more brutal. Charlemagne came to power in the depth of the Dark Ages.

Yet we mustn't think because we say "Dark Ages" that all the world was in darkness. Civilizations outside Europe, such as those in China and India, went their own way regardless of the names we give to various stages of Mediterranean civilization. Even in Europe, darkness was not everywhere. The Byzantine Empire preserved Greek culture throughout the Middle Ages. Moorish Spain developed a high culture. Even in Italy and England, some fragments of learning remained.

It was in the Frankish realm particularly that the light dimmed. It was the Franks, savage and brutal to begin with, whose constant warfare destroyed the lands they conquered.

Ignorance was supreme there. The ruling Frankish nobility had war as their only trade. Life was short in those days under the best of circumstances and all the shorter for the accident of war. To learn the warrior's trade, one had to start early indeed, if it were to be followed for a reasonable number of years. In consequence, the Frankish youngsters had no time for such cultural frills as learning to read and write.

Literacy was confined to the priests and monks and not to all of them, either. In general the warriors came from among the Frankish families, and the priests, for the most part, from the earlier Roman families. Reading and writing became, in a way, a stigma of the conquered. For a Frank to learn to read cast not only doubt upon his manhood but upon his very identity as a Frank.

With literacy confined to the priesthood, it was enough to decide between a cleric and an impostor by opening a Bible and saying "Read!"

The universal illiteracy among the ruling classes and their inability to do simple arithmetic made it difficult or impossible for them to administer their lands sensibly. They probably told themselves that only a milksop would be interested in accounts and petty administrative details. Control had to be passed on to the only educated class, the clerics, and this greatly increased the power of the Frankish priesthood. (To this day, anyone who keeps records is considered a "clerk," which is a form of the word "cleric." We have a town clerk and a bank clerk, for instance. Then, since those tending stores must keep records of sales and make change, we have shoe clerks.)

As roads crumbled, and as prosperity sank under the weight of continuous wars, the cities that had flourished under Roman rule shriveled and decayed. They stood, largely desolate, shadows of their old selves, populated in odd corners, with the rest of the buildings serving as quarries for building materials. If the cities had been strong, they might have served as reservoirs for wealth and in alliance with the king they might have upheld the central authority against the anarchy of the lords, but that was not to be.

What miserable remnant of wealth existed was dispersed over the rural countryside and placed under the power of the lords. The land had to revert to the kind of economy it had had a thousand years before — before the Romans came. Once again it was subsistence farming, where each village grew what it needed on neighboring farms, for there was little hope of getting much from anywhere else.

Indeed, so poor was transportation that there was no hope of carting food back and forth in large quantities even in dire emergencies. If the local harvest failed there was local famine and cruel death by starvation.

And even if the harvest was good, the primitive methods of agriculture of the time produced little surplus, and since lords and warriors, who did not produce at all, helped themselves to the best, the peasantry sank into a misery that never rose much above starvation. Naturally the population declined steadily.

In the disintegration of the times, each lord could operate pretty much on his own, without regard to the king or even to greater lords closer to home. The land became a chaos of petty authority, and the endless quarrels and bickerings between neighboring lords added still further to the unhappiness of the peasantry.

Not surprisingly, any peasant with half a mind, finding himself under the control of a particularly ignorant and brutal lord, might consider leaving his farm and attempting to get established under the somewhat more enlightened rule of a neighbor. This, the landowners, in general, disapproved of, for with the population decline, there were actually too few men to till the earth. No one would feel safe if his peasants, from whose misery he extracted the food he ate and the clothes he wore, could leave at will. If peasants were free in this manner, the landowners might have to bid for their services.

Instead, the custom grew to declare the peasants bound to the soil; that is, they were forbidden to leave the lord in whose territory they were born. In this way, the lords formed a kind of union against the peasants, forcing the latter to accept whatever conditions were imposed upon them.

The peasants were not exactly slaves, for they had certain rights. The lord had to protect them and take from them only what the custom of the land allowed him to take. Still, they were certainly not free in any decent sense of the word. Such bound-to-the-soil peasants are called serfs (a word related to "servant" and coming from the Latin word for slave).

It was only under Charlemagne that the Frankish heartland had a long enough period of peace for some people to become aware of the degeneration of the times. Charlemagne himself was aware of it. Perhaps his early trips to Italy, where the times were somewhat bright (by comparison), enlightened him in that respect.

He therefore began to labor hard to reverse the long-standing trend and managed to establish the best administration the West had seen since the time of Theodoric the Ostrogoth three centuries before.

Disputes, for instance, had in these hard days come to be settled by primitive tribal methods. A man suspected of crime might be put to the "ordeal." He might be asked to grasp a red-hot piece of metal or to lift a stone from the bottom of a kettle of boiling water. If his burned or scalded hand healed in three days, as it was very unlikely to do, he was judged innocent. Such methods were used for individuals low in the social scale and probably only for those concerning whom guilt seemed sure. Still, if a man happened, by accident, to be innocent, he stood no chance.

At a higher level was the trial by combat, where two men fought, with right judged to belong to the victor. Naturally, this meant that the side which was the bigger and stronger bully (or which could hire him) was sure to be right.

Under Charlemagne something better began to appear. A system was developed whereby disputes over land were settled by a panel of local men of good repute who were under oath to deal honorably. The opportunities of corruption still existed but there was a much better chance of finding men who were honest than finding red-hot metal that didn't burn. Our modern jury system slowly developed from this Carolingian innovation.

Charlemagne was badly hampered by the fact that he had no sensible system of taxation any more than the Merovingians had had. He had to depend on the lords, which gave them far too much power. He also had to abandon the coining of gold, which had become too rare for the West to use. What he could do, he did, however, and established a standardized and sensible silver coinage. He divided a pound of silver into 240 equal parts, each called a denarius. (That system lingers today in England, where there are 240 pennies in a pound and where the abbreviation for penny is still *d*. for denarius.)

Charlemagne tried to beautify Aachen, build churches, and make it something of a worthy capital for the great Empire of the West. He recognized also that he would never get anywhere with ignorance everywhere and tried to establish schools where at least a few might learn and, in time, pass on their learning to others, and where non-clerics might even learn to read and write.

Who, however, would be the first teachers? Certainly, nowhere in the Frankish dominions could any decent ones be
found. Charlemagne therefore tried to attract to his court
learned men from foreign parts — from Italy, England, even
Spain.

The chief of these was the Englishman Alcuin (al'kwin),
who had been born in York at just about the time Charles Martel was turning back the Moors. The school at York (a kind of
primitive university) was the most famous in western Christendom at the time, and in 778, Alcuin was made its head. In 781,
he was in Rome, and there met Charlemagne. His reputation
was high and the great king asked him to come to Aachen. Alcuin accepted and founded a school in Charlemagne's court.

So enthusiastic did Charlemagne become about this great adventure of schooling that he insisted on attending classes himself and got various members of his family and court to attend
as well. Everyone used assumed names so that the complica-
tions of rank could be avoided. Charlemagne called himself
David, for instance. (One can't help suspect that other members of the family and court found the schooling a terrible bore,
but naturally no one could say anything.)

Charlemagne knew Latin very well and Greek pretty well,
but there wasn't much else he knew. His secretary, a Frank
named Einhard, wrote a short biography of Charlemagne, and
he describes with great satisfaction the progress made by the
mighty king.

"He learned the art of reckoning by numbers," says Einhard,
which means he learned what we would now consider third-
grade arithmetic. Of course, in those days, only Roman numerals were used, so third-grade arithmetic wasn't as easy as we
might suppose.

He also learned to read after a fashion and he desperately
tried to learn to write, but without success. Einhard reports
that he would take his tablets, with their samples of writing,
and his copybooks, on which he could copy that writing, to bed

with him. He would keep them under his pillow, and in the morning, or if he woke during the night, he would laboriously try to trace out the letters. But it was difficult for his large, war-worn hands, and he never quite managed.

This is the period of the so-called Carolingian Renaissance ("rebirth"), a time when a small candle was lit in Aachen in the hope that gradually all the land would be filled with its light.

Alcuin, in the attempt to accomplish this, wrote all he could and founded other schools. He modified the Church law as practiced in Italy, adding practices common among the Franks and doing it so reasonably and well that the modification was accepted in Rome.

He abandoned the Merovingian style of writing, which was so sloppy it could scarcely be read. Instead he devised a new system of writing small letters (the "Carolingian minuscule") so that they took up less room and so that more words could be squeezed onto a piece of precious parchment. The design of the letters was so good that despite their small size, they looked good and were easy to read. Six centuries later, the first printers used this style in preparing their type. It has served as the model for the "small letters" in use to this day. (The Romans had only "capital letters.")

Alcuin was also Charlemagne's adviser in practical affairs. He urged him to avoid responding too hastily to Pope Leo's pleas for help in order to make the Pope come to the king a suppliant. It was also Alcuin's view that forced conversions to Christianity were wrong and that the Saxon policy should be changed. This bit of enlightenment was, however, too much for Charlemagne and the other men of the time to swallow.

If Charlemagne had been followed by others like himself and Alcuin, perhaps the light of the small candle might indeed have spread and Western development might have hastened forward by some two centuries.

However, after Charlemagne, the dreary round of civil war, made worse by a new and dreadful round of barbaric invasions,

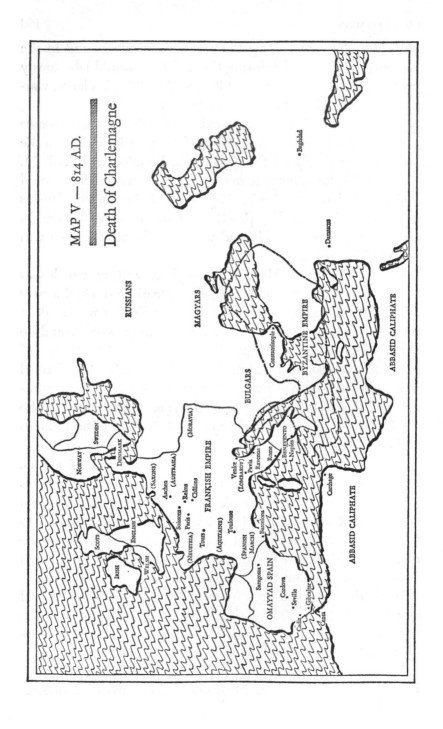

MAP V — 814 A.D.

Death of Charlemagne

ruined matters, and the small light flickered low again. But it
never went completely out. Alcuin's work lingered and the
worst was over. Western Europe was not to forget that bit of
light or to lose entirely the small respect that had been gained
for learning.

8

THE SUCCESSORS OF CHARLEMAGNE

THE LEGEND OF CHARLEMAGNE

Charlemagne finally died in 814 at the age (enormous for the medieval period) of seventy-two. He had reigned for forty-six years, longer than any true Roman Emperor had ever ruled. (Augustus held the record with a forty-five-year reign.) Charlemagne's realm was at its peak in size and strength at his death; he had been almost uniformly successful in warfare; and, most of all perhaps, his enormous frame and natural dignity gave him the posture of a great king at all times, a great and conquering king.

Few at his death could remember any other king, and they must surely have felt that another like him could not come soon. If they felt so, they were right, for seven centuries would pass before any other king would so dominate the West as Charlemagne had. (That other was to be another Emperor

Charles, Charles V, but even he was to be only a pale imitation of Charlemagne.)

Considering, too, that it was a time when no one wrote history in the modern sense; when chronicles were sparse; when hardly anyone could read in any case, so that all information had to be passed along by word of mouth; and when everyone was used to biographies of saints with a content of wild and implausible miracles — it is no surprise that no sooner had the great king died then legends began to be concocted and spread about. Nor is it surprising that the legends bore little or no relation to truth.

Charlemagne became, in the imagination of men, a superhuman, white-haired leader surrounded by twelve great knights who were the "paladins." The term originally meant an official of the palace, but because it was applied to Charlemagne's warriors, it came to mean any hero of the medieval mold.

The most famous of the paladins was Roland, supposedly a son of Charlemagne's sister (with, according to one story, Charlemagne himself as the father). Second only to him was Oliver. So alike were Roland and Oliver in strength and high heroism that whatever one could accomplish the other could do as well. Finally, they met in direct combat on an island in the Rhine River and fought for five hours without decision. After that, they became close friends.

The most famous of all the Charlemagne legends was inspired by Charlemagne's first expedition into Spain. It was written at a time when Europe was hurling itself against the Moslems along the eastern shore of the Mediterranean Sea (three centuries after Charlemagne's death) and anti-Moslem feeling was at its height. Naturally, then, Charlemagne's earlier and somewhat successful fight against Moslems was revived in glamorous style as a source of inspiration.

The tale was written as a 4,000-line poem called *The Song of Roland* and it pictured Charlemagne as having conquered all of Spain but Saragossa. (This glorious picture is quite wrong, of course. Actually, on his first expedition into Spain, Charlemagne was indeed turned back at Saragossa, but he had captured none of the land. To the end of his life he never held any part of the peninsula but the narrow strip south of the Pyrenees.)

In the poem, Charlemagne is persuaded to make peace at this point and sends Ganelon to the Moslems to arrange the terms while he himself leads his army back across the Pyrenees. Ganelon is the stepfather of Roland and there is an undying feud between these men. Roland had proposed Ganelon as ambassador, and Ganelon, feeling certain that Roland hoped the task would mean his death, decided to arrange Roland's death instead. He therefore informed the Moslem ruler of Saragossa of the route Charlemagne's forces were to take, and urged him to ambush the rear guard in the mountain passes.

Roland and Oliver, leading the rear guard through Roncesvalles, become suddenly aware of an overwhelming force of Moslems all around them. Roland has a magic horn which he can sound to recall the main Frankish force. Oliver urges him to do so in view of the vast disparity of numbers, but Roland vaingloriously refuses to call for help. His small army fights with superhuman strength, killing five for one, until only fifty Franks are left alive. And then Moslem reinforcements come on the scene.

Now Roland blows his horn but it is too late. The little band is killed to the man, with Roland himself the last to fall. Charlemagne returns to bewail the corpses and get his revenge by inflicting an enormous defeat upon the Moslems. He then places Ganelon on trial and ends by executing him.

Clearly, The Song of Roland is based on the actual historical destruction of Charlemagne's rear guard at Roncesvalles and, as mentioned in the previous chapter, there seems even to have been a Roland among its officers. Still, it was not, you will remember, the Moslems who defeated and destroyed the Franks, but the Christian Basques. However, with the great period of the Crusades starting at the time of writing, that would have spoiled the whole point of the poem.

A cycle of fanciful medieval tales were also woven about another of the paladins, Ogier (oh'jee-er) the Dane. He was reputedly the son of a king of Denmark, for no particular historical reason. In Charlemagne's time, the Danes remained outside the Frankish Empire. Indeed, they helped the Saxons fight Charlemagne and offered refuge to the Saxon leader Widukind when he was in flight.

Despite this, Charlemagne made no attempt to go beyond the Saxons (a hard enough enemy) and tackle a still more distant group of fierce warriors. He contented himself with a defensive stance on the Danish frontier. Nevertheless, the Danes had adopted the mythical Ogier as a kind of national hero, whom they call Holger Danske.

The Song of Roland gave birth to numerous imitations dealing with the great deeds of Charlemagne and his paladins and they are known, collectively, as the Chansons de gestes (songs of great deeds). These degenerated into the fictional tales of knight-errantry which the Spanish novelist Miguel de Cervantes, eight centuries after the death of Charlemagne, satirized and killed in his great book *Don Quixote*.

THE SON OF CHARLEMAGNE

While he was still alive, Charlemagne fully intended to follow the good old stupid Frankish custom of dividing the realm at his death and laying the groundwork for the inevitable civil war. He had three sons, Charles, Pepin, and Louis, and he wanted each to inherit a kingdom.

All three had had their share of fighting. Pepin, as king of

Lombardy under Charlemagne, had conducted the fighting against the Byzantines, while Charles fought against the Avars in the east. As for Louis, he was born in 778 and was made king of Aquitaine in 781, when he was only three. He was in charge of the war that brought the Spanish March under the Frankish scepter and he led the army that took Barcelona.

Of course, the division of the realm raised the problem of the imperial title. If all three sons inherited, which was to be the Emperor? To Charlemagne that was a problem not worth worrying about. He thought nothing of the title anyway, so in 806 when he formally provided for the eventual partition of the Empire, he formed three virtually independent kingdoms for his sons. There was to be no Emperor at all.

But Charlemagne lived long enough to see two of his sons die before he did. In the last year of his reign, he had only one remaining son, Louis, who was already a middle-aged man of forty-five. That solved the problem of the imperial title, anyway. Louis, as the only surviving son, would inherit the entire Frankish realm intact, so he might as well have the title of Emperor, too.

But Charlemagne was determined not to perpetuate the mistake of his own coronation. Leo III, who had crowned Charlemagne over a decade before, was still Pope, but he was not welcome at the new ceremony. Louis was brought to Aachen, and there, in the presence of Charlemagne but not the Pope, the heir to the throne crowned himself and served as Emperor along with his father. The implication was clear. An Emperor could be crowned without the Pope; and Pope Leo dared not object.

When Charlemagne died the next year, Emperor Louis I was sole ruler of the realm. Nor was there the slightest trouble about the succession. Who would dispute the right to the throne of the only son of the great king?

Louis had been brought up under the awful shadow of his father, however, and he had had a life of security. He had not had to learn, through the rough-and-tumble of court life in the Frankish realm of civil war and literally cutthroat competition, how to be a monster. As a result, he was genuinely religious and tried to live a life according to the dictates of Christianity. He is therefore known, in German, as Ludwig der Fromme, which in English translation is "Louis the Pious." In French, it is *"Louis le Débonnaire,"* which might be translated as "Louis the Good-Natured."

Louis was indeed both pious and good-natured and that made his reign a particularly difficult one for himself. The Frankish nobility, accustomed to forceful kings and not gentle ones, didn't know whether to laugh at the new Emperor or despise him. Probably, they did both.

For one thing, Louis's piety caused him to pay a great deal of deference to the Church and to allow himself to be dominated by the priesthood, who certainly knew how to play on his piety. (He was not a blind puppet, though, for he carried through certain reforms, especially among the monasteries, which could not have been popular with all clerics.) To the nobility, however, such deference to the priesthood was womanish. Nor was this nobility to be taken lightly, for Charlemagne had lived a little too long in this connection, too. In his later years, authority had begun to slip from his aging fingers into the hands of the great nobles who, in any case, controlled the land and held the key to the men and money without which wars could not be fought.

One thing Louis did, out of sheer piety, was a clear mistake from the standpoint of selfish imperial interests. He went out of his way to subordinate himself to the Pope.

Pope Leo finally died in 816, in the second year of Louis's reign. Stephen V succeeded to the Papacy but he was an unpopular choice with the Roman people. Pope Stephen knew that, like his predecessor, he might be evicted from the city by the unruly Romans and he set about at once making sure that he had the Frankish crown behind him. He swore fidelity to the Emperor and made the Roman crowd do so likewise. He then offered to visit Louis at any appointed place.

Pope and Emperor met in August of that year, at Reims, a city eighty miles east of Paris. A shrewd monarch, not unduly troubled by piety, would have recognized that Stephen was in a weak position, needing badly to insure the help of the Emperor against any trouble he might have in Rome. Louis might have granted the help but only after receiving concessions in return, concessions that might have made it clear the Emperor was not beholden to the Pope for his title.

No such idea occurred to Louis; rather it was he who strove, unaccountably, to surrender. He greeted the Pope with the utmost humility, prostrated himself before him, and asked to be crowned by him. Louis had already crowned himself three years earlier, before the austere eyes of his aged father; that crowning had been recognized everywhere, even by the Pope. It had established a precedent that was all to the good of the Emperor — and now Louis threw all that away.

Stephen crowned Louis a second time in the cathedral at Reims, in the city where Clovis and his followers had been converted to Catholic Christianity three and a quarter centuries before. The city was thus doubly hallowed and the crowning of monarchs was to take place there for a thousand years.

Louis not only gave away the imperial bargaining position by kneeling to the Pope, he valued the empty imperial title. He called himself only "Emperor," never using the title of "King of the Franks and Lombards" which his father had proudly borne to the end.

As became a pious man, Louis was a good husband and father. His beloved wife Irmingard had given him three stalwart sons: Lothair, Pepin V and Louis.

Soon after his coronation by the Pope (when he felt, perhaps, really Emperor for the first time), he decided to make arrangements for the division of the Empire in case of his death.

What Charlemagne had been saved by fate from doing, Louis now proceeded to do. He divided the kingdom among his sons, but, to give him his due, he did so as sensibly as possible. There was no division into truly separate and independent kingdoms as Charlemagne had contemplated. There couldn't be, for Louis, unlike his father, had to decide how to dispose of the imperial title. If the realm was to give sovereignty to each of his sons as kings, it had to remain united under a single Emperor.

At a meeting of the nobility of the Frankish realm in 817, then, he officially made Lothair, his oldest son, co-Emperor and chief successor. Since the Emperors are numbered, we can call him Lothair I. Louis and Pepin he made subsidiary kings at opposite ends of the Empire; Pepin was to rule over Aquitaine and Louis over Bavaria. Since the younger Louis consistently ruled over areas that are now part of Germany he is distinguished from his father by being called Louis the German.

This was perhaps as decent an arrangement as one could make; the desirability of the posts was in due order of age and all seemed fair. Louis's three sons accepted it amicably.

Lothair took up his own duties as co-Emperor in Italy and there his position was further confirmed when he was anointed in 823 by Pope Paschal I, the successor of Stephen.

But in 818, Queen Irmingard had died, and Louis's genuine grief did not prevent him from marrying again, within four months, a Bavarian princess named Judith. She was young and beautiful and Louis quite doted on her. In 823 she bore him a son, who was named Charles after his grandfather.

Here came the germ of trouble, for Judith saw no reason why this fourth son of Louis (and her own only son) should not be considered the equal of the other three. Why should he not have a little kingdom all his own?

By 829, she had won out. The poor Emperor, unable to resist, called a new gathering of the nobles and ordered that a third subsidiary kingdom be carved out of the Empire for the young boy Charles.

And that was the beginning of disaster.

THE GRANDSONS

OF CHARLEMAGNE

The co-Emperor Lothair greeted this new division with horror. He saw himself deprived of direct rule over another large part of the realm and knew that the value of the imperial title would decline accordingly. He objected strongly, therefore, and Louis found himself faced with a whole nest of hostile sons.

It was, perhaps, only natural. It is not likely that grown sons are ever going to feel very kindly toward a stepmother as young as themselves. Nor are they likely to have much brotherly feeling toward the son of such a second marriage. Rather, the new youngster would surely be viewed as a stranger and interloper.

What's more, the nobility threw themselves into these suddenly troubled waters. Many saw their chance to profit. In any civil war, their support would be valuable and they could sell that support in return for concessions that would further increase their own power at the expense of central authority. (It was this that had been the ruin of the Merovingians and even Charlemagne had only partially reversed the trend.) The noblemen related to the wives of the various sons saw a chance, in particular, of growing strong if their own relative won a particularly choice portion of the kingdom.

There were not wanting, then, advisers to urge Lothair not to endure the injustice but to assert his rights by force. Lothair succumbed to the unfilial temptation and, in 830, with his brothers joining him, he led an army to war against his father.

He won initial successes, captured the aging Emperor and his young wife and son, and sent them off to separate convents. (This shows the advance of humanity. A Merovingian monarch would at the least have killed the wife and son out of hand, and perhaps the Emperor, too.)

As it was, the sons were content to hope that the king's piety might cause him to decide to become a monk. If he did, he would renounce the throne forever and in that case Judith and Charles could be taken care of easily and all would be well on the lines of the old agreement of 817.

Louis, however, would not play the game. He still had what power was left to the name of Emperor; there were still warriors on his side out of respect for the son of Charlemagne; he was popular with the people; and, most of all, the clergy were entirely on his side.

The Emperor was therefore able to arrange to have himself freed and to call a new meeting of notables. These convened in a section of Austrasia where Louis was strongest. The meeting at Nijmegen (nigh-may'gen), in what is now the southern Netherlands, confirmed the arrangement whereby Charles was to have a kingdom for himself. Judith was restored to her position and the initial victory of the three sons was entirely canceled out.

Louis was much embittered by his imprisonment and by the conduct of his sons. What he had done, originally, in reluctant fashion, he now maintained with energy. Indeed, in 833, in a fit of petulant anger over what seemed to him to be the particular hostility of his second son, Pepin, he disinherited him and added Aquitaine to Charles's kingdom.

That just meant a second rebellion of the sons and this time Louis's position was worse off than before. Even the clergy were upset with Louis, for it seemed clear that his stubbornness and peevish acts would cause the Frankish realm to break up and this they did not want to see happen. Western Christianity, the Pope's spiritual dominion, they rightly felt to be in danger of being caught between the closing jaws of a nutcracker — the Moslems on the west and the Byzantines on the east — if the strong Frankish Empire vanished.

Lothair, the oldest son, still ruling in Italy, tried to take advantage of this clerical displeasure by convincing a new Pope, Gregory IV, to urge Louis to abdicate. The Pope, who had done his best to mediate between father and sons, was not willing to go that far. He was not entirely a free agent, however. Lothair had raised an army and intended to join his brothers in battle against his father once more. The Pope was invited to accompany the army with a show of armed urgency that made the invitation impossible to refuse. The Pope came along, albeit with reluctance.

It was still 833, when the two armies met near Colmar (in what is now Alsace) in just about the geographical center of the Frankish Empire.

The men of Louis's army found, to their horror, that among the opposing forces was the Pope himself. Could arms be raised against the Pope? Would that not lead to instant damnation? The imperial army deserted poor Louis, therefore, and the Emperor was taken without a fight. As a result of this failure of Louis's troops in loyalty to their overlord (a terrible crime in the medieval view), the site of the non-battle was called the Field of Lies ever after.

For the second time in three years, Louis was a captive. This time he was held more tightly. He was accused of a horrifying list of crimes, was made to confess his faults in a humiliating ritual of penance, and was even forced to renounce his throne. He was also urged to become a monk but this he strenuously refused to do. As long as he refused the monk's cowl, he might still somehow regain the Emperor's crown.

The old Emperor's calculations were by no means illfounded. The three sons were in power now and had divided the realm among themselves according to the old system of 817, with Lothair as Emperor. But then, as Louis the Pious had perhaps expected, the sons found out that while it was easy to work together against a common father, it was not so easy to work together after victory.

As Emperor, Lothair expected to be complete master and took the view that his brothers, Pepin and Louis, were merely his subjects. Pepin and Louis, who only lately had been fighting alongside Lothair as his equals, were by no means ready to bow before him.

A new civil war broke out and the clergy, who had turned against Louis the Pious in the hope that by so doing peace could be brought to the Empire, turned back when they found that peace was still absent.

Louis the Pious was absolved of the crimes he was supposed to have committed and was declared by a party of bishops to be Emperor again. His two younger sons promptly joined him against their older brother, Lothair, on whom they eagerly placed all blame for unfilial conduct.

Louis returned to Aachen in the spring of 834, and was rejoined there by his wife Judith and their son Charles. Things were not exactly quiet, but they were better than they had been. The sons were all forgiven; Lothair was once more back in Italy, and the other two sons were in their respective dominions. If they were not entirely reconciled to the situation, they at least made no further open war on their father.

In 838, in fact, Pepin died, and Louis saw his chance to settle everything. Now they could go back to the settlement of 817, which everyone had accepted; except that Charles, his youngest son, could take the place of the dead Pepin in Aquitaine to the exclusion of Pepin's own heirs. Was that not a reasonable solution? Lothair, with a sullen reluctance, agreed. After all, he may have thought, his father was old now — over sixty — and there might not be long to wait.

There wasn't. In June, 840, Louis the Pious died, after a more or less disastrous reign of a quarter of a century. He died with the Empire intact, at least in appearance, but on the point of crumbling under the impact of civil war, past and future.

Worse still, the prestige of the imperial title was destroyed. Where Charlemagne had ennobled the title of Emperor, his

son had given the world the sight of an Emperor abandoned, an
Emperor imprisoned, an Emperor forced to confess to crimes,
an Emperor deposed.

But now the situation was almost as it had been after the
deposition of Louis the Pious seven years before. Once again
the eldest son, Lothair I, reigned as Emperor at Aachen. Once
again two younger brothers ruled at opposite ends of the kingdom. Louis the German ruled in Bavaria. Pepin was dead, so
now it was the teen-aged Charles, his half-brother (and eventually to be known as Charles the Bald), who was king of Aquitaine.

But Lothair still thought that as Emperor he was lord of all,
and his two younger brothers still felt that they were not going
to bow down to any brother. The death of the old Emperor was
thus merely the occasion for one more civil war.

Lothair was forced to fight a two-front war, forever caught
between the forces of Louis on the east and Charles on the
west. He was not the kind of general who could so arrange
matters as to defeat each separately. The two younger brothers
managed to unite their forces and on June 25, 841, almost exactly a year after the death of Louis the Pious, Lothair had to
meet the united armies of the brothers at Fontenoy, about sev-
enty-five miles southeast of Paris.

Lothair was supported by the clergy, who saw in his victory
a last chance at the unity of the realm, but the stars in their
courses were fighting against this. The western and eastern
portions of the Frankish realm had grown so far apart in a thousand ways that nothing could cement them together for long.

The best evidence for this rests with the oath of alliance
sworn by the soldiers of the allied brothers, Louis and Charles,
in 842, after the battle at Fontenoy had proved a defeat for
Lothair. The hunted Emperor was rapidly being brought to
bay and only a split between the victorious brothers could now
save him. The oath was an attempt to prevent that split. This
oath, sworn at Strasbourg, had to be drawn up in two lan-

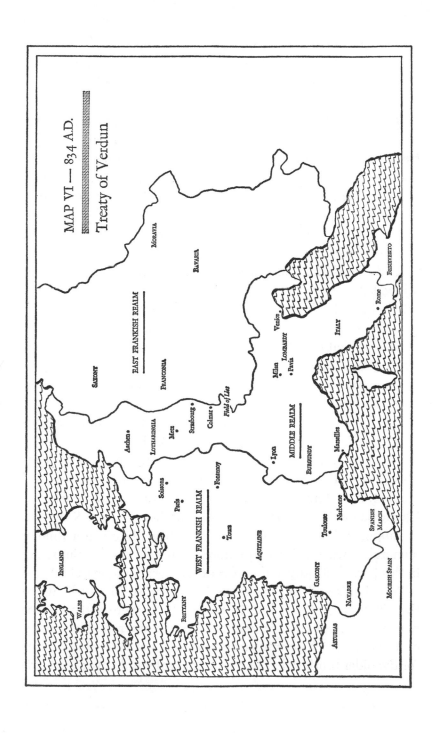

MAP VI — 834 A.D.

Treaty of Verdun

ENGLAND

WALES

BRITTANY

WEST FRANKISH REALM

AQUITAINE

GASCONY

NAVARRE

ASTURIAS

MOORISH SPAIN

SPANISH MARCH

Narbonne

Toulouse

Tours

Paris

Soissons

Fontenoy

Aachen

LOTHARINGIA

Metz

Strabourg

Colmar

Field of Lies

Lyon

MIDDLE REALM

BURGUNDY

Marseilles

SAXONY

EAST FRANKISH REALM

FRANCONIA

BAVARIA

MORAVIA

Milan

LOMBARDY

Pavia

Venice

ITALY

Rome

BENEVENTO

guages, in an early form of German for the soldiers of Louis
and in an early form of French for the soldiers of Charles. The
Franks of the east and the Franks of the west could no longer
understand each other's language.

In that same month, Lothair was forced to give up. Repre-
sentatives of the three brothers met at Verdun and signed a
treaty that was to be the first of the great treaties of modern
Europe. Indeed, it was a treaty which, without actually intending any such thing, set up something in which we can begin to
recognize the germ of the Europe that now exists. By its terms,
both younger brothers expanded their own kingdoms at the
expense of the Emperor Lothair.

Louis the German was to rule not only over Bavaria, but over
all the lands between the Rhine and the Elbe. His lands consti-
tuted, indeed, almost exactly the territory now covered by
modern Austria and West Germany. It was viewed then as
something that might be called the "East Frankish Empire" but
looking back upon it from the vantage point of historical per-
spective, we can see that it is the nucleus of what we would
now call Germany.

Charles the Bald ruled not only over Aquitaine but over Neustria as well. This "West Frankish Empire" is even more clearly
the nucleus of what we would now call France. In later centuries, in fact, Charles the Bald was included in the official
numbering system for French kings and was called Charles II,
Charlemagne having been Charles I both as French King and
as Emperor. (Louis the German is not usually given a Roman
numeral, however. Those are more often used for the Emperors
in this period of history than for other German monarchs.)

Both Louis and Charles were, in theory, still subordinate to
the Emperor Lothair, but in reality both were independent
powers and both knew it, and so did the Emperor. The Treaty
of Verdun, which scrupulously reserved the title of Emperor
for the older brother, left him as actual ruler only over the terri-

tory lying between the two swollen kingdoms of the younger brothers.

Lothair's kingdom was a straggling strip of land extending from the North Sea to central Italy, including the cities of Aachen and Rome, the new and the old capitals of the Empire. The strip was not viable. It was awkward geographically and it had no unity of language or culture. It served only as something that was neither French nor German and therefore something that strongly resembled a bone thrown between two dogs — a cause for eleven centuries of warfare between France and Germany.

MOSLEMS AND VIKINGS

After 843, relative peace descended on the Frankish kingdoms as far as internal war was concerned. Through all his troubles, Louis the Pious had attempted to keep the Carolingian Renaissance going, and scholars were still to be found at the court of his sons, especially at that of Charles the Bald. Nevertheless, the light was dimming, for with one civil war following another, the atmosphere for calm scholarship was absent.

What was worse was that in the generation during which the Frankish energies had been consumed in the fratricidal struggle, new dangers had arisen without.

The Byzantine Empire was going through another period of weakness after the death of Nicephorus, who had fought against Charlemagne. It no longer had any sea power to speak of and the Franks had none either. The Mediterranean was left, by default, to the Moslems, who occupied the entire African coast.

To be sure, the Moslem world was also breaking up, but even its pieces were stronger than the Christian power.

For instance, Moorish Spain, after sustaining its losses at the hands of Charlemagne, was ravaged by a series of civil wars. Fifteen thousand Moors were forced to flee Spain in consequence. They made their way to Egypt, seized Alexandria, and would not leave until their departure had been sweetened by a large sum of money. With that safely in their war chest, they sailed north in 826 to the Byzantine island of Crete, took it, and set up a kingdom that for a century and a half served as a haven for pirates and a center for the slave trade.

Worse still, a Byzantine governor of Sicily, aspiring to the imperial throne, called for help to the Moslem rulers of Tunis (the region that had once been Carthage). These rulers were the Aghlabites, named after the chieftain who had established his rule there a quarter century before in defiance of the Abbasids.

The Aghlabites answered the call eagerly and a Moslem army landed in Sicily in 827. They had no intention, of course, of playing the role of hirelings. They were in it for themselves. (Probably, the most-often-repeated lesson in history is that foreigners who are called in to help one side in a civil war take over for themselves. It is a lesson that seems never to be learned despite endless repetition.)

Little by little, the Moslems took over the island against desperate, but always failing, Byzantine resistance. The Franks, involved in their civil wars, could do nothing about this and by the time of the Treaty of Verdun, Moslem forces were in control of almost all the island.

(Nevertheless, lest the Byzantines — who always tend to be unfairly downgraded in Western histories — be thought of as too easily defeated, it should be pointed out that they held on to isolated Sicilian regions for over a century. It was not until 965 that the last Byzantine stronghold in Sicily was taken. Thus, four and a third centuries elapsed between the time that

Belisarius took Sicily and the last Byzantine soldier departed.)

Sicily remained Moslem for nearly two and a half centuries, and significant portions of Sicilian culture today, like that of the Spanish, stem from the centuries of Moslem rule each endured during the Middle Ages.

The Moslems did not confine themselves to Sicily. Once well established there, they began to raid the Italian coast. In 837, they pillaged Naples and, in 839, they struck far up the Adriatic coast at Ancona, which was Carolingian territory and part of the realm soon to be assigned to the Emperor Lothair himself.

In 840, they conducted more than a raid. They took advantage of their sea power to establish themselves in the towns of Bari and Taranto, forming permanent bases there and becoming virtual masters of the Italian "heel." The Byzantines, hanging on to the Italian "toe" and the once-Lombard duchy of Benevento, were in immediate danger, and the Moslems even established bases at the mouth of the Rhone River in what is now southern France.

If the Moslems were a danger to the south, an even more savage danger appeared in the north. The Moslems were, after all, quite civilized, certainly more civilized than the Franks in this period. Warfare with them was cruel, but no crueler than warfare anywhere.

In the north, however, there appeared a group of pagan sea raiders who had not as yet felt the softening touch of civilization. They were no worse perhaps than the Goths and Franks had been some centuries before, but the descendants of those old barbarians no longer remembered the ways of their ancestors and these new barbarians terrified them.

The raiders came from Scandinavia — the lands we now call Denmark, Sweden and Norway and which are, these days, models of peace and decency for all the world. In Carolingian times, however, overpopulation drove some out of the land; civil war and defeat drove out others; and the sheer lust for travel and adventure sent still others.

They were from the north, as far as the Franks were concerned, and to them they were "Northmen" or "Norsemen."
The Scandinavian raiders called themselves Vikings, meaning
"warriors."

The Vikings raided west and south in the summer, searching
out coastal cities at first, then, more boldly, penetrating rivers
in their light boats. They were after women and loot, and in-
dulged in orgies of killing and destruction with a lighthearted
abandon that utterly horrified and broke the spirit of their victims.

In the time of Charlemagne, the Viking raids fell chiefly on
the British islands, much more exposed to Norse plundering
than the European continent was. There is a story, though,
that Charlemagne once, when at the seashore, saw a Viking
ship sail by on the horizon and broke into tears at the thought
of the destruction the Vikings would some day wreak on the
Franks. (This is undoubtedly a later invention intended to
add to the drama of history — as though history needed inventions in this respect.)

Louis the Pious and his sons had plenty of opportunity, if
they had had the foresight attributed to Charlemagne, to fortify their northern cities, to set up sea watches, to develop a
navy. They did none of these things. They fought each other
instead, and when the Vikings probed beyond England and Ireland, they found a helpless Frankish coast to the south, inhabited by people who could only pray: "From the fury of the
Norsemen, good Lord deliver us." The good Lord did not deliver them often.

Almost immediately after the Treaty of Verdun, the full fury
of the Vikings descended upon the coast of the Frankish kingdoms. In 845, a fleet of Viking ships moved up the Elbe River
to Hamburg, virtually destroying the city and killing everyone
not quick enough to get away. Another fleet sailed up the Seine
that same year and served Paris in similar fashion.

From that year on, for over half a century, every summer saw the Viking ships sailing along the coast and leisurely choosing their targets. The West Frankish Empire with its long coastline and its greater riches was particularly favored. The Vikings even penetrated the Mediterranean.

The Carolingian kings who, after the Treaty of Verdun seemed gradually to lose all their ancestral warlike qualities, dared not face these fierce barbarians in open battle. They fought back with silver weapons instead, buying the Vikings off whenever possible, but never for more than a year at a time.

The Norse raids destroyed the last remnants of central authority. People were thrown upon themselves for protection. Here and there a member of the nobility would fortify a castle in order to be able to fight off the next raid that might come his way. Surrounding peasants would beg for protection, offering to serve him in return.

The tendency toward decentralization that had been going on ever since the fading of the Roman Empire in the West now reached a maximum. The king had become no more than a distant rumor to the average man. The ruler he feared, respected and, on very rare occasions, loved was whatever nearby lord had a castle strong enough to serve as protection.

In later centuries, when this period of utter decentralization was looked back upon, a complicated theory was developed to explain how it worked. In the eighteenth century, French political theorists even gave the system a name — feudalism. This word came from an old German word meaning "property" and, as one can tell from the name, feudalism represented a system of the ownership of land, where that landownership represented virtually the only source of wealth.

The land in a kingdom was supposed, in theory, to belong to the king, who was its lord. He in turn divided that land into fiefs (portions) and invested them in the care of the leading nobles, who were his vassals. (The latter is from an old Celtic word meaning "servant.")

Each vassal then divided up his fief among lesser nobility,

who were his vassals, and so on. Each vassal owed his own lord certain duties, such as having to supply a certain number of men-at-arms on demand. Each vassal was also supposed to show his lord absolute loyalty; failing this, their fiefs were forfeit (if the lord was strong enough to take them).

This feudal system was highly practical in one sense. It required a concrete type of loyalty — loyalty to a specific person rather than to an abstraction such as the people or the nation, or even the royal family.

In theory, too, it seemed to imply a whole hierarchy of levels, with no confusions, extending from the serf at the bottom of the scale to the Emperor at the top. It even moved up beyond the Emperor into Heaven, where God was looked upon as ruling feudally over angels in serried ranks and hierarchies.

In actual fact, though, the feudal system never worked out as it was ideally supposed to. The vassals fought against each other and against their lords, in defiance of theory and entirely in accordance with the laws of each for himself and all for the strongest. Many vassals had fiefs in different places, each derived from a different lord. The confusing checkered network of fiefs was such that A might be B's lord in connection with one fief and his vassal in connection with another.

The system, which seemed so theoretically neat in later centuries, was never workable. It served only as one more excuse for war.

In a way, this was a shame, for if feudalism had worked exactly as the theorists thought it should have, there would be a certain psychological comfort in it. Every man would have a definite place in the social and economic hierarchy, and there would exist an integrated society in which mankind would be a single family.

Though feudalism might suit a disintegrated society in which each local group had to get along as best it could by feeding and protecting itself, it was an exceedingly inefficient system under more favorable circumstances.

When the Viking raids ceased and governments grew more stable, it became essential that there be centralization, so that larger areas, through internal cooperation, might properly exploit the earth's resources and increase their own prosperity. By that time, however, the traditions of feudalism had struck deep and had come to seem the natural way of things and as something ordained by God. (There has never been any custom, however useless it may become with changing conditions, that isn't clung to desperately simply because it is something old and familiar.)

As a result the history of Europe for many centuries consisted very largely of attempts on the part of central governments to impose their will on a turbulent nobility holding firm to their feudal rights.

THE MIDDLE KINGDOM

With enormous troubles on all sides, the three Frankish kingdoms actually attempted to maintain a kind of united front. The Emperor Lothair was the leading spirit here. He was worn out with his attempts to assert his supremacy and was satisfied to maintain a bare equality. The Treaty of Verdun had been a stunning defeat for him and he realized that any resumption of warfare would lead only to further losses for him.

He therefore arranged a series of "summit meetings," whereby every once in a while, the brothers would get together and argue out any differences that arose. This worked well, in Lothair's time at least.

For the middle kingdom, which he directly controlled, he arranged another subdivision among sons, making what was already nonviable, even more so. The more important portion, Italy itself, went to his oldest son, Louis. Louis was in charge there after 844.

In that year, Sergius II became Pope and it occurred to him that with the new Emperor by no means a Charlemagne, the Papacy might well declare its independence of Aachen as it had long since declared its independence of Constantinople. He did not, therefore, bother to go through the formality of seeking imperial approval for his election.

The storm that promptly broke about his head convinced him he could not yet resist the armies of even a weakened Emperor and he retrieved the situation by anointing Louis as king of the Lombards.

Sergius had other troubles, too. The Moslem raiders, operating from their base at Bari in the Italian heel, were having it all their own way. In 846, they even managed to reach Rome itself and to occupy part of it, destroying some of the most venerated churches in Western Christendom.

It may come as a shock to those who think that Charles Martel's victory at Tours in 732 forever ended the Moslem menace to Western Christendom to learn that over a century later, Moslem troops sacked Rome itself, but nevertheless that was the situation. Nor were the Christians in any way capable of reacting appropriately. If the Moslems left, it was not because they were forced out by heroic counterattack, but because they were merely a small raiding party which did not plan an extended stay in the first place.

Sergius II died at about this time and Leo IV became the new Pope in 847. His reaction to the Moslem problem was purely defensive. He built a wall about a small part of Rome, including the Vatican and the Church of St. Peter. So far had the city population declined that the small "Leonine city," so walled about, was sufficient to guard it all in an emergency. Leo also took pains to remain on good terms with Louis, the Frankish monarch in Italy. He crowned him co-Emperor in 850.

Then, in 855, Lothair, Louis's father, eldest grandson of Charlemagne, recognized that death was coming. He abdicated and became a monk just in time to die in the odor of sanctity, and his son became Emperor Louis II.

But the imperial title was now worth very little. The Emperor Lothair had been an eldest brother and nearly the equal of his younger brothers in power. Emperor Louis II controlled only Italy and could not for a moment match himself against his powerful uncles. Being Emperor gave him a certain social status; it gave him nothing else.

Nevertheless, he controlled the military forces of Italy and it was on him that Pope Leo depended for action against the Moslems. Slowly, Louis began to organize an expedition against them. The Byzantines, who were even more threatened by the Moslem presence in Italy, contributed ships to that expedition.

The struggle went on for a long time and was, in a way, a further disgrace to the title of Emperor, for where once an Emperor had been able to take on the full power of Moorish Spain, now an Emperor had great trouble with small piratical outposts. Nevertheless, in 871, Louis managed to reconquer the city of Bari and to drive the Moslems out of the Italian heel that they had occupied for a generation. He got little good out of it directly, for the Byzantines reoccupied the conquered territory (which was what they had had in mind when they joined the expedition).

Louis had the notion, too, that while he was in the south, he might settle matters with the once-Lombard duchy of Benevento, which had held out even against Charlemagne. There he was not successful. He won some victories but not decisive ones, and for a while even had to endure capture and a brief imprisonment. He withdrew to the north, leaving the duchy still independent of the Franks.

The portion of the middle kingdom of Lothair that lay beyond the Alps was even less fortunate. The southern half (the southeastern section of modern France) went to Charles, Lothair's second son, and the northern half (including the present-day Rhineland and Netherlands) went to his youngest son,

Lothair II. When Charles died in 863, his kingdom was divided between Lothair II and Emperor Louis II.

Lothair's portion of the kingdom now included the strip between the two halves of the Frankish Empire, running from the North Sea to the Alps. It was called "Lotharii regnum" or "Lothair's realm." This became Lotharingia — which in turn became Lothringen in German, and Lorraine in French.

Lothair II was enmeshed in an unfortunate domestic triangle. He had both a wife and a mistress, not an uncommon situation at all, but the situation was complicated by the fact that his wife had no child. If he remained married to his wife and ended without children, the entire middle kingdom would come to an end, for his brother, the Emperor Louis, had only a daughter, who couldn't inherit.

As it happened, Lothair did have a son by his mistress and he wanted that son to inherit. All that was required was that he divorce his wife and marry his mistress, thus legitimizing his son.

In theory, this was easy to do. According to the custom of the time, one merely had to draw up a list of terrible crimes against the wife, get a group of bishops to annul the marriage in consequence, and that was it. It was just a matter of form.

But there was one trouble. The very reason that led Lothair desperately to want a divorce, led his uncles, Louis the German and Charles the Bald, not to want him to have a divorce. If he died without an heir, why then the two brothers ruling the Frankish Empire could divide the middle kingdom between themselves.

Therefore, when bishops under Lothair's influence decreed the divorce, other bishops, under the influence of the uncles, denounced the proceedings. An official gathering had to be called and both sides battled with bribes. The uncles won, and Lothair's divorce was declared invalid, although Lothair had already placed his wife in a monastery and married his mistress with great pomp.

In 863, the whole issue had to be turned over to the Pope.

The Papacy had somewhat recovered from its low point in 846 when the Moslems were looting the city, though not before occasion had been given for the invention of a curious legend.

Upon the the death of Leo IV, there was a disputed succession attended by considerable disorder and a kind of miniature warfare. Emperor Louis II supported now one and now the other candidate, but in the end accepted the one who took the name of Benedict III.

The confusion, however, made it possible to create a story to the effect that the actual successor of Leo IV was a very learned monk who was really an Englishwoman. She had entered a Greek monastery to be near her monkish lover. They studied in Athens, but after his death she went to Rome, grew renowned for her learning and piety, and was elected Pope, reigning as "John VIII." She carried off the imposture well, goes the story, until one day in the midst of a solemn procession she was overcome with the pangs of childbirth. She either died in the course of the childbirth or was stoned to death afterward. Ever since, she has been written about as "Pope Joan."

The story was taken as historic throughout the Middle Ages and into modern times, but there seems virtually no doubt now that it is completely mythical. It is one of those dramatic fictions that are much harder to kill than the truth is.

If we stick to history, Benedict III succeeded Leo IV and after a short and undistinguished three-year reign gave way to Nicholas I, who was to prove the strongest pope since the time of Gregory I, two and a half centuries before. He is, indeed, sometimes called Nicholas the Great.

Nicholas was an ardent upholder of papal supremacy over all of Christendom. He seized an occasion to excommunicate the Patriarch of Constantinople, for instance.

He was also the first to use the "False Decretals." These were a list of decrees purportedly given out by early Popes and

Councils. They were supposed to be authentic, of course, and to have been gathered together by the already-legendary Isidore of Seville two and a half centuries before, so that they are sometimes called the Pseudo-Isidorian Decretals. Actually, they are recognized now as forgeries prepared by some Frankish priest not long before Nicholas's time.

The Decretals spoke of a college of cardinals, appointed by the Pope, who were to assist the Pope in legislative matters. All legislation in Church affairs was confined to the Pope and these cardinals. In particular, the various bishops (who had often maintained a haughty and intransigent independence of papal authority) were given no legislative voice.

In this way, Nicholas performed an important service for the Church. In an age when decentralization was spreading everywhere, Nicholas held it away from the Church. He not only kept the Church from turning feudal, but, rather, centralized it further. In doing so, he was strengthened by the wholehearted support of the lower clergy (from whose ranks came the Frankish forger of the Decretals). They much preferred the authority of the distant Pope to the unappealable dictates of a nearby bishop.

It was Nicholas I, also, who first made strong use of the Donation of Constantine to its full propaganda value.

It was the misfortune of Lothair II, then, that when the bishops of the Frankish kingdoms disagreed about his divorce, he had to face this particular Pope.

He did his best. He forced the archbishops of Cologne and of Trier (both of his own kingdom and therefore subject to his pressure) to back him to the hilt. He also got his brother the Emperor (who did not want the middle kingdom left without an heir, either) to present a show of military force that might influence Nicholas in his decision.

The Pope never flinched, however, either before Lothair's bishops or Louis's army. Secure in the knowledge that he had abstract principles of justice and morality behind him, he probably got a grim pleasure out of being able to sit in judgment on Lothair. Sixty-three years before, Charlemagne had sat in judgment on a Pope, and now a successor of that Pope sat in judgment on the great-grandson of Charlemagne.

The judgment was against Lothair II and he was forced to give up his mistress and take back his wife. His son remained illegitimate and unable to inherit. What's more, the archbishops who had decided in Lothair's favor were summarily deposed. In this way, Nicholas not only demonstrated the power of the Pope to decide how kings were to behave, he also displayed his power over two mighty bishops.

Lothair maintained a stubborn refusal to take even a papal decision as final, however. Popes might not change their minds, but Popes must die, and in 867 that is what Nicholas did after a momentous and hectic nine-year pontificate. Lothair promptly made a trip to Italy in order to discuss the matter with the new Pope, Adrian II.

Adrian temporized and agreed to look into the matter once again. For a while, hope must have sprung in Lothair's heart, but it was too late. On the way home, in 869, Lothair II died, and, as he had so desperately feared, left his realm without a direct heir.

9

THE END OF THE CAROLINGIANS

THE LAST OF THE GRANDSONS

The dead Lothair's closest relative was his one remaining brother, the Emperor Louis II. He, by that relationship and by virtue of his position as Emperor, ought certainly to have inherited the land and, temporarily at least, restored his father's middle kingdom in its full extent. At least, so the Emperor himself argued.

The man to decide was Pope Adrian II, who was right in Rome, under Louis's eyes, and uncomfortably aware that Louis was in the process of fighting the Moslem foe to the south, and that upon that victory the security of Rome might depend. He therefore very naturally agreed with Louis and tried to bestow upon him his brother's kingdom.

Adrian was not, however, Nicholas. He was not forceful enough to impose his will. The two uncles, Louis the German and Charles the Bald, were not going to accept the papal decision for a moment. They had gone to a great deal of trouble to keep Lothair from getting his divorce and they meant to get their profit out of it.

Of the two uncles, Charles the Bald was the more capable. Although his West Frankish realm was badly damaged by Norse raids and although the West Frankish nobility were restless, Charles managed, by adroit handling, to hold his own and even to increase his strength.

He succeeded in keeping Brittany attached to his kingdom, although the stubborn Bretons were tempted to join the Vikings in a strike for complete independence. (That may have been bluff; the Vikings would have made uneasy allies.)

He also managed to beat off one Viking raid against the Aquitanian coast. That helped him hold Aquitaine against the intrigues of his nephew Pepin (son of his older half-brother Pepin, who before his death had been king of Aquitaine in the time of Louis the Pious).

Despite all he could do, the lords continued to grow stronger during his reign and the advance of feudalism continued to fragment the land. At times, when the West Frankish nobility rose against him outright, as in 858, and his half-brother Louis the German seized the opportunity for a nonfraternal attack, it seemed as though Charles would lose his crown. That he held on was largely due to the loyalty of the clergy, led by Hincmar, archbishop of Reims.

It was at the court of Charles the Bald that the Carolingian Renaissance continued to flicker dimly. Like his grandfather Charlemagne, Charles established a school at the palace. It was under Johannes Scotus Erigena (eh-rij'ih-nuh), an Irish-born scholar.

Erigena was one of the most important philosophers and theologians of the Dark Ages. His most influential deed was to translate the "pseudo-Dionysian treatises" into Latin. They had been written by some unknown monk in the East in Justinian's time, but were attributed to Dionysius the Areopagite, an Athenian who is briefly mentioned in the New Testament in connection with St. Paul's unsuccessful missionary stay in Athens. A copy of the Greek version had reached Louis the Pious and in good time Erigena put it into Latin. The treatises are a farrago of mystic notions which deal, for instance, with the divisions of the angels into numerous classes, ranked one below the other. Since this seemed to transfer the principles of feudalism to Heaven, the treatises proved popular and influenced medieval thinking greatly.

Erigena also wrote on behalf of Hincmar in various theological disputes in which that powerful archbishop was engaged. Hincmar attempted to establish his own authority over the bishops of the land, and disciplined one of them without any pretense of consulting the Pope or allowing him to be appealed to. This was a mistake, for Nicholas the Great was Pope then. Nicholas insisted that the Pope had the final word on all matters of discipline and Hincmar was forced to bow to that. Erigena might introduce feudalism into Heaven, but to introduce it to Rome against Nicholas's desire was beyond his power.

By 864, Charles the Bald had won out over all difficulties and held his kingdom as firmly as the times permitted. On the death of his nephew Lothair, therefore, he was able to move quickly. In defiance of Emperor Louis II and Pope Adrian II, he seized all of Lotharingia.

But Louis the German let out a bull-roar of displeasure and demanded his share of the loot. Charles the Bald thought a moment and decided that to get part in peace was better than perhaps losing everything in war.

On August 8, 870, agents of the two kings met at Mersen, only about twenty-five miles north of Charlemagne's imperial city of Aachen, and cut Lotharingia right down the middle. (In modern terms, the Rhineland and the northern Netherlands went to Louis, while Belgium and the southern Netherlands went to Charles.)

Five years later, in 875, came another kind of prize. The Emperor Louis II died also, leaving only a daughter, Rothilde, who didn't count. That left the imperial crown empty and waiting.

Louis the German, as the oldest remaining grandson of Charlemagne, was the logical choice. Presumably, he thought the new Pope, John VIII, would see this, and therefore took no extraordinary pains to press his candidacy.

Charles the Bald, however, did not depend on reason and logic. He seized Provence (that portion of Louis's realm just west of the Alps) and kept right on going till he was in Rome and face to face with Pope John.

Here was Charles, right on the spot, with his men-at-arms around him and an open purse in his hand. John VIII welcomed this and had, according to some accounts, invited Charles to come to Rome. Perhaps he reasoned that if he granted the imperial crown to Louis the German, he would but follow the logic of affairs and it might seem that the Pope merely confirmed what was going to happen anyway. If, however, he gave it to Charles, then he would demonstrate that the Pope could give the imperial crown to anyone he chose.

This was indeed what happened. On Christmas Day, 875, exactly three-quarters of a century after the crowning of Charlemagne, the imperial crown was placed on the head of Charles the Bald as an outright gift of the Papacy. He became Emperor Charles II as well as King Charles II, the number being the same in the two cases.

It is amazing, really, to think of the career of Charles the Bald. Born in 823, he had been the infant son of a second wife. He had three older brothers (the youngest of whom, the later Louis the German, was seventeen already at the time of his birth). His half-brothers viewed him and his mother with enmity and he was the focal point around which civil wars raged. For fifteen years, his life could not have been worth a straw, for by the mere slitting of his throat the whole reason for the civil war would have come to an end.

Yet somehow he had ended up with an inheritance. By the fortunes of war, that inheritance was enlarged until it was nearly half the Frankish realm. And, by the accidents of death, here he finally stood, fifty-two years after his birth, the hated infant half-brother, with nothing less than the crown of Charlemagne upon his head.

To Louis the German, this last event must have seemed unbearable. He was approaching seventy himself, but the memory of all the wars against his father and older brother, initially caused by the mere existence of the man who now was crowned Emperor, drove him to the only possible counterstroke.

He got ready for war, but Fate had prepared a last joke. In August of 876, just about half a year after Charles's coronation, Louis the German died, having reigned thirty-six years after the death of his father, Louis the Pious.

Charles the Bald, having outlived all three of his half-brothers, felt he ought now to take measures to reunite all the Frankish dominions under himself. To begin with, he attempted to seize the portion of Lotharingia which Louis the German had absorbed, and to do it at once while the East Frankish realm lay under the usual confusion of a succession.

Unfortunately for him, Louis the German's son (another Louis, eventually called Louis the Younger, to distinguish him from his father) reacted vigorously. He met Charles at Andernach on the middle Rhine in 876 and defeated him. Charles was planning further moves, with undiminished resolution, when he died in October of 877. He had ruled the West Frankish kingdom for thirty-seven years and had been Emperor for less than two.

He was the last of the grandsons of Charlemagne.

REUNION AND DISGRACE

The question now was: Who was to be the next Emperor?

The decision was up to Pope John VIII, and he was in a dreadful bind. Throughout his entire period on the papal throne, the Moslem forces in Italy remained a danger. In fact, in the year of the death of the Emperor Charles the Bald, the Pope was compelled to pay the Moslems tribute to keep Rome safe from attack.

To the Pope, then, the award of the emperorship, which he had within his gift, would be useless unless the new Emperor were one who could drive the Moslems from the papal throat, as once Pepin the Short and his son Charlemagne had driven the Lombards.

Since Charles the Bald had been previous Emperor, one might expect the next one to be among his heirs. Charles, however, was not fortunate in this respect. Two of his sons had died in his lifetime and his sole survivor was Louis II (according to the later system of numbering French kings, a system which counts Louis the Pious as Louis I).

Louis II, however, who is better known as Louis the Stammerer, began his reign with instant discomfiture. He attempted to dominate the lords of the realm by redistributing the offices in such a way as to give power to those he felt to be his allies. The lords he tried to replace contemptuously refused to budge and Louis had to withdraw the attempt in an ignominious confession of defeat.

Nor could there be hopes for the future, for although only thirty, Louis the Stammerer was a sick man. He died in 879 after a two-year reign, leaving the kingdom to two teen-age sons, each too young to serve as the kind of Emperor that Pope John needed.

What about the sons of Louis the German? Here there seemed better prospects. Louis's oldest son, Carloman, ruled over Bavaria and had distinguished himself in war against the Slavs, for instance.

The Slavs, once the Avar yoke was lifted, had begun to make their presence felt in central Europe. They had quietly remained tributary to Charlemagne but in the constant struggles that attended the rule of his son and his grandsons, they gradually slipped out of the Frankish grasp.

In particular, the Slavs who dwelt along the March River, a northern tributary of the Danube, had consolidated themselves into the first powerful Slavic kingdom in Europe. The March River was so called because it formed an eastern boundary of the Frankish realm. To the Slavs the river was the Morava, they themselves were called the Moravians, and their kingdom, Great Moravia.

This was first established in the reign of Louis the Pious and it eventually included what, in modern terms, would be called Czechoslovakia, Hungary, and the southern portions of East Germany and Poland.

Culturally, the Franks remained dominant, and in 862, the Moravian monarch Rostislav, in a deliberate attempt to counteract Frankish influence, turned to the Byzantine Emperor and asked him to send missionaries. Two missionaries were sent — two Greeks named Cyril and Methodius, to be known forever after as the Apostles to the Slavs.

Cyril and Methodius went about their work vigorously. They invented an alphabet for use in the Slavic languages, one based on the Greek alphabet. This is the Cyrillic alphabet, still used today in the eastern Slavic nations, notably in Russia. (Those Slavic nations which eventually came under the religious domination of Rome, such as Poland and Czechoslovakia, eventually adopted the Latin alphabet that is the common possession of the west European languages.)

Pope John VIII, fearing that the labors of Cyril and Methodius might tie the Slavs firmly to Constantinople, associated himself with the venture, calling the Greek missionaries to Rome a couple of times, supporting their work, and even agreeing to allow the Slavs to use their native language rather than Latin in the liturgy. In this way, John laid the groundwork for the eventual absorption of the western Slavs into the Roman Church.

John's labors on the spiritual side were reinforced by Carolingian efforts on the temporal side. In 869, Carloman (already referred to as the oldest son of Louis the German) led a Frankish army against Great Moravia and by 874, the Moravians were forced to acknowledge Frankish overlordship, even though they retained self-government. Rostislav's strategy had thus utterly failed and, indeed, for over a thousand years the Slavs of the region were to remain dominated by German-speaking masters.

Carloman seemed, to himself, to be the natural candidate for the imperial title once Charles the Bald died. He was ruling over Bavaria at the time and it seemed the logical thing to move southward over the Alps and place the Pope under the gentle pressure of a large body of soldiers.

Pope John, however, did not wish to award the title until the candidate made some guarantee concerning the Moslem menace. Before any such agreement could be reached, Carloman sickened, had to be carried out of Italy on a litter, and, after lingering for a while, died in 880.

What about the second son of Louis the German? This was Louis, distinguished from his father by being called Louis the Younger.

Louis the Younger also showed himself to be a capable soldier. It was he who quickly took up arms against Charles the

Bald and defeated him at Andernach. He, however, seemed
more interested in looking westward than southward.

When poor Louis the Stammerer died, the Western Franks
were ruled by two teen-agers named Louis III and Carloman.
There were doubts as to their legitimacy and some of the nobles were only too glad to trade on those doubts and to invite
Louis the Younger into the land for the purpose of further
weakening the central power and increasing their own.

The young brothers, hobbled by treason within, could not
withstand the armies of their East Frankish cousin and soon
after their accession were forced to sign away that portion of
Lotharingia that Charles the Bald had won. It was to take
nearly a thousand years for the later French kings to win back
what the brothers had now been forced to give up.

But while Louis the Younger was busily engaged in fighting
west of the Rhine, he was of no use to Pope John, who was still
desperately holding off the Moslems and still looking for an
Emperor.

Louis the German had yet a third son, the youngest. What of
him? This one was Charles, usually known as Charles the Fat.
When Carloman died in 880, Charles the Fat became king of
Italy. He was on the spot and Pope John could wait no longer.
There had been no Emperor for four years, since the death of
Charles the Bald. John therefore crowned Charles the Fat as
the Emperor Charles III.

The Pope did not live long enough to see what an utterly bad
choice he had made. He was assassinated the next year in a
palace conspiracy. His brains, according to the story, were
beaten out with a mallet.

Charles the Fat was ill and, apparently, an epileptic. He was
completely unfitted to rule and yet the accidents of death
brought him more than a monarch with ten times his ability
might otherwise have won. The death of his oldest brother,
Carloman, in 880 had brought him the kingdom of Italy and the
imperial title. The death of his next brother, Louis the Youn-

ger, in 882 made Charles the Fat ruler over all the East Frankish realm.

Nor was that the end. His young cousins, Louis III and Carloman, who ruled over the West Franks, were peculiarly unfortunate. Louis III had led his army to an unusual victory over
the Vikings in 881, when he was still only eighteen, and he
might well have turned out to be a capable king, but he died in
an accident in 882. Carloman succeeded as sole king but died
in his turn in a hunting accident in 884.

Neither Louis III nor Carloman had any heirs, but they had
a young half-brother named Charles, who was born of Louis
the Stammerer's second wife, after the death of the father. He
was only five years old, and this did not seem to be the time to
have a child on the West Frankish throne.

The West Frankish lords therefore turned to the only remaining member of the Carolingian dynasty — Charles the Fat. He
was invited to become king of the West Franks and in 884,
therefore, all the Frankish realm was united — for the last time
— under one Emperor and king.

But what a comedown from the united Frankish realm of
Charles I (Charlemagne) to that of Charles III! It was, in fact,
what one might expect in passing from a monarch who was
great to one who was merely fat.

Charles the Fat, partly due to his illness, no doubt, was a
monument of inertia. His Empire crumbled about him in all
directions, yet he lacked the energy and perhaps the will to do
anything about it.

He could or would do nothing about the Moslem menace in
Italy, so that old Pope John's search had gone for nothing.
Worse yet, he could or would do nothing about the Norse dep-
redations.

The climax came in 885, when a strong Norse raiding party
ascended the Seine and made for Paris itself. Charles the Fat
remained torpid and did nothing. The defense of the city fell
upon Eudes, who had large holdings in Neustria and who held

the title of Count of Paris. He was the son of a magnate known as Robert the Strong, who had been the right hand of Charles the Bald and who had died fighting the Norsemen.

Eudes, count of Paris, took over the defense of the city. For a whole year, Paris lay under siege and held out valiantly. The mere fact that a city could hold out against the dreaded Vikings offered hope to a despairing population. As month after month passed without its fall, the Norsemen began to seem something less than supermen and Count Eudes became the darling of the nation. Paris became a kind of Stalingrad of the Dark Ages.

Finally, long after Paris and its defenders had clearly established themselves as heroes, the laggard Emperor arrived on the scene. But he came not to attack the Norsemen but to buy them off with money and with an offer to let them winter in some fixed section of the land — that is, to give them a region to plunder.

The contrast between the heroic count and the contemptible Emperor was too great to be endured. The nobles were virtually unanimous in refusing to have so incompetent and disgraceful a ruler, even if he was a great-grandson of Charlemagne.

Nor did Charles the Fat make any effort to hang on. Undoubtedly, he felt the burden of the throne to be too great for him anyway. He was deposed in 887, retired into seclusion, and died the next year.

With the deposition of Charles the Fat, the Frankish kingdom broke up finally and forever. Never again were its eastern and western halves to be united under a single rule accepted by both halves.

THE ITALIAN EMPERORS

What next? Was the Carolingian line through? Not quite!

The magic of legitimacy and the memories of the glories of Charlemagne lingered. The leader of the nobles who had deposed Charles the Fat was one Arnulf, an illegitimate son of Carloman, who had fought the Moravians. Arnulf was therefore a nephew of Charles the Fat, a grandson of Louis the German, and a great-great-grandson of Charlemagne.

If one were willing to overlook the illegitimacy, Arnulf was a Carolingian. There was no better candidate, so the illegitimacy was overlooked and he was accepted as king of the East Franks by the lords of that section of the realm.

He was not, however, accepted in either Italy or the West Frankish realm. Italy had split up into several dukedoms, which quarreled among themselves, each trying to dominate the Papacy. The various attempts at domination canceled each other out and left the Papacy at the mercy of the Roman aristocracy. As Popes and Franks alike sank into weakness, it fell to the Byzantines in the south to control the Moslems. Fortunately for Rome, the Byzantine Empire was entering another period of relative strength. Its holdings in southern Italy expanded and the Moslem menace was held somewhat in check.

As for the West Franks, they (at least temporarily) abandoned the Carolingians altogether. To many of the West Franks, Paris was the city and Count Eudes was the man. Enough of the magnates supported him to make him the first non-Carolingian king of the West Frankish realm since Pepin's crowning a century and a quarter before.

Eudes was to find, however, that running the nation was not as easy as heroically defending Paris against the Norsemen. As king, he had no power except over his own Neustrian estates. He had no reasonable system of taxation, no public funds, and no way of making any noble obey him unless he could defeat him in war. The West Frankish lords outside Neustria simply would not submit to him.

In the end he was forced to do what Charles the Fat had done — buy off the Norsemen. Still worse, he had to search for added strength by doing homage to Arnulf, thus acknowledging his overlordship and, presumably, hoping for the help of his armies.

Arnulf, however, was far too busy with his own military problems to help Eudes and that was the end for the count of Paris. If he could not maintain himself without Carolingian help, then why not return to the Carolingians altogether?

There was still a Carolingian of the West Frankish branch who was available. This was Charles, posthumous son of Louis the Stammerer. When Louis's older sons had died, Charles was only five years old and he had been passed over for the unspeakable Charles the Fat. Now he was fourteen years old, old enough in the eyes of those eager for legitimacy, to rule. In 893, the archbishop of Reims anointed the youngster in traditional fashion, and he became Charles III of the West Frankish kingdom. Once again, after a six-year hiatus, Carolingians ruled over both halves of the realm.

Indeed, Carolingians of a sort even reigned in Italy. Louis the Pious had had a daughter in addition to his four sons. She had married the marquis of Friuli, a region just north of the Adriatic Sea. They had had a son named Berengar, also marquis of Friuli.

To be sure, it was not the Frankish custom to allow monarchy to pass down through the female and Berengar was great-grandson of Charlemagne only on his mother's side. In the confusion that followed the deposition of Charles the Fat, however, all sorts of irregularities could be glossed over. At least Berengar thought so and he did not hesitate to aspire to the imperial title.

Nor was he the only woman-descended candidate in the field. Lothair, oldest son of Louis the Pious, had had in addition to his sons a daughter, and this daughter married Guido (gwee'doh) of Spoleto (a duchy near Rome). Their son, another Guido of Spoleto, was great-great-grandson of Charlemagne on his mother's side, and Guido, too, aspired to the imperial title.

It might seem that such minor princelings could not become Emperor when the powerful Arnulf, king of the East Franks, was the logical candidate. In fact, Arnulf was recognized as Emperor by many of the lords.

However, recognition by the nobility was not enough. The title could be awarded only by the Pope, in line with a tradition now a century old. To get the Pope's blessing and anointing, Arnulf would have to go to Italy where the Pope was and this he couldn't do. He was busy fighting off the Norsemen in the west and putting down a revolt of the Moravians in the east.

Berengar and Guido, on the other hand, were on the spot. Moreover, the Popes of the time were no longer of the heroic mold. They could be easily and rapidly made and unmade by the decadent and corrupt Roman aristocracy and after being made could be forced into anything. The century and a half that followed the death of Pope John VIII is sometimes called the "night of the Papacy."

The princelings fought each other and Guido won. One of the downtrodden Popes of the period, Stephen VI, was forced to declare him Emperor in 891. When Guido died in 894, his son Lambert was declared Emperor in his turn.

This marks the complete degradation of the imperial title. It had become a kind of plaything of Italian politics, to be awarded to any minor individual who happened to control Rome. So far had Charlemagne's crown tumbled in the course of a single century.

Arnulf, meanwhile, had disengaged himself. He had defeated the Norse, whose raids were beginning to taper off in any case, as the century drew to its close. He had also made peace with the Moravians.

Arnulf decided to keep the Moravians in check by allying himself with a new people. These were the Magyars, also called Ugrians, a people who had been living in what is now the Urkraine for some two centuries.

The westward push of new tribes from Asia drove the Magyars westward into the lush plains east of Moravia, the plains which had formed the power center first of the Huns and then of the Avars.

The word "Ugrian" has become "Hungarian" in English, and the plains the Ugrians occupied have become Hungary. The conversion of the first syllable from *u* to *hun* may be the result of the memory of the Huns, who in similar fashion, from the same region, had threatened the Germans. (The word "ogre" is also thought to come from "Ugrian," a sharp indication of the time when the Magyars were the fearful menace of central Europe.)

The people we call Hungarians call themselves Magyars to this day and the official name of the land we call Hungary is Magyarorszag or "land of the Magyars." At this early stage in their history, when they were a group of tribes rather than a settled people, it would be just as well to call them Magyars.

With the Magyars in alliance with Arnulf, the Moravians were caught in the middle. By 906, indeed, the Moravian territory was completely taken over by the Magyars, and the first Slavic kingdom came to an end in a return of the Slavs to their usual fate — that of an oppressed peasantry under the heel of a conquering war band.

However, Arnulf was not to live to see this and at the moment, with the Norse raids fading and Moravia in check, he could turn his attention to the matter of the imperial title.

It required two expeditions, but Arnulf finally took Rome in 896 and drove out Lambert. Once that was done, he had no trouble whatever in persuading the Pope of the moment, Stephen VII, to crown him Emperor. It was just a title. It did him no good, lent him no power. Troubles at home were bound to force him to leave Italy. When he did, Lambert regained power and insisted he was still Emperor.

However, both Lambert and Arnulf died in 899.

THE LAST OF THE EMPERORS

Arnulf left a six-year-old son, Louis. After some hesitation, he was accepted, chiefly because there seemed no alternative. Louis was crowned in February, 900, and the value of his reign can be judged from the fact that he is known as Louis the Child.

He was utterly powerless and represented only the living body on which the title "king" might be placed and around which some show of unity might be demonstrated. The actual power of the kingdom was now entirely in the hands of some half a dozen dukes ruling over the larger sections of the kingdom: Franconia, Saxony, Swabia, Bavaria, Lotharingia, and so on.

What central power could actually be exerted on occasion was in the hands of Hatto, the archbishop of Mainz. He had been a right-hand man of Arnulf, who had, in turn, left him as tutor of his son. Hatto therefore served as regent.

In order to exert power, Hatto had to place himself at the side of one of the dukes. He chose to side with the Franconians against their chief rivals, the Saxons. Later, when the Saxons were in power, they wrote the histories and Hatto figures most disreputably in them as a monster of duplicity and treachery, much more so, probably, than he deserves.

One story associated with him (or, possibly, with another Archbishop Hatto of Mainz who lived a century later) states that during a famine, he gathered many poor people into a barn on the pretext of feeding them, then burned the barn, stating that the poor were good for nothing but, like mice, to devour corn.

Not long after, the story goes, the wicked archbishop began to be plagued by mice, which drove him to a tower at Bingen on the Rhine. They followed him there in uncounted numbers, eventually trapping him and eating him alive.

A tower at the supposed site is still called the Mouse Tower in consequence. Actually, it was built some centuries after the event, which in any case never happened, and is familiar to us today chiefly because the English poet Robert Southey wrote a well-known ballad on the subject.

In any case, the lack of a real central government in the East Frankish realm and the absorption of the dukes in mutual rivalries made it quite impossible for the land to withstand the Magyars, who, having destroyed Moravia, now went on to attack the land of their erstwhile allies.

The Magyar raiders, using the same hit-and-run tactics of the Huns and Avars in their day, bit deep into Germany, leaving not a duchy untouched. In 910, peace was bought at the price of heavy tribute and in 911, Louis the Child died, still only eighteen.

He was the last Carolingian to rule over the East Franks, though monarchs of the line were to continue to rule over the West Franks. By now the two portions of the realm had grown so far apart in language and culture that neither one was truly Frankish in the old sense. The only thing that held them together in a kind of pseudo-Frankish unity was the Carolingian house.

When the Carolingians disappeared in the east, it was as though the Frankish name could be applied only to the west thereafter, even though the west was far the less Frankish of the two halves. It is for this reason that the western half is called Frankreich ("realm of the Franks") in German, and France in French and English.

The Carolingians lingered on in Italy for a while, too.

The old Emperor Louis II, who had died in 875, had left a

daughter who, in turn, had a son, another Louis, who was a great-great-grandson of Charlemagne on his mother's side.

This young Louis had been passed over for Guido of Spoleto and his son Lambert, who were no better descended, for they, too, were Carolingian only on the female side. Now that Arnulf had come and gone, that left Berengar of Friuli, who was also Carolingian on the female side.

Berengar's enemies therefore turned to Louis at last. He was then reigning over Provence, just west of the Alps, but he came with alacrity in answer to the siren song of the completely worthless imperial title. In 901, he was invested by Pope Bene-dict IV with the imperial crown and became Emperor Louis III. It was the only deed of note in that Pope's three-year reign and was not much of a deed at that, considering how meaningless the title now was.

Berengar, however, who had been pushing for that same meaningless title for ten years, was as avid for it as ever. He fought Louis and drove him out of Italy. Then, when Louis tried to return, Berengar captured him and, in an unusually barbarous moment, blinded him and forced him into permanent retirement in Provence. Louis III lived on a quarter of a century after that and is known to history as Louis the Blind.

Now the Papacy hit rock bottom. Pope followed Pope in idle procession, made and unmade for the most trivial reasons. Later annalists tell with grisly delight how a Roman noblewoman, Theodora, and her daughter Marozia dominated Rome during the early part of the tenth century, making Popes of their lovers and relatives. Thus, Sergius III, who was Pope from 904 to 911, was the lover of Marozia and the father of her son, who later reigned as Pope John XI from 931 to 936. Between these two was John X, who became Pope in 914 and, it was reputed, had at one time been the lover of Theodora.

John X, whatever his private faults, was at least of vigorous and martial character. For nearly a century now the Moslems had held Sicily and had been raiding Italy. Rome itself had been under the constant shadow of these raiders for over two generations and to this John X hoped to put an end.

He gathered various Italian nobles under his banner and, furthermore, called in Berengar, and gave him what he had wanted for so long. In 915, Pope John crowned him Emperor Berengar I.

For the first time in history, a Pope led an army to battle. Leading his miscellaneous host, he met the Moslems in 916 on the banks of the Garigliano River about a hundred miles southeast of Rome and completely defeated them. The Moslems remained in Sicily for another century and a quarter to be sure, but the threat to Italy itself and to Rome in particular was lifted.

The Emperor Berengar now had the title, for what pleasure it gave him, but he had no power. The Italian nobility rebelled against him and he had to fight as constantly with the title as he had had to fight without it. In 924, he was killed by his own men. He was the last of the Emperors of the line of Charlemagne. The imperial title had remained Carolingian for just a century and a quarter and for nearly half the time it had remained without a vestige of glory.

THE LAST OF THE VIKINGS

Only in the West Frankish realm did Carolingians remain. There Charles III reigned. He was the son of Louis the Stammerer, the grandson of Charles the Bald, and the great-great-grandson of Charlemagne. He was not a very effective king, as can be seen from the name by which he is known to history — Charles the Simple.

He had been crowned king in 893, but it was not till 898,

when Count Eudes of Paris died, that the nobility really rallied about him. Even then it was clear that he would remain king only as long as he didn't offend the very easily offended lords.

This condemned Charles III to a reign of frustration that was made the keener for the fact that in his years there came the last great raids by the Vikings, or (as it is better to call them in this case) the Norsemen.

Their leader was Hrolf (or Rollo) the Ganger (or Walker). He was called this, according to the story, because he was so tall and heavy that no horse could carry him and he had to walk.

Rollo had served with the Norse raiders at the siege of Paris that had made Eudes famous, and after the lifting of the siege, he continued to lead marauding parties into the territory along the lower regions of the Seine River (on which Paris is situated).

Charles the Simple, hampered at every turn by want of money and by the factiousness of his chief subjects, could do very little about the Norse raids. Besides, something else now attracted his attention.

In 911, his distant cousin, Louis the Child of the East Frankish realm, died without an heir. Charles the Simple was now the only remaining member of the Carolingian line who inherited on the masculine side. It seemed to him that he was the only possible successor and that the entire Frankish realm would be united under him as in the days of Charles the Fat a quarter century before.

The East Frankish lords showed no disposition, however, to saddle themselves with what, by now, they considered a "foreigner." If Charles the Simple was to gain his end, it would have to be by force. That meant turning his attention totally to the east and he could not do so without settling matters first with the Norsemen. He would have to buy peace with them at any price.

What the Norsemen demanded was permanent ownership of

the region at the mouth of the Seine, the region which, in any case, they occupied.

Charles the Simple agreed, requesting only that Rollo go through the motion of accepting Charles as his overlord. That would in no way decrease Rollo's power but it would save face for Charles and make the treaty look like a compromise instead of what it was — an unconditional and disgraceful capitulation.

There is a story that although Rollo agreed to accept Charles as overlord, he drew the line at going through the symbolic gesture of kissing Charles's foot. He ordered one of his lieutenants to do so. The lieutenant, finding the task no less degrading for himself, seized Charles's foot and roughly raised it so that he might go through the motion of kissing it without stooping. Charles fell over backward in an undignified sprawl, a sad indication of what the line of Charlemagne had come to less than a century after that monarch's death.

The Norsemen were official masters of a broad section of north-central France, from 911 on. The region became known as Nortmannia, soon slurred to Normandy, while the Norse inhabitants became Normans. Rollo, the last of the Vikings, is supposed to have been converted to Christianity soon after the treaty and to have taken the name of Robert.

With the Viking question solved, however disgracefully, Charles could turn to the east. He did indeed manage to acquire what had once been Lotharingia, but no more. The eastern lords would not have him, nor could Charles force them to change their minds.

Almost defiantly, under the leadership of Archbishop Hatto, they turned to one of their own, Conrad of Franconia, and elected him as King Conrad I. Only Lotharingia denied him.

Conrad's seven-year reign was a gloomy one. The Magyars continued to devastate southern Germany, and the lords, having elected him king, were not minded to give him anything beyond the title.

The Saxon duke led the opposition and, in fact, had the eye on the succession. He succeeded. In 918, Conrad died and the election fell upon the Saxon duke, Henry. According to the tale, the deputation sent out to inform the new monarch of his election came upon him as he was engaged in hunting birds (or fowl) with a hawk. He is consequently known to history as Henry the Fowler.

Thus it came about that little more than a century after Charlemagne had bloodily conquered the Saxons and imposed Christianity upon them, a Saxon sat upon the throne of Germany.

Henry the Fowler proceeded to strengthen his position in every direction. He indicated his independence of the Church by refusing to make a religious ritual of his coronation and pointedly avoiding anointment by his enemy, the archbishop of Mainz.

Furthermore, he beat down the other lords and forced the return of Lotharingia. In 933, he won the first great victory of the Germans over the Magyars. It did not wipe out the Magyar menace but it stopped them for a while.

What's more, he took care to have the kingship remain in his family. Carefully, he saw to it that the lords would vote for Otto, his eldest son by his second wife, to succeed him as king. This came to pass and when Henry died in 936, Otto became king in his place.

THE LAST OF THE FRANKS

As the non-Carolingians in the east grew more successful, the fortunes of the Carolingians of the West Frankish realm continued to sink.

Charles the Simple's eastern adventure had temporarily

netted him Lotharingia, but his prolonged absence encouraged
those who wanted to be rid of him altogether.

Eudes, who had been king after the death of Charles the Fat,
had a younger brother Robert, who succeeded to the title of
count of Paris. Robert did not claim the throne on his older
brother's death, since it seemed at the time that the forces behind Charles the Simple were too strong to withstand. He
waited.

By 922, he had the support of enough of the other lords, including that of his own son-in-law, Rudolf of Burgundy, to take
the plunge. At Reims, he had himself declared king. To make
that stick it was necessary to defeat Charles, whose forces were
still in Lotharingia.

In 923, Robert's army met the army of Charles at Soissons,
where four and a half centuries before, Clovis had started his
career of conquest. The result was double-edged. Charles the
Simple was defeated, but Robert of Paris was killed.

Robert had a son, Hugh, who was too young to rule effectively, and Rudolf of Burgundy therefore claimed the kingship
and was elected by the lords. There followed a confused period, during which civil war and intrigue made no one king in
reality and during which Henry the Fowler was able to reconquer Lotharingia.

Things looked a bit clearer in 929, when Charles the Simple
died in captivity, and by 935, Rudolf was recognized as king by
virtually all the realm — and then he himself died within the
year.

By this time Robert's young son Hugh, the nephew of old
Count Eudes, was no longer as young as all that and was perfectly capable of ruling. Hugh, however, was not minded to
give up the very real power he held in his own lands for the
shadowy title of king that had lured his uncle, father, and
brother-in-law into endless and useless fighting. Perhaps he recalled the history of Charles Martel, who held the real power
under a Merovingian puppet.

Might there not be someone of the old royal line somewhere who could fill the role of puppet and leave Hugh himself possessing all the power but much less of the trouble?

As it turned out, Charles the Simple had had a son, Louis, who still survived. After the lost battle of Soissons in 923, Louis, then a child of two, had been hastily spirited away to England, the home of his mother, there to be kept safe. He was still there in 936, a likely young lad of fifteen.

Hugh, who was now the greatest power in the kingdom and who is generally known, with little justification, as Hugh the Great, brought Louis back. In 936, he was elected king as Louis IV or, as he is usually known, Louis d'Outre-Mer ("Louis from Overseas").

Louis IV showed surprising spirit. He clearly had no intention of playing the supine role of puppet for Hugh's benefit. He even tried to strengthen himself by forming an alliance with Otto I in what had once been the East Frankish realm and pinning down that alliance by marrying Otto's sister.

It was a standoff. Louis IV could never really assert himself against Hugh, but at least he managed to save the dynasty for a few more years. When Louis died in 954, his son, with the good old Frankish name of Lothair I, became king.

Hugh the Great could not stop the accession of Lothair but he made sure that his own holdings would be passed on to his own son so that the battle between king and count would be carried through another generation. Hugh died in 956, and his eldest son, another Hugh, succeeded as count of Paris.

This new Hugh came to be known for the cape he constantly wore, so that he was called Hugh Capet ("Hugh of the Cape").

Patiently, Hugh Capet opposed Lothair, not so much by open warfare as by a quiet undermining of his policies. Lothair frittered away his own strength by repeated and useless attempts to regain Lotharingia, and died in 986 with Lotharingia untaken. He had lived through a long and completely unremarkable reign of thirty-two years.

His son succeeded as Louis V, but reigned only for a year, dying in 987 in a hunting accident. Having had little time to do anything, he is known in history as Louis le Fainéant ("Louis the Do-Nothing"). Louis V has the melancholy distinction of being the last Carolingian to reign anywhere in Europe, so that the line came to an end three and a half centuries after Pepin of Landen had first brought the family into prominence and two and a third centuries after Pepin the Short became the first Carolingian monarch.

Louis V might, in fact, be called the Last of the Franks, for after him there were no Franks, only Frenchmen and Germans.

10

THE DARKNESS BEGINS TO LIFT

THE PLOW

The period from 900 to 950 might be said to mark a turning point, the beginning of an upward climb at last.

The centuries of history that have been covered in this book seem to have been one of unalloyed decline for western Europe. The great culture brought to it by the Romans had been beaten and smashed to bits under the blows of the German tribes, then the Asian Huns and Avars, then the Moslems, Norse and Magyars.

The moment of Charlemagne, when it seemed the decline might be halted and a new Empire established, had passed and

under his increasingly unworthy descendents the Frankish
realm had disintegrated again. The darkness seemed darker
than ever.

And yet that is not the whole story. The great thing about
the Franks, the enormous contribution they made to later culture, even at their most abysmally brutal and barbaric, was that
they *survived!*

They stopped the Moslems; they stopped the Norsemen.
They were caved in and broken here and there, and they tore
themselves apart in suicidal civil war, but they never collapsed
completely. And then between 900 and 950, the darkness
reached bottom.

By 950 a faint dawn began to appear; barely visible at first;
not clearly visible for a long time, perhaps; but it was there.
What happened was nothing sudden or dramatic; nothing anyone noticed at the time.

To begin with, it was a slow emergence of a new way of
farming that caused changes to spread wider and wider in areas
far outside farming.

Agriculture, had been invented thousands of years earlier in
relatively dry areas where the problem was to make sure that
enough water got to the crops. It was best developed in areas
near the great rivers, such as the Nile and the Tigris-Euphrates,
where the water supply could be controlled by a canal system.

The land in northwest Europe, the heartland of the Frankish
power, was not at all like this. It was forested; it was rainy.
The soil was not the dry, light soil of the Mediterranean shores,
but was heavy and waterlogged.

The old methods of agriculture handed down from ancient
times were suitable only to certain places, and agricultural
productivity in the Frankish territories was very low in the
Dark Ages. (That helped keep the period dark.)

The problem was how to drain the waterlogged soil and the
way out was to use a moldboard plow. This had been invented

long before by some unknown individual or individuals, but it was only after 900 that it began to come into widespread use.

The old plow that merely scratched the surface could not do the job. Instead, there was a plow with a knife-edge in front that dug deep, deep into the soil, dragged it up and shoved it against a curved moldboard so that it turned over into a heap. The plowed field became a line of deep furrows with soil heaped up high between. The water drained out of the heaps and along the furrows and the soil could now be used to much better effect.

Why wasn't the moldboard used earlier? Because inventions are useless in isolation. The moldboard plow is much harder to pull than the earlier plows. One ox is not enough; a team of oxen is required, and there were then few peasants with a team at their disposal. Furthermore, it is hard to turn a moldboard plow; it is best used on long strips of land, narrow perhaps, but long.

What was needed then, to put the new plow to its best use, was a sort of cooperative procedure: many men working together, pooling their land and animals. This was exactly what was made possible by the feudalism that developed after Charlemagne's passing. The serfs that clustered about the castle might work on individual plots but more important, they worked together for the whole manor. The manor of the Middle Ages was rather similar to what we would today call a "collective farm."

A second invention came in to spur the agricultural revolution further ahead. It was even simpler than the moldboard plow; it was the horse collar.

The horse can pull much more efficiently than the ox can if it is harnessed properly. The peasant of the Dark Ages had the horse but not the harness. If the kind of harness that worked well with an ox were placed on a horse, it would no longer work well. The anatomy of the horse is such that a harness of this

sort puts pressure on his windpipe as he pulls. The harder he
pulls, the more nearly he chokes. Therefore, he cannot and
does not pull hard.

The horse collar is a padded ring that is placed over the
horse's neck and made to rest on his shoulders. The harness can
be attached to it and the horse can pull without danger of chok-
ing himself. In the early 900's, the horse collar started coming
into use and the horse could now pull at his full strength. Suddenly, one horse could do the work of several oxen and more
rapidly, too.

The widening use of horseshoes served further to keep the
horse in good condition.

The horse-drawn moldboard plow meant that agricultural
productivity began to show a steady rise and this meant that
there was an increasing food surplus available to support armed
men.

Northwest Europe could now support more easily than ever
before an increased supply of professional warriors, well
equipped in armor and weapons. The age of the heavy cavalry,
which had begun with Charles Martel, finally came into its
own.

The medieval "knights" had arrived.

THE KNIGHTS

The new European heavy cavalry, or knights, did not serve
instantly to place into the hands of European monarchs a new
and irresistible weapon with which they could conquer the
world.

The knights, unfortunately, were an unruly force, poorly disciplined and rarely utilized to anything like their full potential.
Besides, they were involved for the most part in civil wars that
wasted their strength endlessly.

Nevertheless, they gave the new Europe a colorful weapon in which it could take pride and which, however inefficiently, could sometimes bring victory.

Never again (with the single fleeting exception of the Mongol invasion of 1240) were Europeans to feel helpless before onslaughts from the outside. Never again would its civilized centers be reduced to praying for preservation against barbarian fury because nothing but a heavenly miracle could be interposed between themselves and the alien army.

Instead, the tide was turning and the armored knight would soon show his superiority against the barbarian hordes. In a century and a half the armored knights would even be hurled in clumsy, wasteful fight against the Moslems on their home ground. They would be too far from home, too undisciplined, to win in the long run, but they would put on a most magnificent show.

The first clear sign of the dominance of the armored knight came in the reign of the German king, Otto I.

Otto began his rule with the deliberate intention of restoring the great days of Charlemagne. He had himself elected and crowned in Aachen in Charlemagne's palace, and he began at once to bring the German lords to heel, defeating them in battle, deposing them, and replacing them by his own relatives.

Some of the defeated lords, in desperation, called upon the Magyars and the stage was set for the culminating confrontation of armored knights versus nomad riders.

The Magyars gathered together a huge host of a type which, in past centuries, would have been completely unstoppable. Against them, Otto mustered an army of knights from almost every part of his realm. On August 10, 955, the armies met near Augsburg on the Lech River. The site, in what is now southern Bavaria, is known as Lechfeld ("the battlefield on the Lech").

The Magyars crossed the river to attack, a maneuver most dangerous unless victory follows. Victory did not follow. The Magyars felt their charge would be irresistible, but the iron men on their horses were as still as monuments before them. The charge was blunted, then broken, and the Magyar horsemen, disheartened and confused, turned to flee. Now they found they had to cross the river in disorder and this is a fatal maneuver usually. Their losses were enormous. Though undoubtedly magnified by the later chroniclers, the extent of the victory was dumfounding. It was the last time the Magyars ever dared face west in force.

For the Germans, the Magyar menace was ended forever, and not long after that the dreaded barbarians, those "ogres," became good Christians. The magnitude of the victory was enough to cast a great luster upon Otto and earn him the title by which he is known to history, Otto the Great.

Otto now felt it was time for the climax. Even before the battle at the Lech, he had descended upon Italy as Charlemagne had once done. The excuse then was a rather romantic one, at least if we can believe the chroniclers. It seems that Adelaide of Burgundy, a young and beautiful widow, was imprisoned by Berengar II, a grandson of the Berengar who had been the last of the Carolingian Emperors. Otto came to rescue her in 951 and made her his queen.

But Berengar remained at large as the most powerful ruler in Italy and, as such, felt it completely within his right to control the Pope (whichever nonentity the Pope of the time happened to be).

In 955, John XII had succeeded to the Papacy, in the very year of the battle of the Lech. In his eyes as in those of others, Otto must have appeared like Charlemagne reborn. Consequently, in 961, when Berengar's overbearing threats became too much to endure, John XII called on Otto as Leo III had once called on Charlemagne.

Otto answered the call, stopping at Pavia, which two centuries before had been the capital of the Lombard monarchy. In deliberate imitation of Charlemagne, he had himself declared king of the Lombards. He then went to Rome and in 962, in the course of a most festive and splendid ritual, he was crowned Emperor.

The imperial title, which had lain idle for thirty-eight years, since the death of Berengar I, was thus revived. What's more, it was not given to an obscure personage but to the strongest monarch in the West, something that had not been true since the death of Louis the Pious more than a century before. This time the imperial title was not allowed to degenerate. The Emperors that followed Otto were sometimes weak and ineffectual but they were always the leading princes of Europe; never did the Emperor's crown become a disgraceful football, kicked about among minor princelings.

With this coronation begins the history of the "Holy Roman Empire." It was the Roman Empire in theory and Otto was the Roman Emperor, but the adjective "Holy" was applied to indicate its close connection with the Church.

The Holy Roman Empire got under way while the final course of the Carolingians in the West Frankish course had yet a quarter century to go. But that final quarter century was up in due time and Louis V, the last Carolingian, died. He had an uncle, Charles, who might in theory have carried on the Carolingian line, but the lords would have it no longer and Hugh Capet could make his move.

He imitated the technique of Pepin the Short, and had Adalberon, archbishop of Reims and a longtime adherent of his, declare that the throne was elective and was not reserved for Carolingians alone. The archbishop's secretary, Gerbert (zhehr-behr′), the greatest scholar of the age, supplied the necessary argumentation and together they made it possible for Hugh Capet to be elected and anointed king of what we may now call France.

Hugh Capet had little more power than did the last Carolingians and he had to carry on the fight with other lords, but he was a vigorous king and the ancestor of a vigorous line of kings. Every king the French were to have over the next nine centuries was to be a descendant of Hugh Capet.

And so the old Frankish realm was gone and in its place was France and the Holy Roman Empire, little different at first, but with an air of spring about them. The agricultural revolution gave each an army of knights and a supply of food that meant more secure and more prosperous times were coming.

In the atmosphere of the security and prosperity that began to bud, there was time for scholarship — more so than ever before. The dim light of the Carolingian Renaissance, which Charlemagne had striven so hard to set ablaze and which had flickered and smoked as though it would never catch, had not yet entirely gone out after all.

Now it caught and began to burn steadily. It was still not very strong, but it would slowly brighten, and at the beginning of this new era stands the name of the priest who helped Hugh Capet to the throne — Gerbert.

THE BOOKS

This most remarkable change of all involved not Gerbert only, but the Papacy as well.

As the West began to take its first step upward, economically and politically, the Papacy continued feeble and despised. Even its association with the coronation of Otto did not revivify it. Indeed, Otto was almost more dominant over the Pope than Charlemagne had been.

When John XII, annoyed at Otto's domineering manner, decided, within a year of the coronation, that Berengar II was more endurable after all, Otto reacted strenuously. He deposed John in 963 and set up a Pope of his own, Leo VIII. (He also captured Berengar, took him to Germany, and kept him prisoner till Berengar died in 966. The great-great-great-grandson of Charlemagne thus died a prisoner of a Saxon Emperor. Shades of Widukind!)

The dreary round continued in Rome for another generation before Gerbert appeared on the scene. A Frenchman and a marvelous scholar, he was presented to Otto himself in 970 and, for a time, was tutor of Otto's grandson (also named Otto).

He went on to Reims, where he was secretary to the archbishop and where he was deeply engaged in the negotiations that brought Hugh Capet to the French throne. In time he was archbishop of Reims himself and in 999, through the help of Otto III, the grandson of Otto I and the Emperor whom he had once tutored, he became Pope.

As Pope, he took the name of Silvester II. He died in 1003, having served as Pope for only four years, but his influence was tremendous, and one can almost believe that there was something mystically important about his having been Pope in the millennial year, 1000.

He was the most renowned scholar of his age and it was not theological learning in which he was most interested. He was moved in a way unheard of in the West since Boethius had died almost five centuries before, for he was fascinated by secular learning.

He studied and taught what ancient works were available to him. He introduced the abacus for mathematical computation and made use of the newly introduced Arabic numerals as well. He built clocks and astronomical instruments. A superstitious age saw in this a tendency to magic and deviltry, but a few were inspired with interest in secular knowledge themselves — surely there could be no harm in that which interested the Pope.

Most important of all, Gerbert collected ancient manuscripts with loving care and encouraged others to do so. No more was it the more or less official belief that ancient learning was the work of the devil and that only godly works should be studied.

Gerbert began the drive, slow at first, but soon to gain momentum, to rescue the ancient learning. Men turned to the Arabic manuscripts which still preserved that learning and began to translate them into Latin.

Books appeared on the scene. Copies of Aristotle and Ptolemy, of Euclid and Lucretius and many others came into being, and from each new book, additional light sprang outward.

Gerbert's career marks the first clear step out of the darkness at last. To the economic and political moves upward out of the Dark Ages was added the most vital of all, the intellectual move upward.

In summary then, we have in this book glanced over a thousand years of history. We have seen the German tribes grow gradually stronger, then be driven into the Roman Empire under the lash of the Huns.

We have seen them break down the western half of the Roman Empire and set up Germanic kingdoms in its provinces. We have then seen all but one of these kingdoms disappear.

Some were destroyed in wars among themselves, some by what was left of the Roman Empire, some by new invaders. In the end, only a single one was left in existence and this was the greatest and least civilized of them all — the Frankish Empire.

Under the Franks, we watched European civilization sink into a night of darkness and then, at last, slowly begin to emerge into the dawn again.

This slow dawn between 950 and 1000 was not a change, like Charlemagne's, destined to fade — rather it was to be followed by many other changes, one after the other, in quicker and quicker succession, until the accumulation of them exploded into an almost unbearably brilliant civilization that (with its faults as well as its virtues) spread from western Europe through all the world.

And the end of which — we can only hope — is not yet.

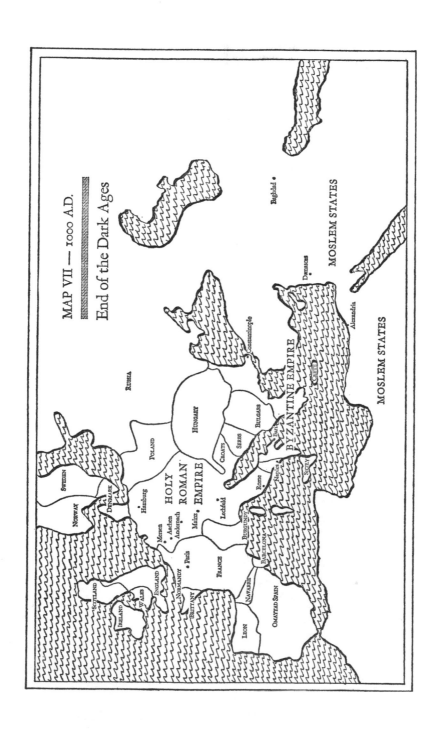

MAP VII — 1000 A.D.

End of the Dark Ages

Baghdad ·

MOSLEM STATES

Damascus ·

MOSLEM STATES

Alexandria

RUSSIA

Constantinople

BYZANTINE EMPIRE

CRETE

SWEDEN

NORWAY

DENMARK

Hamburg ·

HOLY
ROMAN·
EMPIRE

POLAND

HUNGARY

CROATS

SERBS

BULGARS

SCOTLAND

IRELAND

WALES

ENGLAND

NORMANDY

BRITTANY

FRANCE

Meran

Aachen

Anderach

Mainz ·

Lechfeld ·

Paris ·

BURGUNDY

BARCELONA

NAVARRE

LEON

OMAYYAD SPAIN

Rome

Sicily

A TABLE OF DATES

B.C.

1000 German tribesmen inhabit Baltic area

350 Pytheas of Massilia explores northern Europe

115 Cimbri invade southern Europe

101 Cimbri annihilated by Romans

71 German tribal leader, Ariovistus, invades Gaul

55 After defeating Ariovistus, Julius Caesar invades Germany

12 Romans take over Germany, between Rhine and Elbe

A.D.

9 Germans under Arminius annihilate three Roman legions

98 Roman writer, Tacitus, publishes book on the Germans

170 Marcus Aurelius (Rome) fights the Marcomanni

235 Alexander Severus (Rome) fights the Alemanni

251 After Goths migrate to Black Sea area, Decius (Rome) meets them south of Danube and is killed

A.D.

269 Claudius II (Rome) defeats Goths at Naissus

276 Probus (Rome) defeats Franks in Gaul

332 Ulfilas converted to Arian Christianity; begins conversion of fellow Goths

355 Julian (Rome) defeats Franks in Gaul

370 Huns pour westward out of Central Asia

372 Huns destroy Ostrogothic kingdom of Ermanaric; establish Hunnish Empire

375 Visigoths cross Danube into Roman Empire as refugees from Huns

378 Visigoths defeat and kill Valens (Rome) at battle of Adrianople

395 Death of Theodosius I (Rome); Alaric the Visigoth begins his raid

402 Alaric invades Italy; defeated by Stilicho

406 German tribes invade Gaul; enter Roman Empire permanently

410 Alaric takes Rome; dies shortly after

A.D.

419 Visigothic kingdom of Toulouse founded; first German kingdom on Roman territory

429 Vandals under Gaiseric establish kingdom in north Africa

433 Attila, ruler of the Huns; Hunnish Empire at peak

439 Vandals take Carthage

440 Leo I (the Great) as Pope

451 Huns cross Rhine; beaten by Aetius at battle of Catalunian Plain

452 Huns invade Italy; turn back without taking Rome

453 Death of Attila; end of Hunnish Empire

454 Assassination of Aetius

455 Vandals under Gaiseric sack Rome; Vandal kingdom at peak

466 Euric, king of Visigoths; Visigothic kingdom at peak

474 Theodoric, king of Ostrogoths

476 Odoacer dethrones Romulus Augustulus (Rome); rules Italy without establishing any further Emperor in the west; "fall of Rome"

477 Death of Gaiseric

481 Clovis, king of Salian Franks

484 Alaric II, king of Visigoths

486 Clovis takes Soissons; ends last Roman rule in west

488 Ostrogoths under Theodoric invade Italy

492 Gelasius I as Pope

493 Theodoric takes Ravenna,

A.D.

kills Odoacer; establishes Ostrogothic kingdom over Italy

496 Clovis converted to Catholic Christianity

497 Anastasius (Eastern Emperor) recognizes Theodoric as king in Italy

500 Clovis defeats Burgundians

506 Alaric II promulgates written Gothic/Roman law code

507 Clovis defeats and kills Alaric II at battle of Voille

508 Theodoric stops Clovis at Arles; assumes protectorate over Visigothic Spain; Ostrogoths at peak

509 Clovis sole ruler over Franks, establishing Merovingian line

510 Boethius, consul at Rome

511 Death of Clovis; Frankish kingdom divided among four sons

518 Justin I, East Roman Emperor

524 Boethius executed

526 Death of Theodoric

527 Justinian I, East Roman Emperor

533 Belisarius (East Roman general) invades north Africa; end of Vandal kingdom

535 Amalasuntha (daughter of Theodoric) assassinated; Belisarius invades Italy

536 Belisarius takes Rome

537 Belisarius takes Ravenna

543 Death of Benedit, founder

A.D.

Benedictine monastic rule
546 Ostrogoths under Totila retake Rome; beginning of
the Dark Age
551 Narses (East Roman general) comes to Italy
552 Narses defeats Totila at
battle of Taginae; end of
Ostrogothic kingdom
554 East Roman forces conquer
southeastern Spain; East
Roman Empire at peak
558 Clotaire I rules over united
Frankish realm
560 Avars (Asian tribe) invade
Germany
561 Death of Clotaire I
565 Death of Justinian I; dismissal of Narses
568 Lombards, fleeing Avars,
invade Italy; Leuvigild,
king of Visigothic Spain
572 Lombards capture Pavia;
establish Lombard kingdom
in Italy
573 Beginning of Frankish civil
wars over feud between
Brunehild and Fredegund
584 Leuvigild conquers Spain
586 Recared I of Visigothic
Spain converted to Catholicism
590 Gregory I (the Great) as
Pope
596 Gregory I sends mission to
England to convert Anglo-
Saxons
597 Death of Fredegund
600 Lombards converted to
Catholicism; end of Arian
heresy
604 Death of Gregory I
613 Clotaire II, son of Fredegund, captures and kills

A.D.

Brunehild; rules united
Frankish realm; Merovin-
gian power at peak
623 Death of Clotaire II; Dagobert I, last powerful Merovingian king
625 Suintila of Visigothic Spain
captures last East Roman
possessions along coast;
Visigothic Spain at peak
632 Death of Mohammed in
Arabia; Arabs united be-
hind new religion of Islam
633 Suintila deposed by synod
under Isidore of Seville
639 Death of Dagobert I
640 Death of Pepin of Landen;
first Carolingian Mayor of
the Palace of Frankish
realm
649 Martin I as Pope
653 Martin I arrested and sent
to Constantinople
654 Grimwald, son of Pepin of
Landen, unsuccessfully tries
to place son on Frankish
throne
664 Ebroin (not a Carolingian)
as Mayor of the Palace
681 Ebroin assassinated
687 Pepin of Heristal, Carolingian, becomes *de facto*
ruler of united Frankish
realm
698 Arabs, having conquered
western Asia, now take
Carthage and soon control
north Africa
711 Arabs and Berbers (Moors)
invade Spain; defeat Roder-
ick, last king of the Visigoths
712 Liutprand, king of the
Lombards; Lombard king-

A.D.

dom at peak

714 Moors in control of all of Spain; end of Visigothic kingdom; death of Pepin of Heristal

716 Boniface (Winifrid of England) begins conversion of Germans east of Rhine; Charles Martel (son of Pepin of Heristal), Mayor of the Palace

717 Leo III, East Roman (or Byzantine) Emperor, stops Arabs before Constantinople; initiates Iconoclasm controversy

721 Moors raiding Aquitaine; reach Toulouse

728 Liutprand in Ravenna; Pope Gregory II appeals vainly to Charles Martel for help against Lombards

732 Charles Martel stops Moors at battle of Tours

740 Death of Leo III

741 Death of Charles Martel; two sons, Pepin the Short and Carloman, succeed him

744 Death of Liutprand

747 Carloman retires to monastery

749 Aistulf, king of Lombards

751 Aistulf takes Ravenna; Byzantine power in central Italy at end; Pepin the Short comes to an agreement with Pope Zecharias over kingship

752 Childeric III deposed and Merovingian line comes to an end. Pepin the Short becomes Pepin I, first Caro-

A.D.

lingian king of the Franks; Stephen III as Pope

754 Answering pleas of Pope Stephen III, Pepin I invades Italy and defeats Lombards

755 Death of Boniface, "apostle to the Germans"

756 Pepin I defeats Lombards second time; makes "donation of Pepin" to Pope, thus beginning temporal power of Papacy; Desiderius, king of the Lombards; Abdurrahman I, king of Moorish Spain

768 Death of Pepin I; his sons, Charles (Charlemagne) and Carloman, succeed.

771 Carloman dies; Charlemagne sole ruler over Franks

772 Charlemagne begins campaigns against Saxons; Desiderius lays siege to Rome and Pope Adrian I appeals for help to Charlemagne

773 Charlemagne invades Italy

774 Charlemagne puts an end to the Lombard kingdom

778 Charlemagne raids Spain; his rearguard destroyed by Basques at Roncesvalles (giving rise to legend of Roland)

780 Charlemagne visits Rome; hires Alcuin of York to educate his court; beginning of "Carolingian Renaissance"

786 Harun al-Rashid, caliph at Baghdad

788 Death of Abdurrahman I

A.D.

793 Moors raid Mediterranean coast of Frankish realm

795 Leo III as Pope

797 Irene, Byzantine Empress; ends Iconoclasm controversy

799 Leo III driven out of Rome; restored by Charlemagne

800 Charlemagne crowned Roman Emperor by Leo III; Frankish monarchy at peak

801 Charlemagne and Harun al-Rashid exchange presents

802 Irene deposed; Nicephorus, Byzantine Emperor, makes war on Charlemagne

812 Byzantine Emperor, Michael I, recognizes Charlemagne's Imperial title

814 Death of Charlemagne; Louis I (the Pious) succeeds

816 Stephen V as Pope; crowns Louis I as Roman Emperor

827 Moslems invade Byzantine Sicily

829 Beginning of civil war between Louis I and his sons

833 Louis I defeated by his sons at "Field of Lies"

837 Moslems pillage Naples

840 Death of Louis I; Lothair I succeeds as Roman Emperor, with his brother, Louis the German, ruling over eastern third of Frankish realm and another brother, Charles the Bald, over western third; Moslems establish permanent outpost in Italy

842 Emperor Lothair I defeated

A.D.

by his brothers at the battle of Fontenoy; oath at Strasbourg, preceding battle, shows development of Frankish languages in two directions, toward French in west and German in east

843 Treaty of Verdun between Frankish brother-rulers sets up first skeleton of modern Europe, based on division between France and Germany

844 Sergius II as Pope

845 Vikings sack Hamburg; beginning of yearly raids

846 Moslems raid Rome

847 Leo IV as Pope; fortifies part of Rome against Moslems

855 Emperor Lothair I abdicates; one son, Louis II, succeeds as Roman Emperor, but controls only Italy; another son, Lothair II, rules central region north of Alps (Lotharingia, or Lorraine)

858 Nicholas I (the Great) as Pope; makes use of "False Decretals" and "Donation of Constantine" to increase Papal power

862 Rostislav, King of Moravia (first important Slavic power in Europe) welcomes Greek missionaries, Cyril and Methodius ("apostles to the Slavs")

869 Death of Lothair II without an heir

A.D.

870 Charles the Bald and Louis the German divide Lotharingia between themselves

871 Emperor Louis II drives Moslems out of Italian heel which is then reoccupied by Byzantines

874 Franks under Carloman (son of Louis the German) force submission of Moravia

875 Death of Emperor Louis II; Pope John VIII crowns Charles the Bald as Roman Emperor

876 Death of Louis the German

877 Death of Charles the Bald; Louis II (the Stammerer) succeeds

879 Death of Louis the Stammerer; Louis III succeeds

880 Death of Carloman; younger brother, Charles the Fat, becomes king of Italy

884 Charles the Fat rules over united Frankish realm

885 Vikings lay siege to Paris; Eudes, Count of Paris, hero of resistance

887 Charles the Fat deposed; Frankish realm permanently divided

891 Guido of Spoleto (grandson of Lothair I) crowned Roman Emperor by Pope Stephen VI

893 Charles III (the Simple), king of west Frankish realm

894 Death of Emperor Guido; his son, Lambert, crowned

A.D.

Roman Emperor

896 Arnulf (grandson of Louis the German) crowned Roman Emperor

898 Death of Count Eudes of Paris

899 Death of Emperor Arnulf; his son, Louis the Child, succeeds as king of east Frankish realm

901 Louis III (grandson of Emperor Louis II) crowned Roman Emperor by Pope Benedict IV but soon driven out of Italy

906 Magyars conquer Moravia

910 Magyar raids into Germany grow serious

911 Death of Louis the Child, last Carolingian ruler in east Frankish realm; Conrad I (non-Carolingian) succeeds; Hrolf (Rollo) the Ganger founds Normandy

914 John X as Pope

915 Berengar (grandson of Emperor Louis I) crowned Roman Emperor by Pope John X

916 John X and Emperor Berengar defeat Moslems at Garigliano River and drive them out of Italy

918 Death of Conrad I; Henry the Fowler (of Saxony) succeeds as ruler of east Frankish realm

922 Robert (brother of Eudes of Paris) declares himself king of west Frankish realm

A.D.

923 Robert defeats Charles the Simple at Soissons, but is killed himself

924 Death of Emperor Berengar, last of the Carolingian emperors

929 Death of Charles the Simple; Hugh the Great, son of Robert, greatest power in west Frankish realm

933 Death of Henry the Fowler; his son, Otto I, succeeds as king of east Frankish realm

936 Louis IV, son of Charles the Simple, brought back from exile by Hugh the Great, to rule west Frankish realm

954 Lothair, king of west Frankish realm

955 Otto I inflicts overwhelming defeat upon Magyars at battle of the Lech River;

A.D.

John XII as Pope

956 Death of Hugh the Great; his son, Hugh Capet, succeeds to his power

961 Pope John XII asks help of Otto I against Berengar II (grandson of Emperor Berengar)

962 Otto I invades Italy; is crowned Roman Emperor by Pope John XII; founding of the Holy Roman Empire

986 Louis V, king of west Frankish realm

987 Death of Louis V, last Carolingian monarch in Europe; west Frankish realm can now be considered "France"; Hugh Capet elected as king of France

999 Gerbert becomes Pope Sylvester II; end of Dark Ages

The Merovingian Kings

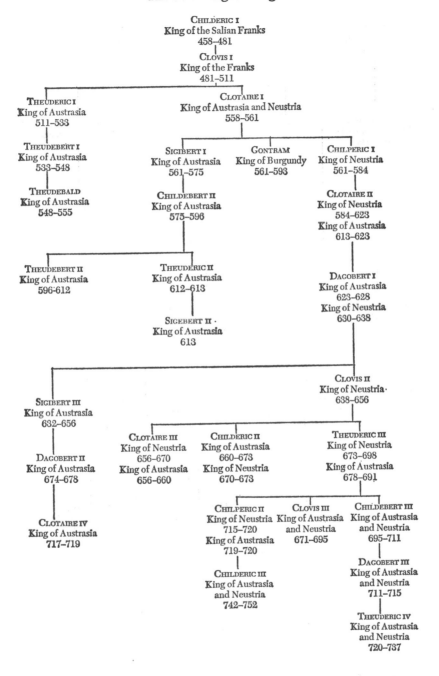

CHILDERIC I
King of the Salian Franks
458–481

CLOVIS I
King of the Franks
481–511

THEUDERIC I
King of Austrasia
511–533

CLOTAIRE I
King of Austrasia and Neustria
558–561

THEUDEBERT I
King of Austrasia
533–548

SIGIBERT I
King of Austrasia
561–575

GONTRAM
King of Burgundy
561–593

CHILPERIC I
King of Neustria
561–584

THEUDEBALD
King of Austrasia
548–555

CHILDEBERT II
King of Austrasia
575–596

CLOTAIRE II
King of Neustria
584–623
King of Austrasia
613–623

THEUDEBERT II
King of Austrasia
596–612

THEUDERIC II
King of Austrasia
612–613

DAGOBERT I
King of Austrasia
623–628
King of Neustria
630–638

SIGEBERT II
King of Austrasia
613

SIGIBERT III
King of Austrasia
632–656

CLOVIS II
King of Neustria
638–656

DAGOBERT II
King of Austrasia
674–678

CLOTAIRE III
King of Neustria
656–670
King of Austrasia
656–660

CHILDERIC II
King of Austrasia
660–673
King of Neustria
670–673

THEUDERIC III
King of Neustria
673–698
King of Austrasia
678–691

CLOTAIRE IV
King of Austrasia
717–719

CHILPERIC II
King of Neustria
715–720
King of Austrasia
719–720

CLOVIS III
King of Austrasia
and Neustria
671–695

CHILDEBERT III
King of Austrasia
and Neustria
695–711

CHILDERIC III
King of Austrasia
and Neustria
742–752

DAGOBERT III
King of Austrasia
and Neustria
711–715

THEUDERIC IV
King of Austrasia
and Neustria
720–737

The House of Pepin

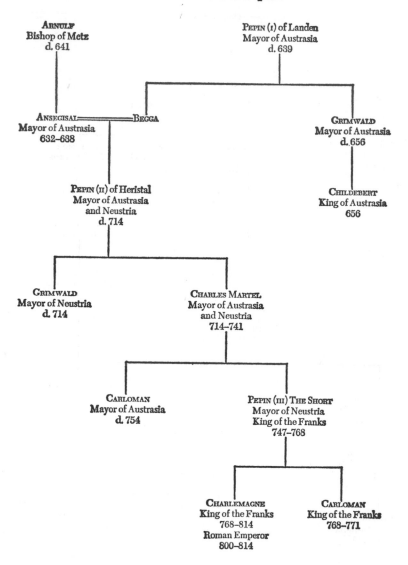

ARNULF
Bishop of Metz
d. 641

PEPIN (I) of Landen
Mayor of Austrasia
d. 639

ANSEGISAL══════BEGGA
Mayor of Austrasia
632–638

GRIMWALD
Mayor of Austrasia
d. 656

PEPIN (II) of Heristal
Mayor of Austrasia
and Neustria
d. 714

CHILDEBERT
King of Austrasia
656

GRIMWALD
Mayor of Neustria
d. 714

CHARLES MARTEL
Mayor of Austrasia
and Neustria
714–741

CARLOMAN
Mayor of Austrasia
d. 754

PEPIN (III) THE SHORT
Mayor of Neustria
King of the Franks
747–768

CHARLEMAGNE
King of the Franks
768–814
Roman Emperor
800–814

CARLOMAN
King of the Franks
768–771

The Carolingian Dynasty

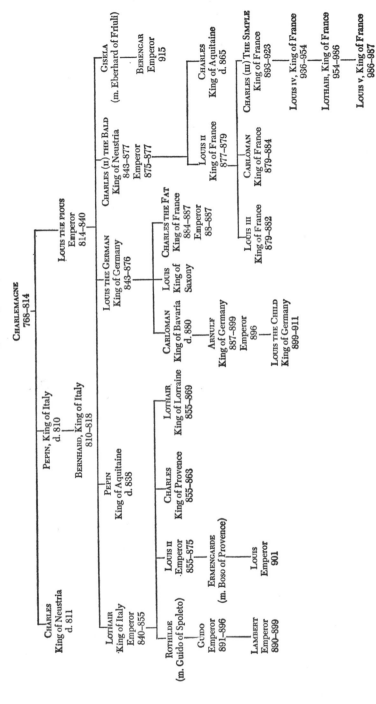

INDEX